Napoleon's Army

Colonel H.C.B. Rogers

Foreword by
Christopher Summerville

Pen & Sword
MILITARY

First published in Great Britain in 1974
by Ian Allan
Published in 2005 in this format by
PEN & SWORD MILITARY
an imprint of
Pen & Sword Books Limited
47 Church Street
Barnsley
South Yorkshire
S70 2AS

ISBN 1 84415 310 X

A CIP catalogue record for this book
is available from the British Library.

Printed and bound in Great Britain by
CPI UK

Pen & Sword Books Ltd incorporates the imprints of
Pen & Sword Aviation, Pen & Sword Maritime, Pen & Sword Military,
Wharncliffe Local History, Pen & Sword Select,
Pen & Sword Military Classics and Leo Cooper.

For a complete list of Pen & Sword titles please contact:
PEN & SWORD BOOKS LIMITED
47 Church Street, Barnsley, South Yorkshire, S70 2AS, England.
E-mail: enquiries@pen-and-sword.co.uk
Website: www.pen-and-sword.co.uk

CONTENTS

FOREWORD

'Troops are made to let themselves be killed,' Napoleon once observed philosophically. And killed they were: between 1792 and 1814 France lost some 1,500,000 of her sons, drowned in a river of blood, for the sake of Revolution and Empire. But what of these soldiers? How were they trained, equipped, organised? As author Colonel Rogers points out: 'Many books have been written about Napoleon and his campaigns, and the great battles fought by his armies have been described time and time again. Much less has been written about the soldiers of those armies and of the organisation and conditions under which they lived and served.' The present volume, then, seeks to plug this gap in our knowledge.

Bonaparte began reforming the French Army in 1802. After years of neglect, the military had fallen into something of a decline, but the energetic first consul set to work to create a new national force: bad officers were weeded out, good ones promoted; intensive training was introduced; shortages in horses and guns addressed; and the basic structure of command and control reorganised and revitalised. Encamped at Boulogne, and ostensibly preparing for the invasion of Great Britain, the French Army was gradually honed into a first class military machine. In the words of Dumas, the camp at Boulogne was 'The best and most complete war school that could have ever been conceived.'

Proclaimed emperor in May 1804, Napoleon required a Grand Army and the work of reform and reorganisation continued apace. This included the appointment of eighteen marshals to oversee the Army, under Napoleon's direct authority. This was followed by a personal inspection of the camp at Boulogne, a scene described Bourrienne, the emperor's biographer:

'When he reviewed the troops, he asked the officers and often the soldiers in what battles they had been engaged, and to those who had received serious wounds he gave the cross [the prestigious Legion of Honour]. Here, I think, I may appropriately mention a singular piece of charlatanism to which the emperor had recourse, and which powerfully contributed to augment the enthusiasm of his troops. He would say to one of his aides-de-camp, "Ascertain from the colonel of such a regiment whether he has in his corps a man who has served in the campaigns of Italy or of Egypt. Ascertain his name, where he was born, the particulars of his family, and what he has done. Learn his number in the ranks, and to what company he belongs, and furnish me with the information." ... On the day of the review, Bonaparte, at

4

a single glance, could perceive the man who had been described to him. He would go up to him as if he recognized him, address him by his name, and say, "Oh! So you are here! You are a brave fellow – I saw you at Aboukir – how is your old father? What! Have you not got the cross? Stay, I will give it to you." Then the delighted soldiers would say to each other, "You see the emperor knows us all; he knows our families; he knows where we have served." What a stimulus was this to soldiers, whom he succeeded in persuading that they would all, some time or another, become marshals of the empire!'

On 5 December 1804, three days after his coronation, Napoleon held a grand festival on the Champs de Mars, and distributed regimental standards–the celebrated imperial eagles–to the regiments that formed the Paris garrison. According to Furse, in *Campaigns of 1805,* 'Napoleon addressed his troops thus: "Soldiers, behold your flags; these eagles will serve you always as rallying points; they will be wherever your Emperor may judge it necessary for the defence of his throne and of his people. Swear to sacrifice your life to defend them, and to keep them always by your courage on the path of victory. Do you swear it?" Thousands of voices replied with enthusiasm, "We do swear it." The army kept its oath, for in less than twelve months the same eagles, after a series of sanguinary combats, were waving on the walls of Vienna and floating in the breeze on the plateau of Pratzen.'

Central to Napoleon's reforms was the subdivision of the Army into corps: big, self-contained units of all arms, which were in effect, separate miniature armies. Each corps was placed under the command of a senior general or marshal, while Napoleon retained the command in chief. The main benefits of this system were speed and flexibility: with several self-reliant forces, capable of fending off large enemy units until reinforced, Napoleon could march rapidly over available roads (40 km per day, according to Georges Blond) without having to concentrate his army into one dense, slow-moving mass. And by keeping his corps within a day's march of each other, Napoleon could rapidly change from dispersion to concentration, as circumstances demanded. The corps system was a major ingredient in the emperor's military success and it was rapidly copied by his enemies.

In *Napoleon's Army,* Colonel Rogers examines the corps system in detail, along with a fascinating array of facts and figures covering all aspects of the Grand Army's organisation and effectiveness in the field. The battles and campaigns are briefly and clearly outlined, to give essential background, but the book is primarily an in-depth study of the hard-marching, hard-fighting Napoleonic war machine, from its birth at Boulogne, through its years of triumph, to disaster at Waterloo. Along the way, the author answers how, as Lord Wavell put it, Napoleon 'inspired a ragged, mutinous, half-starved army and made it fight as it did'.

Fondly regarded by leading Napoleonic scholars and *aficionados* as the book which turned them on to this fascinating period, Rogers' authoritative study is now available in a paperback edition accessible to all. The author was a distinguished military historian and an expert on the campaigns and armies of the Napoleonic Wars. His best-known books are *The British Army in the Eighteenth Century, The Confederates and the Federals at War, Wellington's Army, Artillery Through the Ages, Weapons of the British Soldier* and *Tanks in Battle.*

Christopher Summerville, York 2004

INTRODUCTION

 Many books have been written about Napoleon and
his campaigns, and the great battles fought by his
armies have been described time and time again. Much
less has been written about the soldiers of those armies
and of the organisation and conditions under which
they lived and served. It is the aim of this book to
describe the French Army by staff, arms, and services
as it existed and changed during the long period of a
quarter of a century that separated the Battles of Valmy
and Waterloo. This is not another history of the
campaigns waged under the First French Republic and
the First French Empire, and military operations are
only cited to illustrate organisation, tactics, equipment,
and administration. However, the opening chapter is
devoted to a brief narrative of the various campaigns as an *aide-mémoire*
and an historical background to those readers who may require it. It is a
very condensed summary of the most important events and to keep it
reasonably short the less important actions and movements are of necessity
omitted. In addition, two chapters in the book deal with the operations of
an army corps and a third with the experiences of a junior officer to show
how the various matters described in previous chapters were applied in
the joint operations of all arms in the field. Because the book is a study of
the army, naval matters, except in so far as they had a tactical influence of
land operations, are omitted.

The French Revolution inaugurated a form of warfare in which the
long-service armies of the eighteenth century, waging campaigns with
limited objectives, were replaced by national armies of conscripted men
fighting for total victory: a form of warfare with which we have become
all too familiar. That Napoleon, in commanding such armies, was so
successful was due perhaps as much to his understanding of his soldiers

and his personality as a leader of men, as to his brilliant generalship. Field Marshal Lord Wavell wrote, 'If you discover how ... he inspired a ragged, mutinous, half-starved army and made it fight as it did, how he dominated and controlled generals older and more experienced than himself, then you will have learned something.' And Major-General J. F. C. Fuller, in his *The Conduct of War* (1961), draws attention to Napoleon's following Order of the Day: 'A battalion commander should not rest until he has become acquainted with every detail; after six months in command he should know the names and abilities of all the officers and men of his battalion.' Napoleon set out to make every man feel that it was a privilege to belong to the French Army; and he knew that the mentality of the French soldier would respond to such appeals as: 'All men who value life more than the glory of the nation and the esteem of their comrades should not be members of the French Army.' General Fuller quotes him as saying: 'When in the fire of battle I rode down the ranks and shouted: "Unfurl the standards! The moment has at length come!" it made the French soldier leap into action.' And, 'The 32nd Brigade would have died for me, because after Lonato I wrote: "The 32nd was there, I was calm." The power of words on men is astonishing.'

The personality of this remarkable man was so tremendous that he is perhaps the only general in history who was so reflected in the army he commanded that it is impossible to discuss one without the other.

CHAPTER ONE

From Valmy to Waterloo

The First Campaign

The wars with which we are concerned began on 20th April 1792 when the French Assembly declared war on Austria. Hostilities had been threatened from the previous August when the Emperor of Austria and the King of Prussia declared that they were ready to join other Powers to restore the authority of the French monarchy. Revolutionary France hurriedly prepared for war and on 14th December 1791 three armies were formed for the defence of the northern and eastern frontiers, composed of units of the old regular army and a vast number of new volunteer battalions. They were designated, respectively, the Army of the North, the Army of the Centre, and the Army of the Rhine. The volunteer units received their training as soldiers in actual warfare, and at this stage they were untrained and undisciplined mobs; frequently gallant, but liable in a moment to dissolve in panic-stricken flight.

On 28th April 1792 three columns of the Army of the North advanced to invade Belgium. It was a bad start; there was panic in two columns, although neither had come in contact with the enemy, and in one of them the troops murdered their general. Further advances were unsuccessful, and by 30th June the invasion of Belgium had come to an end.

Subsequent events did nothing for the efficiency of the new armies. On 10th August 1792 the Paris mob invaded the Tuileries and massacred the Swiss Guard, and the monarchy was suppressed and the Royal Family imprisoned. Then the Marquis de Lafayette, commanding the Army of the North, was ordered to hand over his command and report to Paris. As this meant execution by that new instrument of republican terror, the *guillotine,* Lafayette fled to the enemy; an event which shook the faith of the troops in their leaders.

General Charles François Dumouriez was appointed to succeed Lafayette in command of the Army of the North. Meanwhile an Allied army consisting of 42,000 Prussians and 30,000 Austrians had assembled at Coblenz under the command of the Duke of Brunswick. On 19th August Brunswick crossed the frontier at Longwy and, after capturing that fortress and the fortress of Verdun, marched slowly in the direction of Paris.

The only really effective French force to oppose Brunswick was the Army of the Centre under General François Christophe Kellerman, a former major-general of the *ancien régime.* Kellerman commanded by far the best of the French armies of the time because it was composed mostly of regular troops. Dumouriez joined Kellerman with part of his Army of the North, which included some regulars but in which most of the infantry units were the ill-disciplined volunteer battalions. In both armies, however, all the cavalry and artillery were regulars.

On 20th September 1792 there took place the Battle of Valmy. The assault of the Prussian infantry was halted by the devastating fire of the French artillery, and, looking at the steady lines of Kellerman's infantry, Brunswick decided to withdraw.

On the day after the battle the monarchy was abolished and the government of France was taken over by the National Convention.

Other Campaigns of 1792–93

The Duke of Brunswick withdrew to Germany and the armies of France assumed the offensive in various theatres. In the south they captured Nice, and from Alsace a force under General Custine captured first Mayence and then Frankfurt. In the north Dumouriez's Army of the North defeated a smaller Austrian force on 6th November 1792 at Jemappes, and ten days later captured Brussels. As the year closed, however, Brunswick drove Custine back to the Rhine, recapturing Frankfurt on 2nd December.

The war spread as 1793 opened. On 21st January Louis XVI went to the guillotine and an outraged England sent the French Ambassador home. France promptly declared war on Great Britain, Spain, and Holland, and at the same time introduced conscription. As if to make sure that the European Powers took the war seriously, the National Convention declared Belgium to be incorporated in France.

The Allied offensive opened on 1st March, when an Austrian army of 40,000 men under the Prince of Saxe-Coburg marched into Belgium, driving back with ease the French forces in front of them and Brunswick's Prussian army invested Mayence. On 18th March Dumouriez attacked Coburg at Neerwinden, but was defeated. Large numbers of his volunteers deserted and on 21st March he was defeated again at Louvain. Dumouriez now planned to march on Paris and overturn the Government, and he opened negotiations with the enemy. Accused of treason, he took shelter with the Austrians. Dampierre was appointed to command in his place but on 8th May he was mortally wounded. His death saved him from the guillotine, to which he was already destined because of his failure in the field. Custine succeeded Dampierre, but he soon incurred the enmity of the Government. He was called to Paris, and, when Valenciennes surrendered during his absence, he was arrested by the Committee of Public Safety and guillotined on 27th August 1793. Houchard now became commander of the Army of the North.

Mayence fell to the Duke of Brunswick in August, and French difficulties were increased by a Royalist rebellion in the Vendée region and by risings against the Government in the towns of Toulon, Marseilles, and Lyons. The Royalists in Toulon were assisted by a British fleet, including a Spanish squadron; and the British presence in the war was also marked by the arrival in Flanders of a small British expeditionary force under the Duke of York which began the siege of Valenciennes and subsequently invested Dunkirk. A Dutch army commanded by the Prince of Orange also took the field, taking post between the British and Austrian armies in the north.

At this stage only lethargy and lack of co-ordination by the Allies saved Republican France from complete defeat. There was a panic-stricken reaction by the National Convention. On 23rd August the Committee of Public Safety ordered the conscription of the entire male population and a host of new regiments were raised in a hurry. A fortnight later, on 6th September, Houchard, with a superiority in numbers of three to one, assaulted the Duke of York's positions east of Dunkirk. The French attacked with spirit and the Duke of York was forced to retreat, sacrificing his siege artillery in the process. On 13th September Houchard defeated the Prince of Orange at Menin. But after these successes the French suffered a series of defeats by the Austrians. On 23rd September Houchard was arrested, and he was guillotined on 16th November. Jean Baptiste Jourdan, a former private of the old army, succeeded to the command. On 15th and 16th October Jourdan defeated the Austrians under Coburg at the Battle of Wattignies, forcing them to raise the siege of Maubeuge and retire.

The last months of the year saw French successes elsewhere. In the area of the Rhine, Hoche struck at the junction of the Prussians under Brunswick and the Austrians under Würmser, and defeated them at the Battle of Fröschwiller on 22nd December; and four days later he beat them again at Geisberg. Mayence fell once more to the French. Meanwhile the situation in Marseilles and Lyons had been restored and the rebels in the

Vendée defeated. On the Spanish and Italian frontiers the French armies maintained their positions. In December the forts commanding the entrance to Toulon were recaptured from the Allies and the British fleet forced to withdraw, the city falling to the Republican forces.

The last four months of the year, therefore, witnessed a remarkable French recovery, and the Republic which had been on the verge of collapse was now in a strong position with its armies improving rapidly in training and discipline.

The Campaigns of 1794–95

In Belgium the French scored successes during the spring and summer of 1794. On 18th May, owing to a faulty Austrian plan, the British and Austrians were defeated at Tourcoing. But on 22nd May the French attacked again unsuccessfully at Tournai, their repulse being completed by a charge of Fox's British brigade (14th, 37th, and 53rd Regiments) and the devastating fire of the British artillery. On 17th June the French defeated an Austrian attack at Hooglede to relieve Ypres, and the town surrendered the following day. On 26th June, Jourdan, in command of the newly formed Army of Sambre and Meuse, defeated the Austrians and Dutch at Fleurus near Charleroi, and as a result of this great victory the French entered Brussels on 10th July and Antwerp on 27th July. This latter date is more noteworthy on account of the fall of the bloodthirsty dictator Robespierre and the end of the 'Terror'. Henceforward French generals could fight without being haunted by the fear of the guillotine as the penalty for failure.

This was the effective end of the campaign in Belgium, for the Austrians soon withdrew across the Rhine and during the ensuing dreadful winter the British force retreated into Germany, whence it was evacuated to England in the following April. This very cold winter was marked by a curious episode, for French cavalry captured the Dutch fleet by riding across the frozen Texel.

As a result of the French successes peace was concluded on 5th April 1795 with Prussia and then with Spain and many of the minor states of Germany. The two principal Powers with which France was still at war were Great Britain and Austria.

In July 1795 a British effort to stimulate a Royalist rising by landing a force of French *emigré* troops at Quiberon ended in failure, for on 21st July the expedition was completely destroyed by the French Army of the West under Hoche.

Two French armies were in the Rhine area, the Sambre and Meuse about Coblenz, under Jourdan's command, and the Rhine and Moselle, commanded by Pichegru, in Alsace. The opposing Allied armies were under the command of Count Charles von Clerfayt. On 5th September

Jourdan crossed the Rhine and started to advance in the direction of Frankfurt. By the end of October he had been outmanœuvred and forced back across the Rhine. Clerfayt now turned on Pichegru, who was besieging Mayence, beat him on 28th October and invaded the Palatinate. On 10th January 1796 an armistice was signed to cover the whole area in which these two French armies were operating.

During the period 22nd–28th November 1795 the Army of Italy, commanded by Schérer, defeated the Austrians at the Battle of Loano.

The Campaigns in Germany 1796–97

On 20th May 1796 the Austrians denounced the armistice and hostilities were to start again on 1st June. At midnight 31st May/1st June units of the Army of Sambre and Meuse began to advance, but on 16th June Jourdan's left wing was defeated at Wetzler and he drew back across the Rhine the following month. On 24th June Moreau, who now commanded the Army of the Rhine and Moselle, crossed the Rhine at Strasbourg. The Archduke Charles, commanding the Austrian army in the Rhine area, left Wartensleben to hold Jourdan in check and marched the remainder of his army against Moreau. However, the Austrians were repulsed in an indecisive action at Malsch on 9th July and retreated across the Danube between Ulm and Donauwörth on 12th August. Meanwhile, on 28th June Jourdan again crossed the Rhine and forced Wartensleben to retreat.

Charles, who had received reinforcements, now left Latour to watch Moreau and turned again towards Jourdan. Uniting with Wartensleben, he defeated Jourdan decisively at Amberg on 24th August. But the Archduke was not thereby relieved of anxiety, for on the same day Moreau beat Latour at Friedberg. However, Moreau did not follow up his victory energetically, and Charles, sending reinforcements to Latour, marched after Jourdan and drove him out of a defensive position near Würzburg on the Main on 3rd September. Jourdan, after this defeat, retreated rapidly towards the Rhine, and then, on 16th September, fought unsuccessfully again on the line of the River Lahn.

Moreau had dithered uncertainly, and after Jourdan's defeats he was dangerously exposed to attack by the Archduke. On 19th September, therefore, he too began to retreat to the Rhine. On 2nd October he repulsed the pursuing Latour at Biberach. Continuing his retreat, Moreau was attacked by the Archduke Charles on the Elz River on 19th October. The Austrians got the better of an indecisive battle and on 26th October the French withdrew across the Rhine at Huningue.

The French offensive of 1796 had therefore ended in complete defeat. In January 1797 Hoche was appointed to the command of the Army of the Sambre and Meuse and in the spring of 1797 the French initiated another offensive across the Rhine. The Archduke Charles had been sent to halt Bonaparte's Army of Italy. Hoche crossed the Rhine and defeated the Austrian General Werneck on the line of the River Lahn on 18th April. Three days later Moreau's Army of the Rhine and Moselle crossed the Rhine near Kehl against bitter Austrian resistance. The operations of both Hoche and Moreau were brought to a halt by the armistice resulting from Bonaparte's decisive victory.

The Campaign in Italy 1796–97

The complete defeat of Austria and the subsequent peace treaty was due to the remarkable campaign waged by Napoleon Bonaparte in command of the French Army of Italy. Bonaparte was appointed to this army on 2nd March 1796 and took over command on 27th March. It was not a promising command because he had only about 58,000 men, short of both clothing and food, and these were strung out along the coast from Marseilles to Voltri, near Genoa. North of them in the hills were a Piedmontese army of 25,000 men under Colli and an Austrian army of some 35,000 commanded by Beaulieu; whilst to the south the Royal Navy blockaded and threatened all the ports through which supplies should have been delivered.

Both Bonaparte and his opponents planned an offensive. Beaulieu attacked first, capturing Voltri on 10th April. But two days later Bonaparte opened his own offensive with the Battle of Montenotte, striking at the junction between the Allied armies and driving a wedge between them. Then on 14th–15th April, at Dego, he defeated Beaulieu's right wing which fell back to Acqui. Now, with the two opposing armies well separated, Bonaparte turned on Colli and beat him so decisively at Mondovi that Colli asked for an armistice and Piedmont was driven out of the war, opening its fortresses to French garrisons.

By 25th April Bonaparte was following up Beaulieu, who was retiring to an extended front along the River Po. Bonaparte feinted at this river line at various points, and then surprised the defence in a crossing of the Po at Piacenza on 7th–8th May, threatening Beaulieu's communications with the great fortress of Mantua. Beaulieu retreated eastwards, leaving Pavia and Milan open to the French. By a remarkable piece of leadership, Bonaparte inspired an assault which resulted in the capture, in the face of fierce resistance, of the vital Lodi bridge over the River Adda, and drove the Austrians into a retreat towards Mantua. The French could now move on Milan without fear of an Austrian attack on their flank, and on 15th May Bonaparte entered the city. The citadel, however, held out till 29th June before it surrendered.

After quelling an insurrection in his rear, Bonaparte began operations against Beaulieu on 28th May. On 29th May the French troops reached the River Mincio, between Lake Garda and Mantua, along which Beaulieu had now deployed his army with, on his left, a strong garrison in the fortress of Mantua. Bonaparte drove through Beaulieu's line at Borghetto, and by 1st June the Austrian general was retreating northward along the Adige River and into the Tyrol with the remainder of his field army, leaving Mantua to investment.

In July Würmser arrived from Germany to take command of a new Austrian army which was being assembled for a counter-offensive against the French in Italy. Würmser organised his army into three columns. He moved south along the east side of Lake Garda with the main body of about 24,000 men, with the object of relieving Mantua; he sent Quasdanovitch with a strong detachment of 18,000 men down the west side of Lake Garda to cut Bonaparte's communications; and he despatched Meszaro with a much smaller body to move well to the east via Bassano and Vicenza to strike Bonaparte's right rear at Verona. All these Austrian columns met with considerable initial success.

To meet this threat Bonaparte was forced to give up the siege of Mantua and he concentrated 47,000 men south-west of Lake Garda. Würmser's preoccupation with relieving Mantua enabled Bonaparte to throw the bulk of his army against Quasdanovitch. On 2nd August Würmser, anxious about Quasdanovitch, sent a division under Liptay to gain contact with him. Bonaparte left Augereau to contain Liptay and on 3rd August he defeated Quasdanovitch at the Battle of Lonato. Two days later he turned against Würmser and beat him decisively at the Battle of Castiglione. Würmser's broken army retired to the Tyrol.

Mantua was invested again on 24th August and on 2nd September Bonaparte advanced northwards east of Lake Garda towards Trent. Würmser, who had been reinforced, had also resumed the offensive. Davidovitch was to hold the Tyrol with about 20,000 men, whilst Würmser, with another 20,000 marched down the Brenta valley to relieve Mantua. Bonaparte's advancing troops encountered Davidovitch's detachment and drove it back through Trent. Here Bonaparte learned of Würmser's move and himself turned west and south down the Brenta valley to pursue the Austrian main body. He caught up with Würmser on 8th September and beat him at the Battle of Bassano. Würmser withdrew into Mantua with the remnants of his army, bringing the strength of the garrison up to 28,000 men.

The Austrians were determined to relieve Mantua and a new army was assembled under Baron Alvintzy. On 1st November Alvintzy again divided the Austrian army into two elements, sending Davidovitch with 18,400 men directly down the Adige valley, east of Lake Garda, whilst he advanced towards Vicenza east of the Brenta with the main body of 28,700 men. He intended to join Davidovitch at Verona and then move south on Mantua. Bonaparte (whose total strength, including the troops besieging Mantua, was only 41,500) again took advantage of this division of the enemy army. He left Vaubois to contain Davidovitch and with his main body moved east to encounter Alvintzy.

On 2nd November Vaubois, with a much smaller force, was driven south by Davidovitch. On 6th November the French encountered Alvintzy's leading troops, but could make no impression and Bonaparte withdrew to Verona. On 12th November Bonaparte struck from Verona at Alvintzy's advanced guard at Caldiero, but was checked and withdrew again to Verona. On 15th to 17th November there took place the fiercely contested Battle of Arcola, when Bonaparte delivered a surprise attack on Alvintzy's flank and rear. Alvintzy's defence was broken and his army forced to retreat. Bonaparte then turned on Davidovitch and drove him north on 19th November.

In January 1797 Alvintzy made another attempt to relieve Mantua. With his main body of 28,000 men he moved south down the valley of the Adige, and sent two small columns, 6,000 and 9,000 strong respectively, from the Brenta valley—the former from Bassano towards Verona, and the latter from Padua via Legnano towards Mantua. As information of the Austrians reached Bonaparte, so he began concentrating his main body on the plateau of Rivoli between the Adige and Lake Garda. There on 14th January, and before the French concentration was complete, Alvintzy attacked him. At the ensuing Battle of Rivoli, Alvintzy was defeated and driven northwards.

At Mantua, Würmser attempted a sortie to link up with the column advancing to the relief of the beleaguered city; but the French covering forces held until Bonaparte arrived from Rivoli and forced the surrender of the Austrian relief force. On 2nd February Würmser capitulated and the French gained Mantua.

In March 1797 the Archduke Charles arrived to replace Alvintzy in command of the Austrian forces facing Bonaparte. Information of the appointment of this much more able general reached Bonaparte, and also that his forces were not yet ready. Bonaparte decided to attack and on 11th March began his advance. With his main body he advanced directly against the Archduke, who was behind the Tagliamento River in north-east Italy, whilst Masséna moved wide on the left towards the Tarvis Pass and Joubert protected the left flank in the Tyrol. The Archduke, who only intended to fight a delaying action, retired east and north through Laibach and Klagenfurt. Masséna, having reached the Tarvis Pass, the Archduke Charles attacked him there on 23rd March and was beaten at the Battle of Malborgetto. On 28th March Bonaparte was at Klagenfurt. Because of his scattered forces and tenuous position he proposed an armistice; but continued to advance in order to demonstrate that he was not suggesting it from weakness. On 7th April he reached Leoben where a truce was agreed, and on 18th April negotiations started which led to the Treaty of Campo Formio on 17th October.

Egyptian Campaign 1798–99

On 12th April 1798 the Army of the Orient was inaugurated with Bonaparte as its commander. On 19th May the main body of the expedition to Egypt sailed from Toulon under a powerful naval escort, and it was joined by convoys from Genoa, Corsica, Marseilles, and Civita Vecchia. On 12th June the expedition reached and captured Malta and on 1st July landed on the Egyptian coast near Alexandria, which was captured the next day.

Bonaparte had selected the best regiments from the Army of Italy and the 36,000 men of the expedition probably constituted the finest fighting force available to France. It was too good for the famed Mameluke horsemen of the Egyptian Army, and on 21st July Bonaparte's victory at the Battle of the Pyramids signified his conquest of Egypt. The next day he occupied Cairo.

On 31st July Nelson surprised and destroyed the French fleet which had escorted Bonaparte's expedition at the Battle of the Nile. The French Army in Egypt was now cut off from France.

On 31st January 1799 Bonaparte invaded Syria with a force of 13,000 men, leaving the remainder of his army to garrison Egypt. On 7th March he assaulted and captured Jaffa, and on 17th March he invested the fortress of St. John of Acre. An attempt by a Turkish army to relieve Acre was defeated at the Battle of Mount Tabor on 17th April. But under the inspiration of the British Commodore Sir Sydney Smith, the defence of the city was too stubborn for Bonaparte, and on 20th May, his army attacked by the plague, he raised the siege and retreated to Egypt, reaching Cairo on 14th June.

On 15th July a Turkish force from Rhodes under British naval escort landed at Aboukir; but it was attacked and defeated by Bonaparte on 25th July.

On 22nd August Bonaparte handed over command to Kléber, and returned to France in a frigate, which managed to elude the patrolling ships of the Royal Navy.

Operations in Italy, 1799

Fighting broke out again in Italy at the end of 1798, the start of hostilities being marked by the temporary capture of Rome in November by a Neapolitan army. The Neapolitans did not enjoy their success for long, for they were expelled again by the French under Championnet on 15th December.

In northern Italy Schérer took over command of the French forces in March 1799. The Army of Italy was not in very good shape, for Bonaparte had taken the best regiments with him to Egypt. Schérer led it against the Austrians at Verona on 26th March and was repulsed, and shortly afterwards, on 5th April, he was defeated at the Battle of Magnano. The formidable Suvarov now arrived with a Russian army and took over command of the Allied forces. Leaving the Austrian Kray to besiege Mantua, he drove the French field army back into retreat.

Schérer was replaced in command by Moreau, but with only 30,000 men to face 65,000, he was unable to stop Suvarov, who entered Milan on 28th April and Turin shortly afterwards. Macdonald, commanding the French army in southern Italy, hurried northwards with 35,000 men to help Moreau. At the Battle of the Trebbia on 17th–19th June Suvarov defeated Macdonald, who retired westwards to join Moreau near Genoa. Suvarov, following up, drove the united French forces back into the Riviera. On 5th August 1799 Joubert replaced Moreau in command. Ten days later Joubert with 35,000 men attacked Suvarov's army of 50,000 at the Battle of Novi. The French were defeated and Joubert was killed. Suvarov's pursuit of the Army of Italy was only halted by the appearance of the French Army of the Alps under Championnet from the Mont Cenis Pass.

Suvarov was now directed to march into Switzerland with 20,000 Russians, handing over command in Italy to the Austrian Marshal von Melas. On 4th November Melas with 60,000 Austrians defeated Championnet, now commanding the Army of Italy, at the Battle of Fossano, and drove the French back across the Alps.

Operations in Germany, March 1799
In March 1799 Jourdan, with the 40,000-strong Army of the Danube, crossed the Rhine at Kehl and advanced against the Austrians commanded by the Archduke Charles, who had twice Jourdan's strength. Jourdan was checked at Ostrach on 21st March. Four days later he attacked the Austrian army at Stockach where he was defeated and forced to retreat to the Rhine. He then resigned his command.

British Expedition to the Netherlands, August–October 1799
In August 1799 a British expeditionary force under the command of the Duke of York landed on the northern end of the peninsula south of Texel. York was reinforced by some 9,000 Russians. At Bergen on 16th September York attacked the Franco-Dutch army commanded by Brune. The attack was unsuccessful due to failures by the Russian command. In a second attack on 2nd October Brune's army was defeated, and he retreated, followed by the Allies. On 6th October York attacked Brune

again, but once more Russian incompetence resulted in failure. On 16th October a convention was arranged by which the Allies withdrew from Dutch territory, but the British retained possession of the Dutch fleet, which had surrendered to them in the Texel.

Operations in Switzerland, 1799

In March 1799 Masséna, commanding the 30,000-strong Army of Helvetia, advanced to cover the right flank of Jourdan's army in its operations of this month. He crossed the upper Rhine near Mayenfeld and captured most of an Austrian force of 7,000 men holding positions around Chur in the Garrisons. Checked, however, on his left, he paused to await the result of Jourdan's offensive. Meanwhile he despatched Lecourbe with 10,000 men on an expedition down the Inn valley into the Tyrol, where he was joined by a small force from the Army of Italy.

As a result of Jourdan's defeat Masséna was thrown on to the defensive and on his right flank Lecourbe had to retreat before superior enemy forces to the upper Rhine.

The following month the Armies of Helvetia and the Danube were combined into a new Army of the Danube under Masséna's command. Faced by an Austrian army of some 80,000 men under the Archduke Charles, Masséna fell back to Zurich with his main body which was about 45,000 strong. On 4th June Charles attacked him, but was repulsed. Nevertheless, three days later, Masséna withdrew slightly to a stronger position.

In August Masséna defeated the Austrian forces in the area of the Rhone and upper Rhine valleys, but was checked at Zurich on 14th. On 16th August the Austrians attacked his left flank at Dottingen. On 25th September Masséna attacked again at Zurich. The Austrians were in considerably weaker strength due to the departure of the Archduke Charles in an attempt to join the Duke of York in the Netherlands and Masséna inflicted a severe defeat on them. Meanwhile Suvarov had pushed through the St. Gotthard Pass with his Russian army, but he arrived too late to assist the Austrians and had to retreat.

The Italian Campaign of 1800

On 9th November 1799 Bonaparte became First Consul and dictator of France. On 25th January 1800 he ordered the formation of a Reserve Army which was to be 60,000 strong and to be formed around Dijon.

Masséna, now commanding the Army of Italy, was attacked on 6th April, and by 24th April he had been defeated and his army split in two; he, with about 10,000 men, was besieged in Genoa whilst Suchet with 13,000 was driven back on Nice.

Following this defeat Bonaparte ordered the Army of the Reserve, which was as yet only about 30,000 strong, to move to Geneva, ready to march into Italy through Switzerland. His intention was to destroy the Austrian army under Melas and to assist this intention Masséna was ordered to hold out at Genoa until at least 30th May. The offensive started in May. Bonaparte led the main body through the Great St. Bernard Pass, whilst diversionary forces were sent through the Mont Cenis, Little St. Bernard, Simplon, and St. Gotthard Passes. After surmounting great difficulties in traversing the pass, the main body was assembling around Ivrea on 26th May. From there Bonaparte advanced to Milan, which he occupied on 2nd June. He had hoped to follow this by marching to Masséna's relief, but after a very gallant defence that tough general, with his remaining men starving, surrendered to his Austrian opponent, Ott, on conditions which allowed him to rejoin the French army with his men, arms, and equipment.

Melas, finding Bonaparte on his lines of communication, turned east to meet him and on 31st May ordered his field army to concentrate at Allessandria. Ott, marching north from Genoa after its fall, encountered Lannes's Corps of the Army of the Reserve at Montebello on 9th June. Lannes was soon reinforced by Victor's Corps and attacked Ott, driving him towards Allessandria.

Bonaparte believed that Melas was unwilling to risk a battle and was withdrawing. Uncertain of the Austrian dispositions, he was advancing with his columns widely separated. On the evening of 13th June the main column encountered enemy forces in Marengo, which withdrew in the direction of Allessandria, a mile away. The Battle of Marengo began the following morning when Melas with about 28,000 men advanced from Allessandria to attack. Bonaparte with the main column had immediately available only the corps of Victor and Lannes, amounting to about 14,000 men, together with three weak cavalry brigades, totalling in all about 2,000 sabres. Melas's attack drove the French back two miles and by the afternoon he thought he had won the battle; but Bonaparte was now reinforced by Desaix's corps, 9,000 strong, and other detachments, and in the evening he counter-attacked. After a bitter struggle in which Desaix was killed, a cavalry charge by Kellerman decided the issue and the Austrian army was routed. The following day Melas asked for an armistice, and by the terms of the subsequent convention he was allowed to withdraw his army behind the River Mincio.

German Campaign of 1800–1801
During May and June Moreau drove the Austrian General Kray into Bavaria, defeating him at Stockach on 3rd May, Möskirch on 5th May, and Hochstadt on 19th June. Operations were then suspended on account of the armistice mentioned above, and which lasted from 15th July till

13th November. When fighting started again Kray had been replaced by the Archduke John. On 3rd December Moreau defeated John decisively at the Battle of Hohenlinden. Moreau then advanced towards Vienna, whilst on his right flank Macdonald invaded the Tyrol from Switzerland, and Brune, who had taken over command in Italy, approached the Julian Alps. On 25th December the Austrians asked for peace terms.

Egypt 1800–1801

On 21st January 1800 Kléber, by the Convention of El Arish, agreed to evacuate Egypt in return for a free passage for his troops to France. This agreement, however, was not ratified by Great Britain. On 20th March Kléber defeated the Turks at Heliopolis and re-occupied Cairo. On 14th June he was assassinated and was succeeded in command by Menou.

On 8th March of the following year a British force under Abercromby landed at Aboukir and defeated Menou's army, but Abercromby was killed. British and Turkish troops took Cairo and Alexandria, and Menou capitulated on 31st August. His remaining 26,000 troops were given free passage to France.

Ulm Campaign, 1805

On 27th March 1802 there was signed the Treaty of Amiens between France and Great Britain. On 16th May 1803 hostilities broke out again, and Napoleon started preparations for the invasion of England. On 2nd December 1804 he was crowned Emperor of the French. The assembly of troops and craft for the invasion attempt was pushed ahead and by the beginning of 1805 the bulk of the French army was concentrated around Boulogne, though some 50,000 men were left under Masséna's command in Italy. However, because of French failure to secure command of the Straits of Dover from the Royal Navy and warlike moves by Austria and Russia, the projected invasion was abandoned.

Austria and Russia were, indeed, about to attack France. The general plan envisaged initial Austrian advances to Milan in Italy and the River Iller in Bavaria. There they would await the arrival of Russian reinforcements; after which the force on the Iller would advance to Strasbourg to engage and destroy the French army. Napoleon learned of the Austrian concentration and on 23rd August the Grand Army of some 200,000 men left the Boulogne area and marched eastwards.

Meanwhile on 2nd September the Austrian General Mack von Leiberich (under the nominal command of the Archduke Ferdinand) marched towards Ulm with 72,000 troops whilst the Archduke Charles prepared to attack Masséna with 94,000. A Russian army 98,000 strong was marching to reinforce Mack and 22,000 Austrians under the Archduke John held the Tyrol.

On 25th September, moving on a wide front, the French army crossed the Rhine. Mack, who was between Munich and Ulm, had not as yet had information of the Grand Army's departure from Boulogne. Because his northern flank was covered by the neutral Prussian territory of Ansbach, he expected that any attack would come from the west. However, whilst Murat with the cavalry encouraged this appreciation by demonstrating before Ulm, the main body of the French Army violated the neutrality of Ansbach and, crossing the Danube east of Ulm, swept round on that city from the east. The Archduke Ferdinand fled from his encircled army and one corps under Werneck managed to break away north to attack the French communications, but Mack with the main body was forced to surrender on 20th October. Four days earlier Murat had caught up with Werneck, and the men of his corps, too, had to lay down their arms, bringing the number of Austrians taken prisoner to about 50,000.

Austerlitz Campaign, 1805

After his victory at Ulm, Napoleon advanced eastwards on 26th October, detaching the corps under Ney and Augereau to prevent interference by Archduke John through the Tyrol.

The disaster at Ulm made the position of the other Austrian armies untenable. On 29th–30th October Masséna was attacked at Caldiero by the Archduke Charles, but this was only to cover the withdrawal of himself and the Archduke John.

The Russian General Kutosov, with 36,000 Russians, and 22,000 Austrians, had deployed along the line of the River Inn between 12th and 25th October. After Mack's defeat and in face of Napoleon's advance, he abandoned the Inn and the fortress of Braunau on 29th October and retreated eastwards. On 9th November he crossed to the north bank of the Danube at Krems, but his Austrian corps was caught on the south bank by the pursuing French and destroyed. On 11th November Kutosov, in greatly superior strength, delivered a surprise attack on Mortier's isolated French corps on the north bank, but although Mortier suffered heavy casualties, Kutosov was driven off.

On 13th November Murat and Lannes, by a staggering piece of bluff, seized the principal bridge across the Danube at Vienna, and French Troops were soon pouring across it on the heels of the retreating enemy.

On 17th December Napoleon decided to pivot his army on Brünn, a fortress and road centre some 70 miles north of Vienna, the latter place being held in strength. The main part of his army (100,000 men) was deployed over a gigantic rectangle of about 70 miles by 50 miles, and so disposed that it could strike in any direction.

The principal enemy force, mainly Russian, was around Olmutz under the command of the Tsar Alexander and was 86,000 strong, whilst the

Archduke Ferdinand with 9,000 men remaining from his army was at Prague. The Archdukes Charles and John, commanding together about 80,000 men, were withdrawing into Hungary, followed by Masséna with 35,000 and with the passes north through the Alps blocked by Ney and Marmont whose corps had a joint strength of 20,000.

Kutosov, the effective commander under Alexander, planned to move round Napoleon's right flank and cut his communications—a move which Napoleon expected. On 27th November the approach march of the Allied troops started. Napoleon immediately began to concentrate his army, taking up a position two miles west of the village of Austerlitz and facing east. Bernadotte's corps, which was widely deployed about 30 miles to the west, and Davout's corps at Vienna, were ordered to join him by forced marches. In order to tempt the Allies to attack, Napoleon had drawn up his troops on low ground, with the right division thinly extended over a front of two miles and exposed so that its weakness could be seen. Most of his army was massed on the left wing with the left flank on the Brünn–Olmutz road.

On 1st December the Allied commanders spotted Napoleon's weak right and, as he had hoped, decided to break through it and cut the French communications with Vienna. The attack was launched the following morning and the French right, now reinforced by Davout, was forced back. By 9 am one-third of the Allied army was attacking this wing and more troops were being moved across to join in the assault. Napoleon then launched Soult's corps in the French centre against the dominating feature of the Heights of Pratzen, splitting the Allied front. Soult then swung right, rolling up the Allied left wing and routing it. Bernadotte's corps then drove through the gap made by Soult and on the French left Lannes's corps attacked the Allied right, which was finally routed by Murat's cavalry. By nightfall the Allied Army no longer existed.

On 4th December the Emperor Francis of Austria surrendered unconditionally, and the remnants of the Russian forces retreated to their own country. On 26th December, by the Treaty of Pressburg, Austria withdrew from the war.

The Jena Campaign, 1806

In 1806 Prussia established a league of North German states in opposition to Napoleon's Confederation of the Rhine. A powerful war party, encouraged by Queen Louise, gained the upper hand, and on 10th August mobilisation of the Prussian army began. On 6th September Prussia invaded Saxony and forced that country into an alliance and on 26th September an ultimatum was presented to France demanding impossible terms.

The French Grand Army was still mainly in South Germany and from here Napoleon planned to strike north in the general direction of Berlin. He assembled his army in north-east Bavaria, close to the Austrian border, and on 8th October the French advance started. In front was a thin screen of light cavalry (because a mass of heavy cavalry in the Thuringian Forest would have caused congestion) and behind it the main bodies marched in three parallel columns on a 30-mile front, at a speed of 15 miles per day. The Prussian left flank was by-passed and the left leading corps under Lannes overwhelmed a small Prussian force at Saalfeld. Having now established that the greater part of the Prussian army was on his left, Napoleon ordered Davout and Bernadotte of his centre, and leading, column to form the right of the army and to move through Naumberg to the West to cut the Prussian lines of communication, whilst the remainder of the army advanced directly on Jena.

The Prussians, learning of Davout's movement, decided that the Duke of Brunswick with 63,000 men should withdraw down the Saale River to join Würtemberg's corps which was marching south to reinforce the main body of the army. Prince Friedrich Hohenlohe was to remain at Jena with 35,000 men and Rüchel at Weimar with 13,000 to cover this withdrawal.

Early on 13th October the French seized the prominent height of the Landgrafenberg immediately north of Jena and overlooking Hohenlohe's army. Here, after dark, the main body of the French army began to assemble; and Napoleon ordered Davout to move up the Saale and attack the left rear of the Prussians, with Bernadotte supporting him if suitably positioned.

At first light on 14th October Napoleon launched his attack on Hohenlohe, and by noon the Prussians were in disorganised retreat from the field. On the same day Davout's leading cavalry encountered Brunswick's advanced guard. The Prussians deployed and attacked, and Davout sustained successive onslaughts by immensely superior forces for over six hours. During this battle around the village of Auerstädt, Brunswick was mortally wounded and King Frederick William took over active command. Bernadotte, who was near Doornburg, about ten miles from Auerstaedt by road, made no attempt to go to Davout's assistance, though the noise of the battle could be heard clearly by his corps. Davout, however, seizing his moment, counter-attacked and inflicted a decisive defeat.

At the end of the day the whole Prussian Army had virtually ceased to exist as a fighting force.

Campaign against Russia, 1807
Faced with Russian hostility, Napoleon decided to advance into East Prussia and to occupy Warsaw, with the object of setting up an independent Poland. On 28th November Murat entered Warsaw and during

the early days of December French troops crossed the Vistula and moved forward against increasing Russian resistance. A Russian counter-attack was repulsed and the French advance continued. On 18th January 1807 Bennigsen, now commanding the Russian Army in this theatre, attacked Ney's corps south of Königsberg and forced it to withdraw. Bennigsen, on 25th January, switched his attack to Bernadotte, who, after crushing the leading Russian troops, withdrew in his turn. Napoleon now concentrated the major part of his army and threatened the Russian communications. Bennigsen retired in the face of this danger and Napoleon, following, caught him up at Preussich–Eylau on 7th February. On 8th February, in a heavy snowstorm, Napoleon attacked with 44,500 men against Bennigsen's 67,000. The first assault against the Russian line in this Battle of Eylau was a failure; Augereau's corps strayed in the driving snow and got badly mauled. Napoleon then ordered Murat to attack with the cavalry reserve, and this, at the cost of heavy casualties, immobilised the Russian centre. Davout now turned the Russian left, but Lestocq's Prussian corps arrived in time to halt Davout's progress. Well after dark Ney's corps started to arrive on the battlefield, and at 8 pm Ney attacked the Russian right flank. Bennigsen withdrew that night and the battle therefore remained an indecisive victory for Napoleon; but both sides had lost about 25,000 men.

On 15th March the French laid siege to Danzig and captured it on 27th April, in spite of Russian and Prussian attempts to relieve it.

On 5th June Bennigsen returned to the offensive and drove Ney back, though Lestocq's corps failed against Bernadotte. Napoleon concentrated his army north of Allenstein and an anxious Bennigsen retired towards a chain of redoubts he had established about Heilsburg. On 10th June the French attacked this line but were repulsed. Nevertheless Bennigsen retreated during the night 11th/12th. By 13th June Napoleon had placed most of his army between the Russians at Friedland and the Prussian corps at Königsberg. He ordered Lannes to seize the town of Friedland, but Lannes encountered Bennigsen's whole army and reported to Napoleon. The Emperor promptly ordered Mortier and Grouchy to march immediately to Lannes's support, and followed them up by despatching also Ney and Nansouty. Bennigsen attacked Lannes early on 14th. The latter, with never more than 26,000 men, managed to hold Bennigsen's 60,000 Russians for nine hours. At noon Napoleon reached the battle area, and he only awaited the arrival of the reinforcing corps to launch a counterattack. In the evening Napoleon attacked Bennigsen's left flank with the corps of Ney and Victor, and Victor's artillery commander, using massed guns as an assault weapon, blasted the defending Russian infantry out of their positions. Unlike Eylau, the Battle of Friedland was a decisive Russian defeat.

On 15th June Lestocq evacuated Königsberg and retreated to Tilsit. On 19th June Napoleon occupied Tilsit and the Russians asked for and were granted a truce. Peace was concluded with Russia and Prussia after a meeting between Napoleon and Alexander on a raft moored in the middle of the River Niemen.

The Campaigns of 1807–1808 in the Peninsula

In November 1807, with Spain's permission, a French army commanded by Junot, invaded Portugal and occupied Lisbon on 1st December. In March 1808 Murat, at the head of another French army, marched into Spain and occupied Madrid. In May Joseph Bonaparte was crowned King of Spain. Later that month insurrection broke out all over Spain. On 20th July a French corps of 20,000 men commanded by Dupont was forced to capitulate to a Spanish army at Baylen. The news reached Madrid on 28th July and on 1st August Joseph withdrew to the Ebro.

Between 1st and 5th August Sir Arthur Wellesley landed with a British army at Mondego Bay, north of Lisbon, and on 21st August he defeated Junot at the Battle of Vimiero. On 30th August Junot capitulated on terms allowing the evacuation of his troops to France by sea.

On 25th September Sir John Moore assumed command of the British Army in Portugal and advanced into Spain. On 9th November Napoleon, having taken over direct command in Spain, began operations to recover control of the country and captured Burgos the following day. On 2nd December he was on the outskirts of Madrid. The city capitulated and he entered it on 4th. On 21st he received news that British infantry were in Valladolid, and started immediately in an effort to destroy Moore's army. Moore soon learned of Napoleon's advance and on 23rd he began to retreat north-westwards.

On 2nd January 1809 Napoleon decided to return to Paris on account of Austrian preparations for war, leaving Soult to continue the pursuit of Moore. At Corunna, on the Spanish coast, Moore turned at bay and on 16th January defeated Soult, though he was mortally wounded in the battle. Freed from French interference, the British troops embarked.

Campaign against Austria 1809

For three years the Archduke Charles had been organising and training a new Austrian army, ready for a fresh trial of strength with France. With a large proportion of Napoleon's army committed in Spain, Austria decided that the time was favourable to strike. On 9th April Austrian armies invaded Bavaria and Italy; the former operation being directed by the Archduke Charles, and the latter by the Archduke John.

On 16th April John's army was attacked by Prince Eugène de Beauharnais at Sacile, east of the Tagliamento River, but Eugène was defeated and retreated behind the Piave. In the Tyrol there was an insurrection and the population waged geurrilla warfare against the Bavarian allies of the French, who supplied the occupying troops.

On 17th April Napoleon arrived at Donauwörth and took over command in Germany, to find that his Chief of Staff, Berthier, had in his deployment dispersed the army dangerously. Napoleon issued orders for a concentration immediately, and after an anxious period and aided by Austrian slowness, this was achieved. On 20th April Napoleon attacked and pierced the Austrian centre at the Battle of Abensberg, driving their right wing towards Ratisbon and their left towards Landeshut. However, the French regiment defending Ratisbon had to capitulate to the Austrians.

On 21st April the left wing under Baron Hiller was defeated again by the French and retreated across the River Isar. Napoleon then turned north to join Davout, whom he had left to contain the Austrian right wing under the Archduke Charles. On 22nd Charles attacked Davout at the Battle of Eckmühl. Davout held him until Napoleon arrived in the afternoon and defeated the Austrians. On 23rd Napoleon launched an attack against Ratisbon, which Charles was holding to cover his retreat across the Danube. The French captured the town but most of the Austrian army escaped. As a result of his victories, Napoleon marched into Vienna on 13th May. Meanwhile Eugène, having heard of the victory at Eckmühl, attacked and drove back the Archduke John on 29th April and by mid-May he had pierced the Austrian frontier defences.

On 21st–22nd May Napoleon fought the Battle of Aspern–Essling against the Austrians, who were holding positions on the north bank of the Danube. This entailed crossing over the main channel of the Danube to the island of Lobau and over the lesser channel separating Lobau from the north bank. On the second day of the battle the Austrians succeeded in breaking the bridge the French had built across the main channel, by sending downstream a huge floating mill. Unable to reinforce or to send artillery ammunition to the troops on the north bank, Napoleon had to withdraw.

Napoleon now vastly increased his bridging train and reinforced his army around Vienna. He had retained possession of the island of Lobau. On 14th June, at Raab, Eugène defeated the Archduke John, who retreated to Pressburg. On the night 3rd/4th July Napoleon began to move troops to the island of Lobau over his new strengthened and protected bridges. The Archduke Charles became aware of this concentration in the island, and in view of the French superiority in cavalry and artillery he withdrew some six or seven miles from the Danube to a line running east and west through Wagram, but he left an outpost line to cover the river crossings from the north of Lobau.

27

Early on 5th July the French crossed the river from Lobau, but by a number of bridges put rapidly into position on the east of the island, thereby outflanking Charles's covering force. The Battle of Wagram was fought on this and the following day. Early on 6th Charles tried to turn the French left and cut them off from their bridges. The attempt failed. Napoleon massed over 100 guns against the Austrian centre, and after the greatest bombardment known up to this time, launched his infantry against the shaken enemy. This attack broke the Austrian centre, whilst Davóut turned their left flank. In this fiercely contested battle the French lost about 34,000 men and the Austrians about 40,000. On 10th July the Austrians requested an armistice.

War in the Peninsula, 1809–1812

In March 1809 Wellesley, once more commanding the British troops in Portugal, was in the Lisbon area. Soult captured Oporto on 29th March but was driven out again by Wellesley on 12th May. On 12th June Wellesley invaded Spain and was joined by a Spanish army. On 28th July he was attacked at Talavera by the combined forces of Victor and Joseph Bonaparte, but he repulsed them and the French retired on Madrid. The Spanish General Cuesta now removed his army, and Wellesley, his lines of communication threatened by other French forces, withdrew into Portugal.

During the winter of 1809–1810 Wellesley, now Viscount Wellington, built a very strong defensive area about Torres Vedras north of Lisbon. In July 1810 the expected French invasion of Portugal started and Wellington retired as the enemy troops rolled forward. On 29th September he took up a strong position at Busaco, where Masséna, the French commander, attacked him. Wellington defeated Masséna's attack and continued his withdrawal to the lines of Torres Vedras, which he occupied on 10th October. Masséna found the lines impregnable to attack and, after sitting down in front of them, he was eventually driven by lack of food to retreat in November.

In April 1811 Masséna attempted to relieve Almeida, which Wellington was besieging and Soult similarly tried to free Badajoz from investment by Beresford. Masséna attacked Wellington on 5th May and was beaten at the Battle of Fuentes de Onoro, whilst on 16th May Soult was defeated by Beresford at Albuera.

On 19th January 1812 the British captured Cuidad Rodrigo and on 19th April Badajoz, the two Spanish frontier fortresses. On 22nd July Wellington defeated Marmont (who had relieved Masséna) at the Battle of Salamanca. On 12th August he occupied Madrid, but after being repulsed at Burgos in November 1812, he had to retreat to the neighbourhood of Cuidad Rodrigo.

The Russian Campaign 1812

During May 1812 Napoleon assembled an army of 430,000 men for the invasion of Russia, with Austria and Prussia as unwilling allies. In the Grand Army about half the infantry and one third of the cavalry were foreign, and they included Spaniards, Poles, Swiss, Croats, Portuguese, Würtembergers, Italians, Dalmatians, Bavarians, Saxons, Illyrians, Neapolitans, Prussians, and Westphalians. The right flank was protected by an Austrian army under Prince Karl von Schwarzenburg.

Opposing the French were the armies of Barclay de Tolly (127,000 strong, north of the Niemen), Bagration (48,000 strong, between the Niemen and the Pripet Marshes), and Tormassov (43,000 strong, guarding the south-west frontier).

On 24th June Napoleon crossed the Niemen above Kovno, which he captured the same day. On 28th he entered Vilna, but on 29th it rained and the Russian earth roads dissolved into mud, bogging down movement and supply. On 8th July Davout occupied Minsk and on 23rd he defeated Bagration at Mogilev. In August the armies of Bagration and Barclay de Tolly were united under the latter's command. Barclay took up a position at Smolensk whilst Bagration moved farther back to Dorogobuzh. On 17th August Napoleon attacked Barclay at Smolensk. He did not capture the town but Barclay retired the next day, dividing his army in half. Rather strangely the half under his immediate command lost its way and was attacked by the French only three miles from Smolensk at Volutino on 19th August. Barclay escaped disaster through French mistakes. On 29th August Barclay was superseded in command by Kutozov. The Russian retreat continued but Kutosov decided to stand and fight at the little town of Borodino. Here, on 7th September, Napoleon defeated the Russians, but the battle was indecisive and casualties on both sides were heavy.

On 8th September Kutosov retreated to Moscow, but he then evacuated the city and marched 60 miles south-east of it to Kolonna. On 14th September Napoleon entered Moscow—an empty triumph, for the Russians had set fire to it and the mostly wooden buildings were almost all destroyed. On 6th September Napoleon had appointed Victor, who was west of Smolensk, to be rear area commander, with his forces constituted as a central reserve.

Because other Russian forces were threatening his line of communications, Napoleon decided on 17th October to withdraw to Smolensk, marching through Kaluga which was the centre of a district rich in food and fodder. On 24th October the French found the road to Kaluga barred at the bridge of Maloyaroslavets and there was an indecisive battle. Napoleon decided to give up the attempt to reach Kaluga and to retire through Mozhaisk. On 4th November the first snow fell and the roads soon became ice-bound. Horses died rapidly, so that guns and wagons were perforce abandoned and much of the cavalry were soon dismounted. Under these conditions morale weakened and in many units discipline collapsed. On 9th November the head of the army marched into Smolensk. On 12th Napoleon decided that the retreat must continue. Four days later Kutozov's advanced guard was encountered, barring the way at Krasnyle west of Smolensk. In a savage fight Napoleon destroyed Ozharovski's corps and cleared the Russians out of his path. In a brilliant operation of 26th–28th November Napoleon defeated the Russian attempts to stop him crossing the Beresina River near Borisov.

On 5th December Napoleon left for Paris to raise a new army and left Murat in command. The army reached Vilna on 4th December and Königsberg on 19th December. During this appalling campaign both sides probably lost over 400,000 men, and Napoleon's Grand Army had practically ceased to exist.

Napoleon's unwilling allies left him as a result of this disaster. The Prussian corps commanded by Yorck, which had been under Macdonald's command at Riga, deserted the French and joined the Russians, and Schwarzenberg's Austrian army marched back to its own country.

Leipzig Campaign, 1813

By April 1813 Napoleon had raised a new army composed of troops from Spain and Italy, conscripts already under training, men from the National Guard, recalled veterans, and new call-ups. Cadres for new units were formed from officers and NCOs of the old Grand Army. However, there was a grave shortage of both horses and trained riders, so that the new cavalry was both small in numbers and poor in quality.

The allied combination which now faced Napoleon consisted of Russia, Prussia, Sweden, and Great Britain, with Austria only waiting till it was safe to join them. The Allies had reached the general line of the Elbe, where they were faced by Eugène with a covering force of some 50,000 men. Napoleon at the head of an army 121,000 strong made contact with Eugène on 30th April. Marching towards Leipzig, his advance guard reached the city on 2nd May and drove the enemy out of it. On the same day the Allied army under Wittgenstein delivered a surprise attack on Ney's corps which was covering the south flank of this advance. Napoleon swung a mass of artillery against Wittgenstein's centre and then broke his front with an infantry attack, driving him from the field. In this Battle of Lützen both sides lost over 20,000 men. Following up the retreating Allies, Napoleon captured Dresden on 9th May. The Allied retreat continued to Bautzen, immediately east of which they had selected a strong position in which they intended to give battle.

During the French advance, Ney had been despatched with four corps to seize Torgau and threaten Berlin. Napoleon now intended to mount a holding frontal attack on the enemy at Bautzen whilst Ney marched south to envelop the Allied right wing. The frontal attack started on 20th May in preparation for Ney's attack the following morning. However, Ney's attack was ill-managed and though the Allies were beaten they were able to withdraw and escape destruction.

On 4th June Napoleon agreed to an Allied request for a seven-week armistice, which was subsequently extended to 17th August. But on 12th August Austria declared war and on 14th August Blücher, who had superseded Wittgenstein, violated the armistice and advanced westwards.

With the advent of Austria, the Allies had three armies in the field: the Northern Army of 110,000 under Bernadotte (now Crown Prince of Sweden), the Silesian of 95,000 under Blücher, and the Bohemian of 230,000 under Schwarzenberg. The last mentioned commander nominally co-ordinated all three armies, but his control was very weak. On 21st August Napoleon attacked Blücher with some 150,000 men and drove him back in retreat, whilst 90,000 faced the Austrian columns winding through the mountains on the Bohemian border and 66,000 under Oudinot contained Bernadotte about Berlin. Davout, advancing from Hamburg, defeated a mixed Allied force and threatened Bernadotte.

Saint-Cyr retired before the greatly superior forces under Schwarzenberg's command, which were advancing towards Dresden, but on 23rd August he counter-attacked and drove Wittgenstein's corps back. Meanwhile Napoleon, leaving Macdonald with the major part of the troops on this front to hold Blücher, hurried by forced marches to Dresden with the remainder; the Imperial Guard covering 90 miles in three days.

On 23rd August Bernadotte and Oudinot met in an encounter battle, and the latter retired to Wittenberg. On 26th August Blücher and Macdonald also blundered into an encounter battle. Heavy rain made the infantry muskets useless and Blücher was thus able to use his superiority in cavalry to defeat Macdonald. Also on 26th August Schwarzenberg attacked Saint-Cyr at Dresden. Napoleon counter-attacked with his reinforcements and drove the Allies back. Next day he continued the attack. Very heavy rain again made it impossible for the infantrymen to fire their muskets and thick mud hampered the cavalry, but Napoleon had every available horse harnessed to his artillery to make it mobile, and defeated Schwarzenberg by his massive firepower. The Allies retired with a loss of 38,000 men against a French loss of only 10,000. After this victory Napoleon rode to Macdonald's army, which was retiring in a demoralised fashion before Blücher, and by his presence restored the troops' fighting spirit and once more made Blücher retreat.

Ney, who had succeeded Oudinot, tried to take Berlin, but his handling of the operation was so inept that he was defeated by Bernadotte at Dennewitz on 6th September.

On 24th September Napoleon began a withdrawal across the Elbe to await attack. He then decided that Dresden was too close to the Bohemian mountains for use as a central position, or point of pivot, and selected Leipzig to replace it. Blücher and Bernadotte had joined forces, but they were sandwiched by the movement of the French forces converging on Leipzig, and at Blücher's suggestion they escaped westwards across the Saale instead of trying to retreat eastward across the Elbe.

In the middle of October all three Allied armies moved towards Leipzig to engage Napoleon's main army and the Battle of Leipzig opened on 16th. On this first day the Allies suffered local defeats from the French forces, but on 17th Napoleon decided to withdraw westwards and that night, as a preliminary step, the French Army retired into a perimeter nearer Leipzig. The withdrawal began at about 2 am on 19th, and would probably have been successful if sheer incompetence had not led to a bridge being blown whilst the troops were still crossing and thousands were still on the enemy side. Both sides in the Battle of Leipzig lost about 50,000 men.

Bavaria had now joined the Allies and an army from that country was manoeuvring to block Napoleon's retreat until the pursuing Allied forces could reach him. But at the Battle of Hanau on 30th–31st October Napoleon, again employing a massed artillery, routed the Bavarians. Late on 31st he crossed the Rhine at Mayence with formed bodies of about 80,000 men, but another 40,000 stragglers came along behind.

Campaign in the Peninsula, 1813–14

In 1813 Wellington assumed the offensive and on 17th May Joseph left Madrid and fell back to the Ebro. On 21st June Wellington attacked and defeated Joseph's army at the Battle of Vitoria, and Joseph retired into France. Soult now took over command.

On 25th July Soult mounted a counter-attack, but after six days fighting the French were defeated at the Battle of Sorauren and driven back over the Pyrenees. On 31st August San Sebastian fell to the British forces. On 10th November, at the Battle of Nivelle, Wellington's army drove through the Pyrenees and entered the plains of France. In five days of fighting from 9th December Wellington defeated Soult at the Battle of the Nive. On 10th April 1814 Wellington defeated Soult again at the Battle of Toulouse and captured the city.

Campaign in France 1814

By 1st January 1814 Napoleon had assembled an army of about 118,000 men between Antwerp and Lyons, but many of his soldiers were young and untrained. The Allies were already advancing to attack; Schwarzenberg had passed through Basle on 21st December, marching towards Langres, Blücher crossed the Rhine on 1st January and was striking west through Lorraine, and a few days later Winzingerode was approaching Liege. Victor and Ney, supported by Mortier, were directed to oppose Schwarzenberg, and Marmont and Macdonald to operate against Blücher, but there was little effective opposition to the Allied forces during January.

On 26th January Napoleon arrived at Chalons-sur-Marne to learn that Blücher was approaching St. Dizier and Schwarzenberg was at Bar-sur-Aube. He advanced first against Blücher and drove him back at Brienne on 29th January and at La Rothiere on 30th January. However, on 1st February Blücher counter-attacked at La Rothiere and after an indecisive action Napoleon withdrew, reaching Troyes on 3rd February.

Blücher now started to move towards Paris along the valley of the Marne. On 5th–7th February Napoleon, concentrating his main body at Nogent-sur-Seine, ordered Marmont to Sezanne, left Victor at Nogent to contain Schwarzenberg, and on 9th February marched north. On 10th February he defeated Olsuviev's corps of Blücher's army at Champaubert. He then turned west and defeated the corps of Sacken and Yorck of the same army at Montmirail on 11th February. Following them up, he beat them again at Chateau Thierry on 12th February, driving them across the Marne. Blücher with the corps of Kapsevitsch and Kleist was now moving west whilst Marmont retired slowly in front of him. Napoleon returned to Montmirail and beat Blücher on 14th February at Vauchamps.

Meanwhile Victor had had to abandon Nogent which he was unable to hold against Schwarzenberg's superior numbers. Blücher having been disposed of, Napoleon turned south, beat Schwarzenberg at Montereau on 18th February, and re-entered Troyes on 24th February.

Blücher, having reorganised his beaten troops, again moved towards Paris and on 27th February crossed the Marne at La Ferté. Marmont and Mortier were opposing his advance and they attacked and drove back two of Blücher's corps on 28th February. Blücher attacked them with his whole army on 1st March but was repulsed. Leaving Macdonald on 27th February to watch Schwarzenberg, Napoleon marched rapidly north, and arrived at La Ferté on 1st March, but the bridge over the Marne was broken and his crossing delayed. However his advanced guard was north of Rocourt on 3rd March.

Napoleon had hardly left Macdonald before Oudinot's corps was defeated by Schwarzenberg at Bar-sur-Aube, and Macdonald eventually had to withdraw north of the Seine on 6th March.

Blücher, retiring in front of Napoleon, was faced with the problem of crossing the Aisne. He was saved from disaster by the premature surrender of the French garrison of Soissons, giving him the use of the town bridge. Napoleon crossed the Aisne further upstream and Blücher, reinforced by two fresh corps, marched to strike his flank, but he was defeated by Napoleon at the Battle of Craonne on 7th March. Blücher, now much stronger than Napoleon, took up a defensive position at Laon. Marmont, commanding the French right wing, was caught unprepared by a surprise attack, and on 10th March Napoleon withdrew to Soissons.

On 14th March Schwarzenberg succeeded in crossing the Seine against Macdonald's defence. But on 13th March Napoleon turned on an isolated Prussian corps at Rheims, decisively defeating it and recapturing the city. This stopped Schwarzenberg's advance and Blücher, who had moved south to Compiègne and other points, withdrew hastily to Laon. On 17th March Napoleon left Marmont and Mortier to watch Blücher and marched against Schwarzenberg. At Arcis-sur-Aube he repulsed an attack by Schwarzenberg in greatly superior force and withdrew to St. Dizier. Winzengerode followed Napoleon whilst the main bodies of the Allied armies advanced towards Paris. On 26th March Marmont and Mortier, trying to delay this advance, were defeated at Fère-Champenoise on 25th March. On 27th March Napoleon gained his last victory by beating Winzengerode at St. Dizier.

On 31st March Marmont surrendered Paris. Napoleon, who had arrived at Fontainebleau, abdicated on 11th April and retired to Elba on 4th May.

Waterloo Campaign 1815

On 1st March 1815 Napoleon landed at Cannes and marched to Paris, where he arrived on 20th March. In amazingly short time new armies were ready to take the field. The alarmed Allies hastened to assemble their own armies, and by June Wellington's British/Dutch army and Blücher's Prussian army were in Belgium, whilst the Austrians under Schwarzenberg were on the Rhine and a Russian army commanded by Barclay de Tolly was marching westward.

On 11th June Napoleon left Paris for the north, aiming to defeat his nearest enemies before the others were ready. On 14th his army had concentrated near Charleroi. On 16th, sending Ney to seize Quatre Bras with the left wing, Napoleon attacked and defeated Blücher at Ligny. Ney was checked at Quatre Bras by Wellington's troops. On 17th Napoleon sent Grouchy in pursuit of the Prussians and directed the remainder of his army against Wellington, who had fallen back to a defensive position that he had selected at Waterloo. On 18th June Napoleon attacked Wellington but was unable to break his defence. When the Prussians, marching to Wellington's assistance, began to arrive on the French right flank, Wellington counter-attacked. The French army dissolved in defeat.

CHAPTER TWO

CAVALRY

General

The cavalry of the French army suffered much less than the infantry from the upheavals of the Revolution. One would have expected this aristocratic arm to have been the worst affected, and it was certainly regarded with great suspicion by the unpleasant demagogues who seized the reins of civil power. However, it was impossible to improvise mounted troops rapidly, and it was necessary, therefore, to retain those cavalry officers who were prepared to serve under the Republican Government.[1]

In 1791 a step was taken to eradicate the Royalist traditions; regiments were deprived of their old distinctive titles and were allotted numbers. The step was not entirely successful, because the old names were so popular and were a source of such pride amongst both officers and men in many regiments that they continued in unofficial use. Marbot records[2] that when he joined the 1st Hussars he found that it had retained all its customs and traditions of pre-Revolutionary days when it had been the Berchény Hussars. (A large number of both officers and men had, however, emigrated.) Marbot draws the following picture of a *maréchal des logis* (cavalry sergeant) who had been detailed to undertake his instruction: 'Shako over the ear; sabre trailing; face disfigured and divided into two by an immense scar; upturned moustaches half a foot long, stiffened with wax, and losing themselves at the ears; two great plaited tresses of hair hanging from the temples, which appeared from under the shako and fell on the chest; and with all this what an air!—the air of a swaggering ruffian, emphasised by a speech which was jerked out in a most barbarous Franco-Alsatian jargon.'

Nevertheless, in spite of a tremendous *esprit de corps* in many regiments, the French cavalry at the start of the revolutionary wars was generally poor. Most of the old units were gallant enough and fought well, but discipline and morale had suffered and the tactical handling of the cavalry was bad. In 1793 the cavalry in the Army of the North, for instance, was quite ineffective; and on the Rhine, in the following year, Saint-Cyr acknowledged the superiority of the Prussian cavalry, calling it, 'the best military cavalry in Europe'. In the Army of Italy in 1796 Napoleon Bonaparte inherited a cavalry which had had little experience, other than minor actions, and some of his regiments were conspicuously bad. Marmont, in terms probably exaggerated by exasperation, wrote to his family that it was difficult to describe how little courage the cavalry had, adding, 'The cavalry lacked all the intrepidity that the infantry possessed.' However, when the campaign moved from the mountains to flat country where mounted troops could operate effectively, the cavalry improved very rapidly; and Murat soon distinguished himself as a cavalry leader by defeating enemy cavalry in a charge at the head of two regiments of *Chasseurs à Cheval*. Of this incident Napoleon wrote: 'This was the first time that the French cavalry, seeing the bad state in which it had been, measured itself with advantage against the Austrian cavalry. It took nine guns, two colours, and 2,000 men.'[3]

During these early campaigns, the French cavalry learned from the enemy, gaining practical training and experience in the field.

At its peak the cavalry of Napoleon was very good indeed; probably the best in the world on a comparison of regiments and higher formations. In a letter to Lord John Russell of 31st July 1826, Wellington gave the following opinion: 'I considered our cavalry so inferior to the French for want of order, that although I considered one of our squadrons a match for two French, yet I did not care to see four British opposed to four French, and still more so as the numbers increased, and order (of course) became more necessary. They could gallop but could not preserve order.'[4] In other words, the French excelled in battle drill and tactical handling, and the larger the formation the more this superiority told.

Yet Napoleon had no high opinion of his cavalry as late as the start of the campaign against Prussia in 1806, in spite of their successes against Austrian and Russian cavalry in the Ulm and Austerlitz campaigns. The Prussian cavalry had a high reputation due to their performance in the wars of Frederick the Great, but the test of battle showed that Napoleon had overrated them. The cavalry of both sides in this campaign were poor in reconnaissance. General Savary, Duc de Rovigo, says in his *Mémoires* that, 'Our cavalry, so ardent on the battlefield, was directed without intelligence when it was a question of getting news of the enemy.'[5]

On the battlefield the French cavalry was always a most formidable arm, in spite of the serious losses in Russia and the poor performance of some of its new regiments in 1813; indeed on the last field of all—Waterloo—its furious charges showed that it had lost none of its gallantry and *élan*. The cavalry, particularly the light cavalry, attracted the young officer for whom war was a romance and whose code of honour included a gay chivalry and such courtesy to his enemies as circumstances might allow.

Organisation

In 1789 there were 62 cavalry regiments, each of four squadrons. Of these, 26 were heavy cavalry (including two of carabiniers), 6 were hussars, 18 were dragoons, and 12 were *chasseurs*. The headquarters of a regiment included a colonel in command, a colonel as second-in-command, a lieutenant-colonel, a major, a quartermaster, two standard bearers, an *adjudant* (regimental sergeant-major), a chaplain, and a surgeon. In a squadron there were two captains, two lieutenants, two second-lieutenants, a gentleman cadet, a *maréchal des logis chef* (squadron sergeant-major), a *maréchal des logis* (cavalry sergeant), a *fourrier* (quartermaster-corporal), 8 *brigadiers* (cavalry corporals), 2 trumpeters, a clerical brother, a farrier, and 132–152 troopers (depending on the type of regiment). (In the preceding year the commanding officer of the regiment had been entitled *Mestre de Camp de Cavalerie*, instead of colonel.) This establishment should have produced 629 to 729 men in each regiment, but in fact these figures were never realised and the mounted strengths of squadrons varied between 80 and 100. However, the Royalist cavalry was magnificently equipped and mounted, and the NCOs were excellent.[6]

In 1791 there was a change in the regimental organisation. The short-lived rank of *Mestre de Camp de Cavalerie* disappeared and the commanding officer was once more a colonel. The second colonel was replaced by a lieutenant-colonel, so that there were now two of these, and the rank of major was abolished. The remainder of the regimental headquarters was made up by a *quartier-maitre trésorier* (paymaster quartermaster), a surgeon major, a chaplain, 2 *adjudants* (RSMs), a trumpet-major, and 5 *maitres ouvriers* (saddler, armourer, tailor, cobbler, and breeches-maker). The regiment was divided into squadrons, each of two companies consisting of two troops. In regiments of carabiniers, hussars, and *chasseurs à cheval* there were four squadrons, whilst in regiments of dragoons and 'cavalry' (i.e. heavy cavalry) there were only three. A company had a captain, a lieutenant, 2 second-lieutenants, a *maréchal des logis chef*, 2 *maréchaux des logis*, a *brigadier-fourrier*, 4 *brigadiers*, 54 troopers (of which 4 were dismounted), and a trumpeter. The number of squadrons in dragoon and cavalry regiments was increased to four in 1793, but reduced again to three in 1796. The number of troopers in a company varied greatly from time to time but never exceeded 100.[7]

Emigration depleted the corps of officers in cavalry considerably, as one would expect of an arm of the service which included so many noblemen; even two entire regiments—the *Royal Allemand* (15th Cavalry) and Saxe Hussars (4th Hussars)—went over to the enemy, and regimental numbers had to be re-adjusted accordingly.

In 1793 the title of colonel was replaced by *chef de brigade* and lieutenant-colonels became *chefs d'escadron*[8], a title which eventually was equivalent to the British rank of major. There were two *chefs d'escadron* in regiments of heavy cavalry and three in light cavalry.[9]

The numbers of regiments in the different categories were altered in 1791 and again in 1792. In the former year the total number of regiments was increased to 83, of which 29 were (heavy) cavalry (including two regiments of carabiniers), 20 were dragoons, 23 *chasseurs à cheval* and 11 hussars. In 1792 the regiments classified as cavalry were reduced to 27, dragoons were increased by one to 21, and *chasseurs à cheval* and hussars were each increased by two regiments to 25 and 13 respectively.[10] The reduction in the number of regiments of heavy cavalry was due to the difficulty in obtaining large horses. When Napoleon Bonaparte became First Consul he converted many more to light cavalry regiments for the same reason, so that in 1803 there remained only 12 regiments of 'cavalry' (all of which became cuirassiers with steel breast- and back-plates), and 2 regiments of carabiniers.[11]

The 24 new regiments formed in 1791–92 were mostly very bad indeed at first, owing to the lack of experienced officers and of training in horse mastership. Some of the more fortunate obtained officers and men from the disbanded *Maison du Roi* and *Gendarmerie* of the old regime. Others, mostly *chasseurs à cheval*, were formed from the cavalry elements of departmental legions and separate corps of volunteer cavalry.[12]

In April 1792 a company of mounted Guides was authorised for each general-in-chief (i.e. army commander) to provide him with an escort and a pool of despatch riders for the transmission of orders. The establishment was 21 officers and men; but Bonaparte, when commanding the Army of Italy increased the strength of his company to 160 all ranks, and this unit eventually became the nucleus of the *chasseurs à cheval* of the Guard.

In 1797 Hoche, commander of the Army of the Sambre and Meuse, reorganised his cavalry in a fashion that Napoleon, in general, retained in the Imperial Army. Up till this time the cavalry had been split up between the various infantry divisions, except for a few regiments retained in army reserve. Hoche allotted, instead, one regiment of *chasseurs à cheval* to each division for reconnaissance and protective duties; whilst the bulk of the cavalry he organised into divisions according to category (i.e. hussar, dragoon, *chasseur*, and cavalry divisions). He thus had under his direct control as a reserve a powerful cavalry corps. Moreau, commander of the Army of the Rhine and Moselle on Hoche's right, did not like this idea and stuck to the old system; and a typical division in his army (that of Duhesme) consisted of seven infantry regiments, a regiment of hussars, a regiment of dragoons, and a regiment of 'cavalry'. Moreau's cavalry reserve consisted of six cavalry regiments and one dragoon regiment.[13]

As First Consul, Napoleon restored the title of colonel and approved the addition of a second in command of a regiment with the title of *major*, who was to carry out those administrative functions previously the responsibility of the lieutenant-colonel. The absence of a rank between *chef d'escadron* and colonel had created difficulties. Although the old lieutenant-colonels had become *chefs d'escadrons*, they had become essentially squadron commanders, as their rank implied, and an equivalent of the lieutenant-colonel in a cavalry regiment was needed. Napoleon asked some of his senior officers what this rank should be. Berthier and others thought that the grade of lieutenant-colonel ought to be revived; but Napoleon disliked this proposal because under the old regime colonels were great lords who passed their life at court and rarely appeared for regimental duty. Administration and training were carried out by the Lieutenant-Colonel, so-called because he exercised command on behalf of the Colonel of the Regiment. Since the Revolution, however, colonels had carried out their duties of command and an officer styled lieutenant-colonel would be confused with his commanding officer because their juniors would address both of them as 'Colonel'. Napoleon decided, therefore, that the rank of the second-in-command of a regiment should be major.[14]

On 10th October 1801 Napoleon decreed that each cavalry regiment should have an *Elite* company which should always form on the right of the line and would be the equivalent in the cavalry of the infantry grenadier company. The élite company was always the senior company of the two in the 1st Squadron.[15]

By a decree of 24th September 1803 the number of dragoon regiments was raised to 30, and in 1805 24 of them were put on to a mixed organisation consisting of three mounted squadrons and one dismounted squadron—each squadron having two companies. From these 24 regiments Napoleon formed, when required, a dragoon army corps of three mounted divisions and one dismounted division. The mounted division was organised into two brigades each of three regiments. The dismounted squadrons were removed from regiments to form the dismounted division; and these taken from the regiments forming a mounted brigade were grouped into a battalion of six companies. There were thus two battalions from a mounted division, and these together formed a regiment; so that the dismounted division consisted of three regiments, and it was allotted ten guns for its artillery support.

The idea behind this organisation was the provision of a mobile force to cover the landing in England of the invading army. This operation, of course, never took place, but the dragoon organisation was used in the crossing of the Rhine in 1805. The loss of their horses and service in the dismounted dragoons was heartily disliked by both officers and men; even though Napoleon accorded them the privilege of marching with the Guard. In 1808 eight sappers were added to the establishment of a dismounted dragoon regiment.[16]

On 31st August 1806 a fourth squadron was added to each cuirassier regiment. The regiment then consisted of the following officers and other ranks: on regimental headquarters 1 colonel, 1 major, 2 *chefs d'escadrons*, 2 *adjudants majors* (adjutants), 1 paymaster-quartermaster, 1 surgeon-major, 1 *aide major*, 2 *sous-aides majors*, 2 *adjudants*, 1 corporal trumpeter, 1 veterinary surgeon, 6 *maîtres* (tailor, saddler, cobbler, breeches-maker, armourer, and spur-maker); and in each company 1 captain, 1 lieutenant, 1 second lieutenant, 1 *maréchal des logis chef*, 4 *maréchaux des logis*, 1 *fourrier*, 8 corporals, 82 troopers, and 1 trumpeter. The regimental strength varied between 800 and 960 troopers.[17]

Napoleon was impressed with the effectiveness of Polish cavalry armed with the lance, and also with the way the Cossacks wielded this weapon. In 1807 he incorporated a regiment of Polish lancers into the Guard, and in 1810 he added a second regiment, which became known, from their uniform, as the 'Red Lancers'. Satisfied with their performance, on 18th June 1811 he converted six regiments of dragoons (the 1st, 3rd, 8th, 9th, 10th, and 29th) into the 1st to 6th Light Horse Lancers. The two Polish regiments were then renumbered the 7th and 8th Light Horse Lancers. A further lancer regiment, the 9th, was provided by converting the 30th *Chasseurs à Cheval*.[18]

The cavalry of the Ulm campaign provides an example of Napoleon's adoption of the higher organisation of the cavalry as devised by Hoche. There was one division of light cavalry (hussars and *chasseurs à cheval*) in each of the six army corps of the field force; whilst the cavalry reserve under Murat consisted of two cuirassier divisions, four dragoon divisions, and one dismounted dragoon division. In the Jena campaign the organisation was somewhat similar; each of the six corps included a division of light cavalry, and the cavalry reserve (again commanded by Murat) consisted of two heavy divisions (cuirassiers and carabiniers), four dragoon divisions, and two light cavalry brigades.

Horses

The best trained and equipped cavalry cannot be really effective unless it is suitably mounted. This does not infer only that horses should be of good quality and able to carry the cavalryman and his equipment, but also that they should have sufficient stamina to stand up to the hardships of a campaign in the theatre of war concerned. By these standards the French cavalry were by no means always well mounted.

Major G. Tylden[19] says that the heaviest French cavalry encountered by the British in the Peninsula were, 'their Dragoons, medium cavalry and not always very well mounted while in Spain.' British cavalry officers learned, however, the 'tremendous impact of true heavy cavalry, big men on big horses, in a charge knee to knee'. In the British Army the hunter was considered the ideal mount; heavy weight for the heavy cavalry and light weight for the light cavalry. But the heavy type was expensive to produce and needed considerably more feed than lighter horses. For the latter reason the British heavyweight hunter was not suitable for all theatres of war; nor did he take kindly to extremes of climate.

Napoleon took a keen interest in the horses of the cavalry. Marbot records[20] that Napoleon would review an army corps, and that this was a most severe and rigorous inspection. Amongst the questions he would ask the commanding officer of a cavalry regiment were: 'How many Norman horses have you? How many Breton? How many German?' These questions were always made in an abrupt and imperative tone, accompanied by a piercing look; and woe betide the colonel who gave a hesitant reply!

In the campaign of 1806 the Prussian and Saxon cavalry were better mounted than the French, and Napoleon, knowing this, remounted a large proportion of his cavalry on captured German horses after the Prussian defeat.[21]

Nevertheless, many French regiments were mounted on excellent horses and the best commanding officers took great pains over their quality. Regiments were responsible for obtaining their own remounts and a colonel had authority to purchase locally the number of horses he needed to complete his regiment.[22] Parquin, who enlisted in the 20th *Chasseurs à Cheval* in 1803, says[23] that the regiment was excellently mounted, and that the 1st Squadron had black horses, the 2nd Squadron bay horses, the 3rd Squadron chestnut, and the 4th Squadron (as well as the band and trumpeters) grey horses.

There were special standards for the horses of the cavalry of the Guard. In 1810 the Horse Grenadiers were mounted on black Normandy horses, aged from 4 to 5, purchased in Caen, and having full manes and tails; the *Chasseurs à Cheval* had horses of either bay or chestnut; in the Polish Lancers each troop had horses of the same colour: chestnut, black, bay, or dark grey; and the Dragoons of the Guard were mounted on bay or chestnut horses.[24]

The French heavy cavalry rode Norman and Flemish horses which were great weight carriers but very heavy and slow. Launched into a charge in the evening at the Battle of Eckmühl with a long day's work behind them, they were unable to get beyond a trot. The captured German horses all went to the light cavalry regiments, but most of these were mounted on French horses.[25]

Horses in the Russian army are commented on by General Sir Robert Wilson, who was attached to that army during the campaigns of 1806–1807. He writes[26]: 'The Russian cavalry is certainly the best mounted of any upon the continent; and as English horses can never serve abroad in English condition, it is the best mounted in Europe.' (He explains his comment on English horses as follows: 'At least so long as the English cavalry are nurtured to require warm stables, luxurious beds, etc.—so long as efficiency abroad is sacrificed to appearance at home.') 'The heavy Russian horses,' says Wilson, 'are matchless for an union of size, strength, activity and hardiness; whilst formed with the bulk of the English cart-horse, they have so much blood as never to be coarse . . . They are chiefly bred in the plains of the Don and the Volga.' On the other hand, the irregular Cossack cavalry were, he says, 'Mounted on a very little, ill-conditioned horse, which can walk at the rate of five miles an hour with ease, or, in his speed, dispute the race with the swiftest.'

The type of horse on which the French heavy cavalryman was mounted is shown by the following incident. Marbot, having lost his horse, was provided temporarily with one from a neighbouring cuirassier regiment. This, he said,[27] was an enormous animal, heavy and incapable of carrying an ADC rapidly from one point to another. This sounds as if some of the cuirassier regiments were mounted on heavy draught horses, perhaps of the Percheron type. Marshal Lannes noticed Marbot's predicament, and the colonel of the Würtemberg Light Horse directed his orderly to dismount and to hand over his excellent horse to Marbot. This horse bore the regimental brand of stag's antlers on the left leg. (Branding of horses to show regimental ownership was doubtless a very necessary precaution.)

After the disaster in Russia in 1812, the horses obtained by many of the newly raised cavalry regiments were very poor, and, in addition, officers and men all too often lacked any knowledge of horsemastership. Baron von Odeleben, a Saxon officer on Napoleon's staff in 1813, states[28] that a considerable number of horses were taken from various depots and also collected from every part of France to supply the new regiments. Hurried marches and the weight of the saddlery to which they were not yet accustomed reduced many of them to a poor condition—so poor that a new detachment of cavalry could be recognised as such by the smell from the unfortunate horses' saddle sores.

Uniforms and Equipment

The cavalry, before the Revolution, wore blue, with the exception of the dragoons who were dressed in green. Under the new regime the colour of their uniforms remained basically the same (unlike the infantry, most of whom had to change from their traditional white to blue). The blue coat of the Royalist heavy cavalry had facings of a colour distinctive to the regiment; breeches and waistcoat were of leather; the hat was similar to that of the infantry; boots were long; the cartridge pouch was carried on a white leather cross-belt; and the housings on the horse were of blue cloth trimmed with the colonel's colour. Only one regiment still wore cuirasses—the *Cuirassiers du Roi* (which became the 7th Cavalry in 1791). Hussars wore the traditional dress of dolman and pelisse in a variety of colours, together with a high shako without a peak. *Chasseurs à cheval*, like dragoons, wore green, but their headdress was the standard army hat whilst the dragoons had a helmet without visor, topped by a flowing horsehair crest.[29]

There was not much immediate change in the uniforms after the Revolution, but it was simplified and lost much of its former elegance. The insignia of the colonel disappeared and the tricolour cockade adorned the headdress. In 1792 troopers belonging to regiments of heavy cavalry, hussars, and chasseurs were allowed to wear a moustache and to cant the headdress slightly over the right eye. (These privileges were not extended to dragoons.)

Weapons carried by cavalrymen included pistols, carbines (or other equivalent smooth-bore flintlocks), swords, lances, and occasionally bayonets; and these changed little during the whole period of the Revolutionary and Napoleonic wars. Heavy cavalry (later cuirassiers and carabiniers) were armed with a pistol, carbine, and straight sword. After 1812 the carbine was replaced by the musketoon, which had a longer barrel and range, and in the last campaigns the musketoon was withdrawn from the cuirassiers, for issue to new infantry levies, and replaced by a second pistol. Light cavalry (hussars and chasseurs) had pistol, musketoon, and a heavy sabre. Dragoons carried a sword, a pistol, and a light musket (which was suited for their occasional infantry role).[30]

The uniforms of the cavalry, which were worn with minor alterations throughout the Imperial period, were laid down in detail by a decree of 24th September 1803.

Cuirassier regiments were clad in a short blue coat over which were back and breast plates. Their headdress was a steel helmet with a flowing black horsehair crest. For the colours of their facings, etc., they were divided into four groups each of three regiments: the 1st, 2nd, and 3rd *Cuirassiers* had scarlet; the 4th, 5th, and 6th, golden yellow; the 7th, 8th, and 9th, pale yellow; and the 10th, 11th, and 12th, rose. The 13th and 14th *Cuirassiers*, which were formed after 1803, were allotted a colour known as lees of wine.

Carabiniers wore the short blue coat without body armour and a grenadier pattern bearskin as a headdress.

Dragoons retained their traditional long green coat, but they were divided for distinctive facing colours into five groups of six regiments in numerical order; the respective colours being scarlet, crimson, deep rose, pale yellow, and golden yellow. Their headdress was a copper helmet encircled by a tiger skin turban with a black flowing horsehair crest.

Chasseurs à cheval, the original French light cavalry (of which there were 26 regiments at this time) wore a short green coat without facings but adorned with much braid, green breeches, and an infantry pattern shako with plume.

The traditional hussar dress came from Hungary; and in the old French Army the Hussar regiments were composed of foreigners, of whom some were Hungarians but most were Germans. By 1789, however, there were a fair number of Frenchmen in the regiments, and by 1803 both officers and men were mainly French. The ten Hussar regiments of that year had the most showy uniforms in the army, displaying a variety of colours with a unique arrangement for each regiment. The items of uniform to which these colours applied were the dolman (a short close-fitting jacket), the pelisse (an over-jacket, generally slung from the left shoulder), the breeches, the braid on the uniform, and the barreled sash worn round the waist. The 1st Hussars had dolman, pelisse, and breeches of sky blue, white braid, and a scarlet sash. In the 2nd Hussars dolman and pelisse were chestnut-brown, whilst the sash and breeches were sky-blue and the braid white. All the uniform garments of the 3rd Hussars were silver grey with white braid. The 4th Hussars were royal blue dolman and breeches, but the pelisse was scarlet, the sash white, and the braid yellow. The 5th Hussars had a scarlet dolman, dark blue pelisse, sky-blue breeches and sash, and lemon coloured braid. The 6th Hussars had dolman and pelisse of the same colours as the 5th, but breeches and sash were also scarlet and the braid was yellow. In the 7th Hussars the dolman and pelisse were both dark green, the breeches and sash were scarlet, and the braid was pale yellow. The colours worn by the 8th Hussars were exactly the same as those of the 7th, except that the braid was white. The 9th Hussars had sky-blue pelisse, breeches, and sash, but the dolman was scarlet and the braid yellow. The 10th Hussars differed from this slightly in having sky-blue dolman, pelisse, and breeches, with white braid and a scarlet sash. These Hussar colours were not changed during the Napoleonic era, and their distinctive dress became a jealously guarded tradition of each regiment. Hussar generals often liked to wear in action the uniform of the regiment that they had previously commanded.[31]

Men in the élite companies of Chasseur and Hussar regiments wore bearskin busbies, whilst those of Dragoon companies wore bearskin grenadier caps. In addition red epaulettes were worn by chasseurs and dragoons.[32]

In August 1806, just before the campaign in Prussia, men were ordered to cut off their queues and, in those Chasseur and Hussar regiments that wore them, the long plaited tresses. This order was much resented by the men.[33]

For this same campaign *chasseurs à cheval* were issued with bayonets. In Parquin's regiment, the 20th, the only use the men found for them was to dig up potatoes in a field, just before the battle of Jena; and most of the men left their bayonets in that field.[34]

Sometime during or after this campaign the dress of the chasseurs was changed. Their green hussar-pattern dolman and braided breeches were now replaced by a long green coat, and pantaloons garnished with tanned sheepskin.[35]

Marbot, writing of the Wagram campaign, says that the dandies of the Army had taken to wearing trousers of an excessive bagginess, which looked smart enough when mounted but which were a hindrance when on foot. He mentions a young subaltern called La Bourdonnaye, who was attached to the staff of Marshal Lannes. During an action Lannes ordered La Bourdonnaye to dismount and run to a bridge to give an order to the troops in the locality. 'The spurs of this young man,' writes Marbot, 'caught in his trousers; he fell and we believed him dead! He got up briskly, however, and started to run again, but the Marshal cried out, "Isn't it absurd to come to war with six ells of cloth round one's legs?" La Bourdonnaye, who was in action for the first time under the eyes of the Marshal and was anxious to prove his zeal, drew his sword, cut and ripped his trousers off from mid-leg, and, freer of movement, resumed his way with knees and legs bare! Although we were under the fire of the enemy the Marshal and his staff laughed till they were in tears at this new costume, and, on his return, La Bourdonnaye was complimented on his presence of mind.'[36]

In 1812 dragoons stopped wearing the long coat and changed to a short one, also green, with copper convex buttons. With this went breeches and waistcoat which were white for review order and grey for service dress. Breeches were accompanied by long boots, but gradually the former were replaced by grey cloth trousers garnished with leather. The 1803 pattern helmet was retained. These changes in dress reflected, rather belatedly, the change in function of Dragoon regiments from mounted infantry to heavy cavalry; and this was recognised too by the men being given permission to grow moustaches. (In Spain, like the sappers, many of them wore beard and whiskers as well.)[37]

In Spain many regiments were unable to procure cloth of the right colour for their uniforms, and, as depots were unable to supply it, replacement uniforms were made out of the brown cloth found in Capuchin monasteries.[38]

The cavalry of the Guard wore special uniforms. The Horse Grenadiers were clad in a blue grenadier coat with orange aiguilette and shoulder knots, white breeches, long boots, and a grenadier fur cap trimmed with orange cord and without a frontal plate. The housings for the horses were blue trimmed with orange braid. The trooper's cloak was white and was normally carried folded on the valise behind the saddle.[39]

In the *Chasseurs à Cheval* of the Guard officers and men wore busbies and hussar pattern dolmans and pelisses (the former green and the latter scarlet) with an aiguillette on the left shoulder. Officers' horses had panther skin shabraques. This uniform was derived from Napoleon's Company of Guides. (Not all these companies of Guides were dressed alike. When Masséna was commanding the Army of the Danube in 1799 he had his Guides dressed in a leather shako covered with blue cloth and surmounted by a yellow plume, a blue dolman with white lace and high red collar, blue trousers with white stripes, and long boots. Masséna increased this 'company' into a force of 330 officers and men, organised in 24 mounted companies and a light artillery company with two guns!)[40]

The Dragoons of the Guard (created in 1806) had a uniform similar to that of the Grenadiers of the Guard, but the long coat was green and they wore a brass helmet with panther skin turban round it, surmounted by a flowing black horsehair crest and red plume. In 1808 the colonel of the regiment, disliking this uniform, dressed two NCOs in a new uniform of his own design which consisted of a short-tailed green cutaway coat with an aiguilette on the right shoulder (to distinguish them from the chasseurs, who wore it on the left), white buckskin breeches, gauntlets, and a helmet similar to the previous one but with an eagle crest and a red plume. The Emperor approved this new uniform and it was taken into use.[41]

The uniform worn by the seven French Lancer regiments consisted of green jacket and trousers with the piping of the epaulettes and the facings of a colour distinctive to the regiment. These colours were: 1st Lancers scarlet, 2nd golden yellow, 3rd rose, 4th crimson, 5th sky-blue, 6th madder red, and 9th buff. Men of these regiments wore a copper helmet of dragoon pattern with a black coxcomb. The 1st and 2nd Polish Lancers of the Guard, which became the 7th and 8th, retained their old uniform and the square-topped lancer cap. The 7th wore blue faced with crimson, and the 8th a scarlet jacket, trousers, and helmet, with blue facings and trouser stripes. The lance was of straight-grained oak 8 ft 10 in long, topped with a red and white pennant. In 1813 regiments were re-equipped; half the men being armed with lances and always posted in the front rank, whilst the remainder, or rear-rank men, carried sabres and musketoons.[42]

Cloaks in the cavalry were often used as a form of protection. In the Chasseurs, at any rate, it was customary before going into action to roll the cloaks and sling them across the body from the right shoulder (*manteaux en sautoir*), thus giving protection against sword cuts and at the same time leaving the sword arm free.[43]

The busby is an interesting headdress. It was known in the French army as the *colback*, a name derived from the *kalpak* of the Turkish army. Its origin is unknown, but the Turks seem to have introduced it into Europe, for there was a corps of cavalry in the old Ottoman army called the Gunalis who wore a conical cap bordered with fur and having a top which fell over to make a hanging bag. The Gunalis also wore a pelisse. The Turks continued to wear the kalpak, generally with a turban twisted round it, until Sultan Mahmoud the Reformer changed the national headdress to the fez in the nineteenth century. A similar type of cap is worn by the Uzbeks of Bokhara and was also worn by the Cossacks whom Napoleon's army encountered, so that it may have originated somewhere east of the Caspian Sea. The Hungarians adopted both kalpak and pelisse from the Turks, and from them the fashion spread to Germany and then France. The hanging bag became eventually the ornamental flap at the side of the modern busby, which in the British Army is still the full dress cap of the Hussars, the Royal Artillery, the Royal Engineers, and the Royal Signals.[44]

Of the Cossacks, Wilson says[45] that their dress was: 'A blue jacket (with a white frog on the cuff or cape) fastened with hooks; a pair of loose trowsers, plaited so as to cover and conceal the opening in front; a pair of short boots, a black cap made of the unborn lamb from which depends a red pandour sack, a plume on the side of the cap, or, what is more common, except in the Attaman's regiment, merely a cloth cap with a kind of sack hanging behind, in which he stuffs his provisions or other articles—and a white or black hair Circassian short cloak.'

Apart from the Mamelukes, these Cossacks were the only formidable body of irregular cavalry with which the French had to contend. Wilson says that they were armed with a lance, a pistol in the girdle, and a sword, and that: 'The Cossaque is not first armed with the lance when he proceeds to war, or when he attains manhood, it is the toy of his infancy, and the constant exercise of his youth; so that he wields it, although from 14 to 18 feet in length, with the address and freedom that the best swordsman in Europe would use his weapon ... The equipment of the Cossaque's horse is light—a snaffle,—an halter, of which the rein is always held in the hand that he may be instantly attached on dismounting, or be led with facility—the tree of a saddle, on which is bound a cushion stuffed with the Cossaque's property, and on which he rides—form the whole of his accoutrements and baggage.'[46]

Tactics and Tactical Employment

In principle light cavalry (hussars, chasseurs, and, later, lancers) were responsible for reconnaissance and protection (i.e. advanced, flank, and rear guards, and outposts); whilst the heavy cavalry (cuirassiers and carabiniers) delivered the massive mounted attack. Dragoons were originally in a class of their own to be used either as mobile fire power or for shock action; but they generally acted with the heavy cavalry, and gradually the latter role predominated. All cavalry regiments were expected, however, to be able to undertake any of the above duties.

Napoleon's employment of his cavalry was masterly. He said himself: 'The use of cavalry demands boldness and ability, above all it should not be handled with any miserly desire to keep it intact . . . I do not wish the horses to be spared if they can catch men . . . Take no heed of the complaints of the cavalry, for if such great objects may be obtained as the destruction of a whole hostile army, the state can afford to lose a few hundred horses from exhaustion.'[47] These are truths that have escaped not only generations of cavalry soldiers but also commanders of armoured formations and battle fleets.

Unlike so many other generals (notably in the American Civil War) Napoleon did not use his cavalry for large-scale raids, or indeed for any long distant operations away from the main body of the army. The bulk of his heavy cavalry and dragoons formed, as has been shown, the cavalry reserve corps; the reserve attack force of the field army—a battering ram to break a wavering enemy line and exploit the victory.[48]

But the cavalry reserve had other uses besides that in the main battle. In the approach march to the Ulm operations in 1805 the main body of the French Army crossed the Rhine on a seventy-mile frontage from Mannhein to Kehl, sweeping forward in its vast outflanking movement. The cavalry reserve corps preceded the infantry corps on the previous day, using the same roads initially, but then moving towards the entrances to the Black Forest defiles with orders to penetrate some distance into them. The intention was that the cavalry would both cover the army during its crossing of the Rhine and then mislead the enemy as to the real direction of the advance—make him think, in fact, that the attack was coming frontally through the Black Forest. The cavalry corps was not to push on through the Black Forest; once its demonstration had been felt, it was to turn left, avoiding the passes, and move to cover the right flank of the army in its approach to the Danube. Local protection of the infantry corps throughout the march was carried out by their own light cavalry divisions.[49]

Napoleon's employment of the cavalry reserve for deep reconnaissance and protection is well shown by the duties allotted to it during the advance, after the successful completion of the Ulm campaign, through Vienna to Brunn. The division of dismounted dragoons was used to scout towards Pilsen; one dragoon division remained in Vienna with Davout's corps to keep the road clear between Vienna and Brunn; another dragoon division watched the south-eastern frontier of Bohemia; a third dragoon division, after helping to secure Augsburg as a base, was on the march to Vienna; whilst the remaining dragoon division and the two cuirassier divisions formed the vanguard of the army during its advance.[50] The dragoons, with their heavy firepower, were remarkably versatile troops; and a combination of heavy cavalry and dragoons was considered to have sufficient 'punch' to deal with enemy rear guards.

Lack of cavalry could handicap operations severely; and after the virtual destruction of his cavalry force in Russia, Napoleon was unable to plan and conduct the campaign of 1813 as he would have wished. Not only were his cavalry few in numbers, but the new regiments were not trained for their task and he received little information from mounted reconnaissance. He said himself that it is impossible 'to carry on anything but a defensive war, covering oneself by entrenchments and natural obstacles, if one has not a cavalry fairly equal in strength to that of the enemy . . . If you lose a battle your army is lost . . . An army superior in cavalry will always have the advantage of being able to cover its movements, of being well informed as to the enemy's movements, and giving battle only when it chooses. Its defeats will have few evil consequences and its successes will be decisive.'[51]

The effect of this shortage at the start of the 1813 campaign was that Napoleon was obliged to use the River Saale as a screen for his movements because there were too few regiments for this typical cavalry role. In a letter to Eugène, Berthier wrote: 'The intention of the Emperor is to guard the whole of the Saale, in order to prevent the enemy from detaching any party on the left bank of that river.'[52]

The cavalry charge was a frequent and important feature of the Napoleonic battle. At Marengo the decisive stroke was a flank attack by Kellerman's cavalry brigade. At Austerlitz Murat smashed the Russian right by a charge with the reserve cavalry—96 squadrons numbering nearly 15,000 men.[53] At Eylau the charge of the heavy cavalry of the reserve and the Guard saved the battle. And at Waterloo the great French cavalry charges against Wellington's right centre were perhaps the most memorable aspects of the battle.

Napoleon aimed at launching his cavalry reserve into the attack when the enemy was already closely engaged with the French infantry and had no time to form square to meet a massed cavalry charge. If the timing, as at Waterloo, was sometimes wrong, this was due to the fault of his subordinates. The cavalry charge, according to Napoleon's orders, should be carried out in successive lines, with sufficient space between leading and supporting brigades so that, if the leading echelons were repulsed, there was room to rally without disordering the ranks of the succeeding waves.[54]

Some detail of cavalry regiments in action is provided by Parquin and Marbot. At Eylau the regiment in which Parquin was serving, the 20th *Chasseurs à Cheval*, was in the IV Corps, commanded by Soult, and was brigaded with the 7th *Chasseurs à Cheval*. The brigade was drawn up in front of the corps artillery park, with the 20th in front and the 7th in the second line. On their right flank was the 27th Infantry Regiment. All the morning they were under artillery fire, but the enemy's guns were poorly directed and they suffered little harm. It was cold and thick snow was driving into their faces. Parquin says: 'Towards two o'clock in the afternoon an enormous mass of cavalry was set in motion and advanced towards us at a walk; the snow and marshy ground not permitting any faster pace. The enemy filled the air with their "Hurrahs"; some chasseurs replied with cries of "*Au chat!*", making allusion to a play on the pronunciation of the word "Hurrah! (*Au Rat!*)". The allusion was seized upon and in a moment passed from right to left of the regiment. Colonel Castex asked if the carbines were loaded. On the reply being affirmative he ordered, "Present carbines!" (We always on service carried our carbines suspended from the belt hook.) Then he ordered officers to fall back into the ranks. That enormous mass of dragoons continued to advance towards us at the walk. But when the Russians were only six paces away the Colonel gave the order, rapidly, "Fire!" The order was executed by the regiment as if on an exercise. The effect of the discharge was terrible: nearly the whole of the first rank of the dragoons was put out of action; but soon the dead and wounded were replaced by the second rank and there was a general mêlée. Without the presence of mind of Captain Kirmann the regiment would have been in difficulties, because a body of Cossacks arrived to attack our left flank, so that the regiment would have been assailed on two sides. Captain Kirmann, by rapidly ordering, "Squadron, face left!", foiled the enemy's intention. At last this mass of dragoons, who were certainly double the regiment's strength, turned about; but not without having caused us serious loss. More than a hundred men of the 20th Chasseurs had been killed or wounded. The enemy lost at least three hundred men, because the battalion square of the 27th Regiment, by well-directed fire at the Russians, inflicted heavy losses on them during the retreat.'[55]

On another occasion during this same campaign a body of Cossacks harassed the regiment during a whole day. The chasseurs repeatedly charged them but could never gain contact, because the Cossacks, following their usual tactics, retired at the gallop covered by the fire of the Russian artillery, and the sudden unmasking of these pieces caused many casualties amongst the 20th Chasseurs. As these tactics were causing cruel losses, Parquin's colonel, profiting by the infantry seizing a copse on the right of the regiment, sent one squadron to lie in ambush behind it and to charge as soon as they heard a troop open fire. He then despatched a troop to the other side of the wood where they could be seen by the Cossacks, giving the officer commanding the following orders: 'Go off with your troop at a trot; go ten paces beyond the head of that wood. Your front rank will present carbines; the enemy in front of you will charge in mass; you will not give the order to fire till he is six paces from you; he will return to the charge; you will be cut at with sabres, thrust at with lances and overthrown—but you will not turn about. I shall be watching you.' These orders were carried out with precision. As soon as the troop opened fire, the squadron broke from the wood and charged the Cossacks in the rear. Two more squadrons from the regiment then charged frontally, and the Cossacks were completely routed, losing many prisoners and leaving the ground covered with their dead.[56]

Marbot gives two interesting examples showing the strength and weakness of the lance as a weapon. His regiment, the 23rd *Chasseurs à Cheval*, was engaged at the battle of Polotsk, in 1812, with the Cossacks of the Guard, who were armed with the lance. Once having penetrated the Russians' leading rank, all the advantage lay with the French because the lances were too long to compete with the sabre at close quarters. Of the battle of the Katzback in 1813, however, he has the following story to tell: 'The plateau of Jauër and the banks of the Katzbach suddenly became the theatre of a bloody battle, for from every wood Prussian troops were advancing. My regiment . . . soon found itself in front of an enemy infantry brigade whose muskets had been put out of action by the rain and could not fire a single shot. I tried to break the Prussian square but our horses, hindered by the mud which was up to their hocks, could only advance at a walk, and one knows that without some impetus it is nearly impossible for cavalry to penetrate into the closed ranks of steady and well commanded infantry, presenting a hedge of bayonets. We went so close to them that we spoke with them and struck their muskets with the blades of our sabres. But we could not break into their lines, though this would have been easy if General Sebastiani had not sent the brigade artillery to another place. Our situation and that of the enemy infantry in front of us was becoming really ridiculous, for . . . our sabres were too short to reach our enemies whose muskets could not fire! Things were in this state for some time when General Maurin, commanding the next brigade to ours, sent to our aid the 6th Regiment of Lancers, and their long weapons, passing over the enemy bayonets, killed in an instant so many Prussians that not only they but also the 23rd and 24th Chasseurs were able to penetrate into the enemy square . . .'[57]

James Smithies, who charged in the Royal Dragoons at Waterloo, says that when they encountered the French Lancers they found that they had the lance fastened to a foot, 'and when we neared them, they sent it out with all their might; and if the man at which they aimed did not manage to parry the blow, it was all over with him.'[58] It would appear, from this account, that the French Lancer regiments in action against cavalry were leaving the right hand free to wield a sabre.

During its latter years the Napoleonic army included so many different nationalities that there were occasions when regiments of similar origin fought on opposite sides. Marbot cites the following remarkable instance:

'Amongst the extraordinary incidents that occurred during the battle of Wagram, I must mention the fight of two cavalry regiments which not only served in opposing armies but belonged to the same Colonel-Proprietor, Prince Albert of Saxe-Teschen. He had married the celebrated Archduchess Christine of Austria, Governor of the Netherlands. Having the title of Prince in both countries, he possessed a regiment of Hussars in Saxony and one of Cuirassiers in Austria. Both bore his name in their title, and, in accordance with the custom of the two States, he nominated all the officers in the regiments. Because for many years Austria and Saxony had been at peace with one another, when Prince Albert had an officer to place, he put him in whichever of the two regiments had a vacancy; so that one could see members of the same family serving in both Prince Albert's Saxon Hussars and Prince Albert's Austrian Cuirassiers. Now, by a coincidence, which was as deplorable as it was extraordinary, the two regiments were opposite each other on the battlefield of Wagram and, driven by a regard for their duty and as a point of honour, they charged each other. It was also remarkable that the Cuirassiers were driven back by the Hussars, who fought with very great spirit because they were anxious to make up, under the eyes of Napoleon and the French Army, for the double repulse that had been suffered by the Saxon infantry! The latter, although it had proved its courage on many occasions, was not nearly so soundly recruited or trained as the cavalry, which was regarded, with reason, as one of the best in Europe.'[59]

1. Edouard Detaille and Jules Richard, *L'Armee Française*, 1885–89
2. *Mémoires du Général Baron de Marbot*, 39th edition, 1891
3. Colonel R. W. Phipps, *The Armies of the First French Republic*, ed. Colonel C. F. Phipps and Elizabeth Sandars, 1926–1939 (5 vols.)

4. Sir Charles Oman, *Wellington's Army*, 1912
5. F. Loraine Petre, *Napoleon's Conquest of Prussia—1806*, 1907
6. Detaille and Richard, op. cit.
7. ibid.
   Colonel Ruby and Capitaine de Labeau, *Historique de 12me Regiment de Cuirassiers*, 1944
8. ibid.
9. Detaille and Richard, op. cit.
10. Phipps, op. cit.
11. Detaille and Richard, op. cit.
12. Phipps, op. cit.
13. ibid.
14. Marbot, op. cit.
15. Ruby and de Labeau, op. cit.
16. Detaille and Richard, op. cit.
17. Ruby and de Labeau, op. cit.
18. Detaille and Richard, op. cit.
19. Major G. Tylden, *Horses and Saddlery*, 1965
20. Marbot, op. cit.
21. Petre, op. cit.
22. Marbot, op. cit.
23. *Souvenire de Capitaine Parquin*, Introduction by F. Masson, 1892
24. Henry Lachoque, adapted by Anne S. K. Brown, *The Anatomy of Glory*, 1961
25. F. Loraine Petre, *Napoleon and the Archduke Charles*, 1909
26. Sir Robert Wilson, *The Russian Army and the Campaigns in Poland 1806–1807*, 1810
27. Marbot, op. cit.
28. Baron von Odeleben, *A Circumstantial Narrative of the Campaign in Saxony*, French edition, ed. Aubrey de Vitry, English transl., A. J. Kempe, 1820
29. Brig. Gen. V. J. Esposito and Col. J. R. Elting, *A Military History and Atlas o the Napoleonic Wars*, 1964
   Ruby and de Labeau, op. cit.
30. Detaille and Richard, op. cit.
31. ibid.
32. ibid.
   Parquin, op. cit.
33. ibid.
34. ibid.
35. ibid.
36. Marbot, op. cit.
37. Detaille and Richard, op. cit.
38. ibid.
39. Lachoque, Brown, op. cit.
40. Phipps, op. cit.
   Lachoque, Brown, op. cit.
41. ibid.
42. ibid.
   Detaille and Richard, op. cit.
43. Parquin, op. cit.
44. Colonel H. C. B. Rogers, *The Mounted Troops of the British Army*, 1959
45. Wilson, *op. cit.*
46. ibid.
47. Count Yorck von Wartenburg, *Napoleon as a General*, ed. Major W. H. James, 1902

48. Sir Charles Oman, *Studies in the Napoleonic Wars*, 1929
49. Wartenburg, op. cit.
50. ibid.
51. ibid.
52. F. Loraine Petre, *Napoleon's Last Campaign in Germany 1813*, 1912
53. Oman, *Studies in the Napoleonic Wars*
54. ibid.
    Marbot, op. cit.
55. Parquin, op. cit.
56. ibid.
57. Marbot, op. cit.
58. Rogers, op. cit.
59. Marbot, op. cit.

CHAPTER THREE

INFANTRY

General

As in most other armies in the latter centuries of military history, the infantry of the Napoleonic army was popularly regarded as the core or nucleus of its strength. This is probably true, though, as we shall see, Napoleon (an officer of artillery) had certain reservations. But, as a result of the long series of French victories, something of a myth grew up in the minds of Frenchmen; a myth which was typified by the *grognards*, or 'grumblers', of the Imperial Guard— the grizzled old soldiers who, invincible on the battlefield, followed Napoleon, in spite of their grumbling, wherever he might lead. Popular artists of the period have pandered to and reinforced this myth by depicting the Grenadiers of the Guard as middle aged and even elderly men. The myth was of course very far from the truth, because such men could never have stood up to the long marches and hardships of a Napoleonic campaign. Marshal Bugeaud, who had lived amongst the *grognards*, said that old soldiers were old in experience rather than in age, generally being between 25 and 30; and it was such men that were chosen with care for posting to the Imperial Guard.[1]

In the early years of the Republic the infantry fought frequently with great gallantry; but as a large proportion of the units were only partially trained and disciplined, there was insufficient cohesion to counter the effects of a reverse, with consequent panic flights of whole battalions and even armies. On 15th September 1792, before the Battle of Valmy, Dumouriez's whole army was in flight. On 17th May 1793, in the Army of the Rhine, a raw battalion fired at some of its own cavalry, which had suddenly appeared, and then fled, carrying with it into rout a whole supporting column of 6,000 men; whilst in the same army in October

1793 there was a momentary panic during a retreat caused by troops firing at a hare. On 13th June 1793 in the civil war, the opposing sides fired at each other; both became panic-striken and ran from the battlefield, 'so that', as an admiring officer remarked, 'the two forces would have had to encircle the globe in order to meet.'[2] Napoleon had his troubles in this respect in the 1796 campaign. The 85th Demi-Brigade of Joubert's Division, for instance, when ordered to charge at Rivoli, broke and ran. On the other hand the behaviour of this unit was more than counterbalanced by the gallant advance of Masséna's 32nd and 75th Demi-Brigades.

Apart from panic, defeat could result in insubordination and even mutiny. This happened on a wide scale in Italy in 1799, when in some particularly bad units, officers who tried to repress disorder were killed by their own men. General Sérurier wished to resign the command of his division because, as he wrote, murder was the order of the day, he had lost all authority, and two excellent colonels had been threatened by the bayonets of men of their own regiments. 'This manner of serving', he finished, 'cannot be suitable for a man of my age.'[3]

Yet at the siege of Acre, and after continuing failure in the attack, men displayed the most conspicuous gallantry. Special companies of éclaireurs were formed for the most dangerous action, and they were frequently almost wiped out; yet men disputed for the honour of being posted to these companies. One who was there says: 'I have seen men weeping whilst saying to the colonels of regiments: "Am not I as good a soldier and as brave as so-and-so, who goes in front of me?" To calm them the colonels were obliged to promise them that their time should come.'[4]

Marshal Bugeaud, who was born in 1784 and served throughout the Napoleonic wars, says that in the campaigns of 1805 and 1806 the army was magnificent. The years of peace had been put to good use by introducing proper discipline and regulations in place of the previous low standards, which had been due to the neglect and slackness of the Republic and the Directory.[5]

Yet the type of discipline which was adopted seems to have been designed to suit the French character and the individualism generated and fostered by the Revolution and the Republican regime. A French emigré, who was serving in the Bavarian army during the campaign of 1805, wrote amusingly: 'Ulm taken and negligently occupied, the army of Bonaparte, the victorious army, was disbanded, and appeared to me no longer anything but an army in rout; but in rout in advance instead of in retreat. This torrent took the direction of Vienna, and henceforth there was nothing but an arrive qui peut by roads full and encumbered. Our German army alone marched like regular troops.' Later the same officer describes his utter astonishment when at the first sound of alarm, all this apparent disorder vanished, and regiments, divisions, and corps, stood marshalled in perfect order.[6]

The Imperial Guard was always regarded as a *corps d'élite*. In the earlier campaigns its strength was not very great (at Austerlitz it numbered only 7,000 men) and it was always held in reserve and rarely engaged. From this manner of using it and the care with which its men were selected, it acquired a high prestige and consequently its entry into action had a considerable moral effect. Towards the end of the Napoleonic period, the deterioration in the quality of the French infantry led to a large increase in the strength of the Guard, and at the end of 1813 it reached a strength of more than 70,000.[7]

From 1807 to 1809, because of the constantly increasing needs of the war and the ever-extending theatre of operations, the composition of the army was weakened and its constitution altered. To meet these require-ments the quantity of the army's effectives took precedence over its quality. Great efforts were made to retain with the colours old soldiers, who had become too old, and to increase the number of young soldiers, who were too young. The result was that nothing like the nominal strength of a force was ever available for action. An army might have a paper strength of 100,000 men, but after a long and arduous advance there would be left crawling along in rear some 20,000 to 25,000 men, composed of old soldiers who were too old to stand the pace and weak conscripts who formed an army of skrimshankers living on the inhabitants of the country.[8] General the Duc de Fézensac writes, in his *Souvenirs Militaires de 1804 à 1814*, that after the Battle of Eylau in 1807 there were 60,000 men, nearly all marauders, absent from the army 'that one thought nearly entirely composed of *grognards*, unshakable in their duty'[9].

However, provided that he was brave under fire and could stand up to the fatigue of the long marches, the Emperor was prepared to tolerate much in the conduct of his troops so long as disorderly conduct did not compromise the success of his operations. Indeed such toleration was probably a deliberate policy in order to retain the enthusiasm of his soldiers for his military ventures. He was, too, able to instil into the soldiers a feeling of self-respect, so that they themselves would not commit or allow deeds which could be held to tarnish their military glory. The day after a battle men who had absented themselves from the fight, for instance, would be dealt with by unofficial soldiers' courts. It was a loose type of discipline, then, based on a cult of the Emperor and the honour of the regiment, that formed the basis of the French army's capacity for long marches and hard fighting; though generally badly fed, badly maintained, and badly paid.[10]

But Marshal Bugeaud thought the British infantry superior to the French. He fought against them in the Peninsula for a long time and formed the highest opinion of their fighting abilities. Trochu says that he always included in his accounts of the campaign the following phrase: 'The English infantry is the most formidable in Europe; fortunately there is not much of it.' ('*L'infanterie anglaise est la plus redoutable de l'Europe; heuresement il n'y en a pas beaucoup.*')[11]

Against Austrian troops, their most frequent antagonists, the Napoleonic infantry were generally successful. The Austrian infantrymen were steady but very slow and rigid. They could face French infantry on reasonably even terms on open ground, where their parade ground formations could be employed; but in broken or hilly country and in village fighting the quick French soldiers, with their ability as skirmishers, were immeasurably superior. The same comments apply generally to the Prussian infantry, whose methods had not changed since the days of Frederick the Great.

The Russian infantry is described by Wilson[12] as follows: 'The infantry is generally composed of athletic men between the ages of 18 and 40, endowed with great bodily strength, but generally of short stature, with martial countenance and complexion; inured to the extremes of weather and hardship; to the worst and scantiest of food; to marches for days and night, of four hours repose and six hours progress; accustomed to laborious toils, and the carriage of heavy burdens; ferocious but disciplined; obstinately brave, and susceptible of enthusiastic excitements; devoted to their sovereign, their chief, and their country.' In defence Russians were extremely tough troops, but they were inferior to the French in attack.

Organisation

In 1789, when the Revolution effectively started, there were 102 regiments of the infantry of the line (of which 79 were French and 23 foreign), twelve battalions of *chasseurs à pied*, seven colonial regiments, one marine regiment, and provincial infantry. Each of these regiments had two battalions except *Le Roi*, the 28th, which had four. Of the two battalions in a regiment, one had one company of grenadiers and four of fusiliers and the other had one company of *chasseurs* (light infantry) and four of fusiliers. Each company had a strength of approximately 120 all ranks. On the headquarters of a regiment there was a band and a platoon of sappers.[13]

Regular regiments were recruited by voluntary enlistment. A soldier enlisted for eight years and could re-engage after that for two years at a time up to a maximum of twenty-four years. He was then either retired or posted to the *Invalides*. Normally an enlisted soldier did not rise above the rank of sergeant. However, in spite of the barriers which separated officers from NCOs, there were rare instances of men being commissioned from the ranks and even reaching the ranks of colonel and general. Two commissioned appointments were, in fact, reserved for exceptional men promoted from the ranks; those of colour bearer and second lieutenant of the grenadier company.[14]

In the order of seniority, the artillery ranked as the 64th Regiment of Infantry (though it was itself organised into eight regiments) and the provincial infantry ranked collectively as the 97th. These latter were recruited by ballot in parishes and consisted of eight Royal regiments, fourteen provincial regiments, and seventy-eight garrison battalions. In war the provincial troops were called up, taking over garrisons from the regular regiments and furnishing such additional contingents as were required by the field army.[15] Apart from the regiments of the line and the provincial troops, there were six battalions of French guards and four battalions of Swiss guards.

By 1789 the quality of the French infantry had deteriorated. Defeats suffered in the wars of the eighteenth century had lowered its prestige and the troops who had fought in America had been infected by all the talk they had heard of liberty and independence. Morale was adversely affected, too, by bad accommodation, poor food, and a severe discipline. Most of the officers had no contact with their men and little even with the NCOs, though these latter were the backbone of the army. The number of officers was excessive, and most of them were without occupation, for less than a third served effectively with their regiments. Only nobles who had been presented to the King were promoted to the higher ranks; most officers were provincial gentlemen who were too poor to frequent Versailles, and they had little chance of rising above the rank of captain.[16]

Amidst the first agitations of 1789 the innate discipline of the regiments sufficed to maintain good order and correct bearing. But after the capture of the Bastille by 800 men of the French Guards and the revolt at Nancy of the *Régiment du Roi* (showing that even the privileged were no longer loyal) disaffection spread rapidly and many regiments mutinied.[17]

A decree of 1st January 1791 abolished the old aristocratic titles of the regiments and on 4th March the provincial troops were disbanded and replaced by the new and useless levies of the National Guard. Later in 1791 the Assembly decided to raise 169 new battalions of volunteers which were to be recruited and formed by the Departments. These battalions were comparatively good troops because they were largely composed of officers, NCOs, and men of the disbanded provincial troops. In 1792 another batch of so-called volunteer battalions was demanded from Departments, but these were formed mainly by unwilling and untrained men obtained by ballot, and were thoroughly bad and undisciplined. The worst of them were the so-called *Féderés*; a special levy of 20,000 men who were sent to Paris and from whom representatives were 'federated' at the national festival of 14th July in 1792. A battalion of this force from

Marseilles took part in the slaughter of the Swiss Guard at the Tuileries, after the King ordered the latter to cease firing. In 1793 the Convention ordered a *levée en masse*, but the men so swept into the army were of little use and many of them deserted.[18]

It will be apparent that the infantry in the early years of the Republic was very varied in both quality and composition. There were two main elements: firstly the old regular regiments, but with new numbers in place of their old names, and with their two battalions, which used to serve together, now separated and incorporated into different formations; and secondly the volunteers, of both genuine and balloted categories, formed into battalions named after the Departments which raised them (e.g. 1st Vosges, 2nd Vosges, and 3rd Vosges).

To obtain more cohesion and a more even quality, it was decided to form new three-battalion regiments in which, as far as possible, one battalion should be regular and two volunteer. For political reasons the term *demi-brigade* was used instead of regiment. This process, known as the *Amalgame*, was decreed by a law of 21st February 1793; though the order to put it into effect was not given till 8th January 1794. Each regular regiment of the line became the nucleus of two demi-brigades, and a demi-brigade was completed by two volunteer battalions. (If volunteer battalions were below strength, three or more might be joined to provide the two for a demi-brigade.) The demi-brigade then consisted of a centre, or 2nd battalion, which was regular, and a 1st and a 3rd battalion, both of which were volunteer. For instance, on 8th December 1794 the 1st Battalion of the 1st Regiment was joined to the 5th Paris Battalion and the 4th Somme Battalion to form the 2nd Demi-Brigade of the Line. Demi-brigades formed round a line regiment were designated *demi brigades de bataille*, whilst those formed round a regiment of *chasseurs à pied* were called *demi-brigades légères*. Each battalion consisted of nine companies, of which one was grenadier and the remainder fusiliers. In addition there was a regimental battery, which originally had six 4-pr. guns, but in 1795 the number was reduced to three.[19]

There were, on their first formation, 198 *demi-brigades de bataille* and 15 *demi-brigades légères*; but the number of the former was gradually increased to 211 and of the latter to 32, without including a number of provisional and departmental demi-brigades. On 8th January 1796 the Directory ordered a new reorganisation of the infantry which reduced the battle demi-brigades to 100 and the light demi-brigades to 30. The weaker demi-brigades were broken up and their men transferred to other units; for instance, two battalions of the 161st Demi-Brigade were transferred to and absorbed by the 2nd Demi-Brigade.[20] On 30th March 1796, however, the battle demi-brigades were again increased to 110.

The demi-brigade organisation was retained until, by a Consular Decree of 24th September 1803, there was a re-arrangement and all the permanent demi-brigades became regiments. (The term demi-brigade was, however, used during the following years for provisional groupings of battalions.) The number of line regiments in 1803 was fixed at 90, of which 19 had four battalions and 71 had three; whilst of light regiments there were 27, three having four battalions and the remainder three.[21]

The regimental battery was abolished on this reorganisation; but this proved such a disadvantage in practice that in 1809 Napoleon ordered that two 3-prs. or 5-prs., captured from the Austrians, should be allotted to each infantry regiment in the corps of Masséna, Davout, and Oudinot. They were manned by the men of the regiments to which they belonged and always marched with the Eagles. Generally the best officers and men competed for the honour of belonging to the regimental artillery company. But in 1812, probably due to the heavy demands on ordnance, the guns were removed again.[22]

By 1806 the 4th battalions of four-battalion regiments were often removed and grouped to form provisional regiments or demi-brigades.

The organisation of the infantry in 1808 was laid down by Napoleon in a decree of 18th February. The first seven articles of this most interesting instruction were as follows:

'1. Our regiments of infantry of the line and light infantry will in future be composed of a staff and five battalions; the first four will be designated war battalions and the fifth the depot battalion.

2. Each war battalion, commanded by a *chef de bataillon* having under his orders an adjutant and two regimental sergeant-majors, will be composed of six companies, of which one will be grenadiers, one light infantry, and four fusiliers, and all of equal strength.

3. Each depot battalion will consist of four companies. The Major will always be attached to this battalion. A Captain, designated by the Minister from three candidates selected by the Colonel, will command the depot battalion under the orders of the Major. He will at the same time command one of the companies. There will be in the depot an adjutant and two regimental sergeant-majors.

4. The strength of the staff and that of each company of grenadiers of carabiniers [in a light regiment], of light infantry, or of fusiliers is to be as follows:

Staff		*Company*	
Colonel	1	Captain	1
Major	1	Lieutenant	1
Chefs de Bataillon	4	2nd Lieutenant	1
Adjutants	5	Sergeant-Major	1

Staff		Company	
Quartermaster/Paymaster	1	Sergeants	4
Paying Officer	1	Quartermaster Corporal	1
Eagle Bearer	1	Corporals	8
Surgeon Major	1	Grenadiers, Light	
Assistant Surgeons	4	Infantrymen, or	
Assistant Adjutants	5	Fusiliers	121
Regimental Sergeant-Majors	10	Drummers	2
2nd and 3rd Eagle Bearers	2		———
Drum-Major	1		140
Corporal Drummer	1		
Bandsmen (incl 1 Bandmaster)	8		
Master Craftsmen	4		
	———		
	50		

Thus the strength of each regiment will be 3,970 all ranks, of which 108 will be officers and 3,862 NCOs and men.

5. There will be in each war battalion four sappers who will be chosen from the grenadier company of which they will continue to form part, and there will be a corporal who will command all the sappers of the regiment.

6. In battle the grenadier company will be on the right of the battalion and that of the light infantry on the left.

7. When the six companies are present with the battalion it will always march and act by divisions. When the grenadiers and light infantry are absent from the battalion it will always manoeuvre and march by platoon. Two companies will form a division; each company will form a platoon; each half company a section.'[23]

It will be noted that the terms 'division', 'platoon', and 'section', as used in infantry regiments, did not refer to sub-units of the regiment but to tactical formations.

The infantry of the Imperial Guard was on a special establishment. A decree of 16th January 1809 laid down that it was to be composed of the following six regiments: grenadiers, fusilier-grenadiers, skirmisher-grenadiers, chasseurs, fusilier-chasseurs, and skirmisher-chasseurs. A regiment had two battalions, each of four companies of 200 men. The grenadiers and chasseurs were the senior units and were composed of men having at least ten years' service. Admission into them was a reward for services rendered in regiments of the line, and all of the men ranked as NCOs. To be admitted into the Fusiliers of the Guard men had to have served at least two years in the Skirmishers of the Guard and to be able to read and write. All fusiliers with four years' service were eligible for entry into the Grenadiers of Chasseurs of the Guard, but the Emperor's approval was necessary. The regiments of Skirmishers were composed of conscripts selected from all depots, and were treated as soldiers of the line.[24] The organisation of the Guard, however, varied considerably during the Imperial epoch.

On 23rd March 1809 the rank of *Colonel en Second* was instituted by promotion from selected majors. Most of them were infantry officers and they were specially designated to command the *demi-brigades d'élite*. These were formed by grouping provisional battalions composed of grenadier of light infantry companies taken from regiments of the line. Previously such demi-brigades had been commanded by majors.[25]

Uniform, Standards, and Weapons

Before the Revolution French infantry regiments wore white uniforms; but Swiss and Irish regiments in the French service wore madder red and other foreign regiments a dark sky-blue. Royal regiments had blue facings (lapels, collars, and cuffs), regiments of the Princes had scarlet facings, and the remainder were divided into groups wearing facings of respectively sky-blue, black plush, violet, iron-grey, rose, pale yellow, crimson, silver-grey, golden yellow, and dark green. *Chasseurs à pied* wore green with facings which varied according to the regiment. Provisional troops wore white with a collar, only, of royal blue.[26]

After the Revolution blue was laid down as the colour of the infantry uniform. After the *Amalgame*, *demi-brigades de bataille* wore blue coats with red facings and white lining, white waistcoats, white trousers, and long gaiters. *Demi-brigades légères* were clad entirely in blue, relieved by white piping. The uniform was of nearly the same cut and pattern as in Royalist days, and remained without material modification until 1803. In the early days the uniforms were generally of such poor quality that they soon wore out, and soldiers wore anything they could get hold of, including the uniforms of much better material that they captured from the enemy.[27]

Many of the regular soldiers disliked intensely losing their traditional white. As regards the officers, *Cannonier* Bricard records that on 10th August 1793 the Representatives of the People, in a harangue to the troops, complained that officers were retaining their long white coats and white epaulettes which had been forbidden by a Decree of the National Convention, and they gave them a limited time in which to remove them. In the opinion of that stout Republican volunteer Bricard, it was ridiculous to see officers, who had not even been sergeants under the old regime, affecting an air of disdain for the national uniform.[28] But dislike of the blue was not confined to the officers. The old regular rank and file, when

63

they were forced to give up their white coats, frequently either wore them off parade or fixed their old regimental buttons to their new blue uniforms.[29]

However, whatever the cut or quality of their uniforms, it did not affect the fighting ability of the French infantry. (It apparently did not affect, either, the lack of fighting ability amongst the Neapolitan infantry; for the King of Naples is reported to have said to someone who was producing a scheme to reform the uniform of his troops: 'Dress them in blue, red, or yellow; they will run just the same!'[30])

When the new regulations for uniforms were being compiled in 1803, Napoleon first thought of reintroducing white. He may not have pursued the idea for two reasons; firstly, because white got dirty easily, and secondly, because by this time blue had acquired a tradition from its association with victorious campaigns. There were alterations in the pattern of the uniform: the waistcoat was removed from the line; the skirts of the coat were diminished in size and length; and the breeches and long gaiters were replaced by pantaloons. The shako, which was at first limited to light infantry, finally replaced the old headgear—the big cocked hat, worn cross-wise (or *en bataille*, as the soldiers called it) with tricolour cockade in front.

But the most radical changes in the equipment of the infantry lay in the design of their standards. The design and pattern of the colours and standards of the French Army has been the subject of lengthy books, and it is not possible here to do more than indicate the general principles and changes.

Under the monarchy the colour of the first battalion of a regiment was white with a white cross throughout, outlined in gold, and the second battalion had the white cross throughout on a field of the regimental pattern and tincture. At the extremity of each limb of the cross on both colours was a gold fleur-de-lys, and from the top of the colour pike hung a white scarf.

The first change came in 1790, with a decree of 22nd October that the white scarf was to be replaced by one in the new national colours of blue, white, and red. This white scarf commemorated the victory of Marshal Francois de Luxembourg at the Battle of Fleurus on 1st July 1690, and its replacement was widely resented and so strongly resisted that a circular was sent to colonels of regiments on 26th May 1791 directing compliance with the order.

The decree of 1st January 1791, referred to above, allotted new numbers to regiments, so altering the seniority; and regiments were formed into fresh groups, each of twelve regiments, with, of course, new facings. These, in order of seniority, were: black, violet, rose, sky-blue, crimson, scarlet, royal blue, dark green, and light green. As regards the regimental colours, the decree said that these would be distinctive to each battalion and the pattern would be fixed by the regulations which were being prepared for uniform and equipment. It also said that the battalion colour was to be carried by a sergeant-major selected by the Colonel. The regulations were promulgated by a decree of 30th June 1791. This directed, rather vaguely, that the first battalion colour should include the national colours and that all others should bear the new facing colours and regimental numbers. In addition, to remind soldiers of their duties and obligations, the legend *Discipline et Obéissance à la Loi* was to be inscribed on all colours.[31]

On 29th September 1791 the Military Committee brought out more exact orders. The first battalion colour was to have three horizontal bands of blue, white, and red in the upper quarter of the flag next to the pike, and to have a border of these colours. The colour of the second battalion was to have the white cross on a field of the facing colour, arranged in a pattern which differed in each regiment of the group; though the same patterns (with different facing colours) were used in each group. The number of the regiment was in the centre of each colour, within a wreath, and the above-mentioned legend was inscribed on the limbs of the cross. On 28th November 1792, the monarchy having been abolished, regiments were ordered to either remove the fleur-de-lys or cover them with lozenges of tricolour cloth.[32]

The *Amalgame*, of course, necessitated entirely new colours. The senior battalion in each demi-brigade was the second, or centre, and its colour was derived from that of the first battalion of a regular regiment. It was white, with blue, white, and red horizontal bands in the top quarter next to the pike, and it had a blue, white, and red border. But in the centre was a device consisting of a lictor's fasces and axes, surmounted by a Phrygian cap, and enclosed by two branches of oak tied at the bottom. On one side of the flag was the inscription *République Française* and on the other *Discipline et Obéissance aux Lois Militaires*. In each corner was the number of the demi-brigade. The colours of the first and third battalions had the same device and legends, but the field of the flag was a pattern in blue, white, and red, which differed for each demi-brigade.[33]

In Napoleon's Army of Italy differences from the regulation pattern soon appeared. The fasces and cap disappeared from the obverse and inscribed on it were battle honours and such legends as *Le Terrible 57e qui rien n'arrete* which Napoleon had used in his despatches. Light demi-brigades apparently carried colours which did not conform to the standard pattern and which always incorporated a bugle. When Napoleon became First Consul all the light demi-brigades received new colours of complicated design by a consular decree of 10th June 1802. The 9th Light Demi-Brigade, which had particularly distinguished itself at Marengo, had been

2nd Bn. 147th Demi-Brigade 1794

1st Bn. 63rd Demi-Brigade 1794

9th Light Demi-Brigade, 2nd Bn. 1802

3rd Light Demi-Brigade, 1st Bn. 1802

2nd Regiment of Dragoons. 'Eagle' of 1812

12th Regiment of Cuirassiers. 'Eagle' of 1804

presented with colours a month earlier which departed from the common light demi-brigade pattern.

The establishment of the Empire entailed another change in the colours and standards of the army. Napoleon selected an eagle with wings displayed as the Imperial emblem, and a new type of colour was approved with the corners alternately blue and red, and having in the centre a white lozenge emblazoned with a globe inscribed *Napoleon Empereur des Français au —ᵉ Régt d'Infanterie* (or other type of unit) surmounted by the eagle on a thunderbolt, and above the device *Empire Français* and below it *Valeur et Discipline.*[34] However, this colour was never issued to the army because Napoleon suddenly decided that, instead of being borne on a colour, the eagle itself should be the standard by being moulded in metal and placed on the top of a staff. He wrote to Berthier: 'The Eagle with wings outspread, as on the Imperial Seal, will be at the head of the standard staves, as was the practice in the Roman army. The flag will be attached at the same distance beneath the Eagle as was the Labarum.' The flag, in fact, was no longer the regimental colour, but an ornamental ancillary to the eagle.

The eagle was made of gilded copper, and below the thunderbolt on which it stood was a brass tablet bearing in raised figures the number of the regiment. The staff was 8 feet long and painted imperial blue. The silken flag was 35 inches in the hoist and 33 in the fly. The white lozenge and alternate blue and red corners of the proposed colour were retained. On each of the latter was the regimental number within a chaplet. On the obverse was inscribed *Empire Français* and *L'Empereur des Français au —ᵉ Régiment d'Infanterie de Ligne* (or other type of unit), and on the reverse *Valeur et Discipline* with beneath it the number of the battalion, cavalry squadron, etc. Beneath this number again was any battle honour or title of honour.[35]

Every eagle was presented personally by the Emperor, and the inevitable result of the prestige that accrued to them was that they became invaluable prizes in battle. During the Austerlitz campaign, therefore, Napoleon directed that hussars and *chasseurs à cheval* (who, by the nature of their duties were frequently too widely extended in the field to give proper protection to the eagles) should no longer take eagles on campaign. This order was later extended to dragoons and regiments of light infantry.

In 1808, because a number of eagles had been lost in battle, Napoleon reduced the number of eagles from one to each battalion (or squadron) to one to each regiment. The new regulations were contained in articles 17, 18 and 19 of the above quoted decree of 18th February 1808, and were as follows:

'17. Each regiment will have an eagle which will be carried by an eagle bearer having the rank of lieutenant or second-lieutenant and having at least ten years' service, or having made the four campaigns of Ulm, Austerlitz, Jena, and Friedland. He will receive the pay of a lieutenant of the first class. Two good men, selected from illiterate old soldiers, who for that reason cannot obtain promotion, having at least ten years' service, with the titles, one of 2nd Eagle Bearer and the other of 3rd Eagle Bearer, will always be placed at the side of the eagle. They will have the rank of sergeant and the pay of sergeant-major. They will wear four chevrons on both arms. The eagle will always remain where most of the battalions are together. The eagle bearers form part of the staff of the regiment. They are appointed by Us and can only be dismissed by Us.

18. Each war battalion will have a standard carried by an NCO chosen by the *chef de bataillon* from one of the companies of the battalion. The depot battalion will not have a standard.

19. The line regiments alone have eagles for colours; the other corps have standards. We reserve to ourselves the presentation of new eagles and standards to new regiments.'[36]

By the restriction of eagles to line regiments, Napoleon meant that provisional regiments and other units not forming part of the regular establishment would not be issued with eagles. They would carry the appropriate flag attached to an ordinary colour pike or staff.

From October 1811 a much more elaborate flag was issued for attachment to the eagle staff. On a field of blue, white, and red, vertical stripes, were embroidered in gold: in the two top corners an imperial crown, in the two bottom corners an eagle displayed, in the centre of each side the letter 'N' within a wreath, and on each side of the 'N', on the top and bottom sides of the flag, eight bees. The appropriate inscriptions appeared in the centre of the flag. The flag was fringed with gold.

There was an addition to some of the eagles when the city of Paris voted the presentation of gold wreaths to adorn the eagles of all regiments which had fought in the Jena and Polish frontier campaigns. Napoleon thought this an excellent idea and suggested that the regiments of Austerlitz should be included too—a suggestion which was of course adopted; though with some reluctance. To all this glamour of the eagles, however, it must be sadly added that the soldiers commonly referred to them as 'cuckoos'![37]

A number of regiments, before going on service, removed the flag from the eagle staff. Asked after the Peninsular War about the inscription and battle honours on the flag of his regiment, an infantry *chef de bataillon* replied that he had never set eyes on it. He said that the flag had been removed from the eagle staff before he joined the regiment as a lieutenant and had always, he understood, been kept at the depot in France in the regimental chest.[38]

The standard infantry weapon was the flintlock musket of the 1777 pattern, and, later on, a modification of it which was issued in 1801. The bayonet was triangular and was carried in a scabbard on the left hip. Next to the bayonet scabbard was the sword in its scabbard, suspended from a belt which was hung across the body from the right shoulder. Crossing this belt was the pouch belt which was hung from the left shoulder.[39]

Tactics

The infantry of the old regular army fought in line both in attack and defence. In the wars which followed the Revolution, though line in three ranks was still retained for defence, attack was carried out in column— generally in battalion columns with the companies, each in three ranks, formed one behind the other. The original reason for this was that the new levies were too lacking in discipline and training to undertake an attack in line. But because the French copied the Austrians in covering their front with skirmishers and increased the number of these considerably, the attack in column was remarkably successful. The skirmishers, sometimes consisting of whole battalions of *chasseurs*, would move forward in front of the advancing columns in loose order and making much use of cover. When within range they would open fire, from behind cover if possible, on enemy troops in their close line. The latter, therefore, had few targets to which they could reply, though they suffered heavy casualties themselves and by the time the columns arrived they were generally wavering and the weight of the columns was sufficient to break their line.[40]

This method of attack suited, too, the characteristic individuality of the French soldier. It was particularly formidable in wooded hilly country where the broken ground did not favour the rigid line in defence. As they gained in experience, the French learned to vary their method of attack to suit circumstances. An example is provided by the following vivid description given by a French *emigré* officer, de Rison, of an attack which he watched in 1794 being delivered by Ferino's division of the Army of the Moselle:

'We saw the plain suddenly covered by an immense number of soldiers scattered over the ground, who, starting from the crest of the heights occupied by the Republicans, made at full speed for the village of Berstheim. Hardly had they got within pistol-shot when they formed in squads, even in battalions, to rush the attack on this locality which had become so important to them. Our eyes had hardly time to observe this manœuvre when Berstheim was in the hands of the Republicans. This bold stroke nullified in an instant all the effects of our artillery fire. Homage to the soldiers of our country, perhaps the only ones in Europe capable of executing such an attack.'[41]

Under Napoleon, as the French Army came to be composed of well-trained and steady infantry, tactics gradually became rather more formal; and as the hostile armies began to counter the French skirmishers by employing a heavy defensive screen of skirmishers themselves, so the task of shaking the enemy infantry line before the attack was undertaken more generally by artillery bombardment. The column was retained, but not to the exclusion of other formations.

The tactical organisation of infantry laid down by Napoleon in 1809 is given earlier in this chapter: battalion columns could be either by divisions (double companies) or by platoons (single companies). But Napoleon seems to have preferred the *ordre mixte* in which a regiment was drawn up with its centre battalion, or battalions, in line of three ranks, whilst the flanking battalions were in column of divisions. Such a formation could develop a good fire-power, whilst it was effective against a flank attack by cavalry. However, his 'set-piece' attacks against the decisive point in the enemy line seem generally to have been carried out by heavy columns.[42]

Wellington was the first to find an effective counter to the French column attack. He established a strong outpost line of light infantry and riflemen skirmishers which prevented the French skirmishers from approaching his main defensive position. This latter consisted of a line of infantry in two ranks only, so that every weapon could be used, generally stationed initially behind the crest of a hill and so out of view of the French artillery. Marshal Bugeaud, who fought as an infantry officer in the Peninsula, has told what happened:

'I served seven years in the Peninsula. I sometimes beat the English in isolated encounters, and in surprise attacks which, as a senior officer on detached duty, I was able to prepare and direct. But during that long war, to my sorrow, I only saw a few actions in which the English army did not get the better of us. The reason was obvious. We nearly always attacked our adversaries without taking any account of our own experience that the methods that were nearly always successful against the Spaniards nearly always failed against the English.

'The English generally occupied well-chosen defensive positions on rising ground where they showed only part of their men. The customary bombardment ran its course. Then, hastily, without studying the position, without taking time to reconnoitre the routes by which one could mount flank or turning attacks, we marched straight at the enemy taking, as it were, "the bull by the horns".

'When about 1,000 yards from the English line our soldiers got agitated and exchanged their thoughts; they hurried their march which began to get disorderly. The silent English, with ordered arms, looked, in their impassive stillness, like a long red wall—an imposing spectacle which never failed to impress the young soldiers.

'Soon the distance shortened, repeated shouts of *"Vive l'Empereur! En avant! A la baionnette!"*, broke from us; shakos being raised on the ends of muskets. The march became a run, the ranks lost their order, the agitation became an uproar, many muskets were fired. The English line, still silent and immobile with arms still at the order, even when we were within three hundred yards, did not seem to notice the storm which was about to assail it.

'The contrast was striking; more than one of us noted uneasily that the enemy was very slow to fire and reflected that this fire, so long withheld, would when it came be very unpleasant. Our ardour began to abate. The irresistible effect in action of an apparently unshaken calm (even if it did not exist) opposed to dazed and noisy disorder, weighed heavily on our spirits.

'The painful wait suddenly ended. The English line turned a quarter right as muskets were brought to the "ready". An indefinable feeling halted many of our men who opened a wavering fire. From the enemy came a simultaneous and accurate volley which overwhelmed us. Decimated, we staggered, trying to recover our balance; then three formidable "Hurrahs!" broke at last the silence of our adversaries. At the third they were on us, pressing our disordered retreat. But to our great astonishment they did not pursue their advantage beyond about a hundred yards, but returned quietly to their position to await a second attack; which when reinforcements arrived we rarely failed to deliver under the same conditions, with too often the same lack of success and with fresh losses.'[43]

The French, like other armies, adopted the system of forming élite shock battalions by grouping the grenadier companies of different regiments. The result was not always good, because the regiments deprived of their best troops were lowered in quality, whilst the resulting grenadier battalions, lacking cohesion and esprit de corps, were often poorer than the average line battalion.[44] Sometimes, however, they were very good indeed. A British officer wrote from Vittoria on 8th August 1813: 'The 34th Battalion of French Grenadiers was the finest I ever saw, most beautifully clothed and equipped, the whole of them were dressed in sergeant's cloth with fine red shoulder knots. They wore tall bearskin caps and immense long feathers. They made a most formidable show in line. They were the first that were charged by our regiment and a proper example was made of them, they have hardly a man left to tell the story.'[45]

In Germany in 1813 the deterioration in the standard of his infantry resulted in a change by Napoleon in their tactics. The regiments were now drawn up in solid masses with artillery placed in the intervals between them, whilst light troops occupied all the broken ground, villages, houses, and woods. The infantry attack now confirmed the success of the artillery bombardment.[46]

The marches performed by Napoleon's infantry were frequently outstanding, in spite of the apparent lack of march discipline, mentioned earlier. In his first campaign of 1796 Napoleon fought two engagements and one battle in the week 5th to 11th September, and during this period Masséna's division covered 100 miles (including the passage of one river by ferry) and Augereau's division marched 114 miles. Count Yorck von Wurtemberg comments, 'It is only a genius who can compel ordinary human beings to perform such feats.'[47]

In 1805 the corps of Lannes and Soult arrived at Vienna on 13th November, having marched 152 miles in 13 days along rough country roads; and that without including the extra distance incurred by detours. Davout's corps, in 16 days, marched 150 miles as the crow flies, partly over difficult mountain roads. 'Thus', says Count Yorck, 'Napoleon did not, after all, vanquish his enemies so much by the battles of Ulm and Jena, however disastrous these were, as by his incredible marches.'[48] In 1806, when he entered Berlin on 25th October, Davout had fought the battle of Auerstaëdt and marched 166 miles as the crow flies, all in 14 days.

The march tunes of the Napoleonic army became famous. The foremost was probably *Veillons au Salut de l'Empire*, which was played during reviews and attacks. The band of the Grenadiers of the Guard played it when the army marched out of Moscow, and it was heard (perhaps for the last time) when Napoleon reviewed his troops before the Battle of Waterloo. It is said that the Guard were played into the last attack at Waterloo by the 'March of Marengo', a favourite march of the Guard which was played at the Battle of Marengo and had previously been called the 'March of the Consular Guard'. During the Battle of Austerlitz the drums of the Imperial Guard beat a popular army march, which subsequently became known as the 'March of Austerlitz'.[49]

1. General L. J. Trochu, *L'Armée Française en 1867*, 1868
2. Colonel R. W. Phipps, *The Armies of the First French Republic*, ed. Colonel C. F. Phipps and Elizabeth Sanders, 1926–1939 (5 vols.)
3. ibid.
4. ibid.
5. Trochu, op. cit.
6. Comeau, *Mémoires des Guerres d'Allemagne*, quoted by F. Loraine Petre in *Napoleon and the Archduke Charles*, 1909
7. Trochu, op. cit.
8. ibid.
9. ibid.
10. Colonel Vachee, *Napoleon at Work*, transl. G. Frederick Lees, 1914
11. Trochu, op. cit.

12. Sir Robert Wilson, *The Russian Army and the Campaigns in Poland 1806–07*, 1810
13. Edouard Detaille and Jules Richard, *L'Armée Française*, 1885–89
14. ibid.
15. ibid.
16. Colonel J. Revol, *Histoire de l'Armée Française*, 1929.
17. Detaille, op. cit.
18. Phipps, op. cit.
19. Detaille, op. cit., Phipps, op. cit.
    Journal du Canonnier Bricard, Introduction by L. Larchey, 1894
20. Bricard, op. cit.
21. Detaille, op. cit.
22. ibid.
23. Commandant Saski, *Campagne de 1809*, 1899
24. ibid.
25. ibid.
26. Detaille, op. cit.
27. ibid.
28. Bricard, op. cit.
29. Phipps, op. cit.
30. ibid.
31. O. Hollander, *Les Drapeaux des Demi-Brigades d'Infanterie*, 1913
32. ibid.
    Jean Brunon, Amendments to above—letter to author 20th Dec. 1952
33. O. Hollander, op. cit.
34. ibid.
35. Edward Fraser, *The War Drama of the Eagles*, 1912
36. Saski, op. cit.
37. Fraser, op. cit.
38. ibid.
39. Henry Lachoque, adapted by Anne S. K. Brown, *The Anatomy of Glory*, 1961
40. Phipps, op. cit.
41. ibid.
42. Sir Charles Oman, *Studies in the Napoleonic Wars*, 1929
43. Trochu, op. cit.
44. Phipps, op. cit.
45. Lt. R. Garrett, 'A Subaltern in the Peninsular War', *Journal of the Society for Army Historical Research*, Vol. XIII, No. 49
46. Baron von Odeleben, *A Circumstantial Narrative of the Campaign in Saxony*, French edition, Ed. Aubrey de Vitry, English transl. A. J. Kempe, 1820
47. Count Yorck von Wartenburg, *Napoleon as a General*, ed. Major W. H. James, 1902
48. ibid.
49. Major J. Regnault, 'French Napoleonic Marches', *Journal of the Society for Army Historical Research*, Vol. XIII, No. 51

CHAPTER FOUR

ARTILLERY

General

Artillery was the one arm of the service which was left more or less unchanged at the Revolution, and it did not have to absorb large numbers of volunteers. The *Royal-Artillerie* of the old regular army was a very efficient body with a high reputation, and it was realised that any meddling with these technical troops would ruin their effectiveness. The victories of Valmy and Jemappes in 1792 and Wattignies in 1793 were largely due to the efficiency and disciplined bravery of the artillery, and in all the early campaigns it provided a steady core in divisions and armies when many of the infantry battalions were shaky. The blue uniform of the regular artillery was acceptable to the revolutionaries, and their performance in action so impressed the Directory that in 1797 they became first in the order of precedence followed, respectively, by the Engineers, the Infantry, and the Cavalry.[1] (It should be noted, however, that most of the artillery officers sympathised with the Revolution whilst most of the cavalry officers did not!)

Napoleon, of course, was an artillery officer, and his fondness for that arm was often expressed. His various notes and correspondence include the following: 'A good infantry is without doubt the backbone of the army, but if it had to fight long against superior artillery it would be discouraged and disorganised.' 'The artillery, like the other arms, must be collected in mass if one wishes to attain a decisive result.' 'The more inferior the quality of a body of troops, the more artillery it requires. There are some army corps with which I should require only one-third of the artillery which I need for other corps.' 'It is the artillery of my Guard which generally decides my battles, for, as I have it always at hand, I can bring it to bear wherever it becomes necessary.' 'Great battles are won by artillery.'[2]

The esprit de corps in some of Napoleon's artillery is shown by an account given by a Saxon artillery officer of an incident in Dresden in 1813.[3] He saw a battery receive orders to be ready to move into action, and he says: 'The men were dust-stained and untidy after their long march. The moment they heard of the order, each man began to get out of his haversack his parade uniform, which it was thought suitable to don on such an occasion. Comical scenes ensued as men, in the act of changing their trousers, had to skip off as they might to avoid a shell about to burst. All were laughing and cheery, as if about to go to some fête. Such was the spirit of Napoleon's soldiers.'

Organisation

In 1789, as mentioned in the previous chapter, the artillery ranked as the 64th in the order of precedence of infantry regiments; although it was an entirely separate arm. It was first created as a separate corps in 1671, when it was designated *Fusiliers du Roi* with the number 51. In 1693 it became *Royal-Artillerie*, and was numbered 46. Its number of 64 was allotted in 1776, and in 1790 this was changed by a decree of 3rd December to 63.

Before the Revolution the Artillery was divided into seven regiments, with an eighth regiment to provide for colonial garrisons. A regiment comprised two battalions each of two divisions; and there were in a division five artillery companies. In a company there were 2 captains, 2 lieutenants, and 55 other ranks. The staff of a regiment consisted of a colonel, 4 lieutenant-colonels, 2 adjutants, a quartermaster, 2 regimental sergeant-majors, a surgeon-major, a drum-major, a corporal drummer, 8 bandsmen, and 3 master-craftsmen. Also belonging to the Artillery were eight companies of miners (located at Verdun), ten companies of pioneers, eight companies of invalid gunners, and some coast defence artillery companies. On 27th August 1792 the colonial regiment was incorporated in the Royal Artillery.[4]

The seven regiments in France took the titles of the seven artillery schools with which they were linked, and after the Revolution these titles were jealously retained; though like other arms of the service new numbers were allotted. The La Fère Regiment, for instance, became the *1er Régiment d'Artillerie à Pied*.[5]

The equipments of the foot artillery were hauled by horses provided by civilian waggoners, while the gunners marched on foot. Horse artillery, on the other hand, had their own horses and soldier drivers; but this branch was not included in the old regular army. Horse artillery seems to have owed its origin to the Marquis de Lafayette, who had seen and admired the Prussian 'flying batteries'. Early in 1792 General Mathieu

Dumas formed two companies of horse artillery at Metz, in which all the gunners were mounted. In Strasbourg another company was formed, but on the system used in the Prussian army with the gunners carried on the gun carriages and ammunition wagons and in special 'Wurz' light carriages. On 17th April 1792 nine horse artillery companies were formed by decree; and three were allotted to each of the Armies of the North, the Centre, and the Rhine. It was intended that all gunners should be mounted, but owing to the shortage of horses this was initially only possible in one company of each group; the Wurz carriages being used by the remainder.[6]

Apart from their mobility, the great advantage of the horse artillery was that they did not have to use the civilian waggoners. These men frequently panicked, or, in difficult situations, cut the traces of their teams and decamped, leaving the guns to fall into the hands of the enemy. Many guns were lost in this fashion. At the end of 1799, General of Brigade Marmont, who had been nominated as a Councillor of State, at last got rid of the civilian waggoners and replaced them with soldier drivers and army horses.

Besides those manned by the horse and foot artillery, pieces of ordnance were included from time to time on the establishment of infantry units. During the Seven Years War infantry battalions had had their own light guns, but these had been removed when the war ended. Each of the new volunteer battalions of the Revolutionary regime had an artillery company equipped with two 4-pr. guns. In February 1793 the intention of adding a similar company to each regular battalion was announced, but on examination the proposal was found impracticable and was dropped. However, when the demi-brigades were formed they each included an artillery company, and this formed part of the establishment until 1798 when infantry guns were abolished. In 1809 Napoleon re-introduced them and allocated to each regiment two of the numerous pieces of ordnance captured from the Austrians. They were all lost in the disastrous campaign in Russia and no further guns were issued to the infantry.

In 1795 the strength of the artillery was fixed at 8 foot regiments and 8 horse regiments. On 10th October 1801 the establishment of the Artillery was laid down in detail. There were to be 8 foot regiments, each of 20 companies; 6 horse regiments, each of 6 companies; 2 pontoon battalions, each of 8 companies; 15 pioneer companies; 8 battalions of the train; and 1 horse company for the Consular Guard. The chief artillery appointment was an Inspector-General, with the rank of general of division. The other senior officers were 7 generals of division, 12 generals of brigade, 33 *chefs de brigade* (colonels), and 37 *chefs de bataillon*. The total number of all ranks was 28,000.[7]

From 1803 there were successive increases in the artillery establishment, till in 1814 there were 328 companies. Of these, 252 provided 9 foot regiments (28 companies in each regiment), 48 made up 6 horse regiments, and 28 were in the Imperial Guard (6 foot companies and 6 horse companies in the Old Guard, and 15 foot companies and 1 horse company in the Young Guard). Each company was allotted 6 or 8 pieces, according to calibre, which were pulled by teams supplied by the artillery train. Normal quotas were 6 guns and 2 howitzers for a foot company and 4 guns and 2 howitzers for a horse company.[8]

In the artillery train there were 18 companies of artisans, 6 companies of armourers, 3 battalions of pontoneers, and a company of pontoneers of the Guard. On 30th March 1814 the total artillery strength was 80,273 all ranks. (It will be noted that pontoon bridges were the responsibility of the artillery.)[9]

Whilst the battalion organisation was retained for the foot artillery, companies of horse artillery were grouped, when required, in squadrons (normally of two companies). A horse artillery regiment had six war companies, numbered 1 to 6, and, from 1805, a depot squadron. The term 'battery' was originally applied to an emplacement containing a certain number of pieces of ordnance. As it was convenient to allot one company to serve such an emplacement, the terms 'battery' and 'company' gradually became almost synonymous. The term 'division' at this period denoted an arbitrary number of artillery equipments, approximately sufficient for two batteries. For instance, in 1805 Chef d'Escadron Boulart of the 3rd Regiment of Horse Artillery was ordered to form a division of artillery of twelve pieces, to be attached to the Imperial Guard. To serve his division, he was given two companies of his regiment.[10]

In 1815 the allotment of artillery in the Army of the North was, in general, one company of foot artillery to each division, one company of horse artillery to each cavalry division, and from one to four companies of foot artillery in each corps reserve. In III Corps, for instance, the artillery order of battle was as follows:

Commander Corps Artillery—a general of brigade with a major as chief-of-staff.
8th Division—7th Company, 1st Regiment of Foot Artillery.
10th Division—18th Company, 2nd Regiment of Foot Artillery.
11th Division—17th Company, 2nd Regiment of Foot Artillery.
3rd Cavalry Division—4th Company, 2nd Regiment of Horse Artillery.
Corps Reserve—1st and 19th Companies, 2nd Regiment of Foot Artillery.
These companies provided five batteries of foot artillery and one battery of horse artillery, with a total of 46 pieces. They were served by 30 officers and 645 men, with a further 9 officers and 402 men in the artillery train.

(It will be noted that regimental commanders had a purely administrative function, and that the unit in the field was the company.)

In the Imperial Guard, which was the army artillery reserve, there were eleven companies of foot artillery and five companies of horse artillery—a total of sixteen batteries containing 118 pieces, served by 65 officers and 1,605 men.[11]

Artillery Equipments

When the Revolutionary War broke out in 1792, the French field artillery was almost unique in being equipped throughout with 4-pr. and 8-pr. guns. All the other European armies—except the Spanish—had 6-prs., 12-prs. and 24-prs. However, when Napoleon became First Consul he directed that French ordnance should change to the European calibres. The field artillery was to be equipped with 6-pr. and 12-pr. guns and 24-pr. howitzers; whilst siege artillery was to have both short and long 24-pr. guns. But to make the change was a lengthy business, and it was not till the campaigns in Russia in 1812 and in Germany in 1813 that the artillery consisted entirely of the new equipments. It was not to be so for long, because the cumulative heavy losses led to the old 4-prs. and 8-prs. being taken out of the fixed defences to re-equip the depleted field batteries.[12]

Napoleon gave as his reasons for the change that no officer could well decide whether a 4-pr. or a 8-pr. was the proper gun to use, and therefore a 6-pr. could logically replace both of them; but a heavier gun than either was needed in reserve, and for this purpose a 12-pr. gun was suitable. He considered that a 3-pr. gun should be the equipment of mountain batteries. He thought the 6-in. howitzer too wasteful and chose the 5½-in. (24-pr.), which had the additional advantage that 75 rounds of its ammunition could be loaded on an ammunition wagon, as compared with 50 rounds of 6-in. He abolished the 10-in. mortar, but retained the 6-in., 8-in., and 12-in. The 8-in. he thought excellent as a siege mortar, whilst the 6-in. was very useful in supporting the infantry attack and in the defence of certain localities.[13]

Napoleon decided that a battery of horse artillery should have six of these equipments, and a battery of foot artillery eight; and in each battery two of the pieces should be 24-pr. howitzers and the remainder 6-pr. guns. This large proportion of howitzers was necessary for dislodging enemy from villages and other defended localities and for destroying redoubts. Each field battery was to have, in addition, two spare gun carriages, a forge, a divisional wagon (carrying spare axles, wheels, etc), six ammunition wagons (each drawn by from six to twelve mules), and four wagons for shells (each pulled by four mules).[14]

Napoleon would have liked his batteries to be smaller, with only four pieces in each; but this would have entailed almost doubling the number of artificers, spare stores, forges, etc.[15]

All these pieces or ordnance were bronze. The limbers were simple wooden affairs with two wheels, attached to the gun carriage by a pintle bolt fitting into a ring on the trail transom. Gun projectiles were round shot and canister, whilst howitzers had shells and canister. (A canister was a cylinder, fitted with a lid, and filled with small shot.) Complete cartridges were made up by putting the requisite amount of powder into a serge bag; then securing a round shot to a circular wooden plate known as a sabot, and intended to seal the bore behind the shot; and finally inserting the sabot into the mouth of the bag and tying the latter with a piece of string wound round a groove in the sabot. The Guard artillery was supplied with 350 rounds per piece, which was double the normal allotment. This ammunition was distributed between the chests on the gun carriages, the ammunition wagons, and the vehicles of the artillery park.[16]

In the 1809 campaign the artillery of the Imperial Guard had forty-eight pieces of ordnance, consisting of twelve 12-pr. guns, twenty-eight 6-pr. guns, and eight 24-pr. howitzers. For these there were the following spare gun carriages: fourteen 12-pr., thirty-four 6-pr., and ten 24-pr. The ammunition wagons, which were all under artillery control, numbered seventy-two for 12-pr. ammunition, eighty-four for 6-pr., thirty-two for howitzer, and fifty for infantry small arms ammunition. In addition there were sixteen ammunition carts and eight field forges. These guns were organised in ten batteries, each served by one company of foot artillery, and two batteries constituted a division.[17]

Artillery in Action

General Dampierre (who was saved from the guillotine by being mortally wounded in 1793) said that the French soldier depended implicitly on the superiority of his artillery and that there was a noticeable lessening of his courage if he saw that artillery receive a check or draw back. Throughout the wars of the Republic the excellent French artillery made up for many deficiencies in the other arms. The new horse artillery made its first effective appearance of the Battle of Jemappes on 6th November 1792, when several batteries went into action. Although many of the men could as yet hardly ride, the batteries did so well that every general wanted them.[18]

Marshal Saint-Cyr gives in his *Mémoires* an incident at the siege of Kehl in January 1797 which showed the tremendous pride in their arm possessed by men of the horse artillery. One of the siege batteries had been especially allotted to a company of horse artillery. But although the battery came under very heavy enfilade fire the men would not construct any earthworks to protect themselves from it. Their reply to instructions to do so was that they were horse artillery who fought in the open, and not behind entrenchments; and that if they were permitted to do so they would demolish the defences which had been erected against frontal fire. They had their way, and each morning by 9 o'clock their guns had been smashed and half their men killed or wounded.[19]

The superiority of the French artillery was not due to its equipment, but to its tactical handling and to the efficiency and esprit de corps of its officers and men. That superiority was very marked, for instance, in the Jena–Auerstädt campaign of 1806. The Prussian army had a greater ratio of artillery to infantry than the French; but in the artillery, as in the other arms, the Prussian officers were still following the teachings of Frederick the Great. In their time these had been revolutionary, but that student of the art of war, Napoleon, had absorbed the lessons and had superimposed his own system of a massive artillery reserve, in order to achieve artillery superiority at the decisive point.

To take another example, the Russian artillery was excellent as regards its equipment, but it was poorly commanded. Sir Robert Wilson writes:[20] 'The Russian artillery is of the most powerful description. No other army moves with so many guns and with no other army is there a better state of equipment, or more gallantly served. The piece is well formed, and the carriage solid, without being heavy. The harness and the rope-tackling is of the best quality for service, and all the appurtenances of the gun complete and well arranged. The draught horses are small, but of great muscular strength, strongly loined, and with high blood. Four draw the light field pieces, and eight the twelve pounders; the latter have sometimes indeed ten horses.' The extra horses were required for the dreadful Polish roads, before the frost stabilised the bottomless mud and after the thaw some months later. 'The drivers,' says Wilson, 'are stout men: like all other drivers, they require superintendence in times of danger, to prevent their escape with the horses, but on various occasions they have also shown great courage and fidelity; and they have the essential merit of carefully providing subsistence for their horses. Neither gun, tumbril, nor cart belonging to the artillery is ever seen without forage of some kind, and generally collected by the prudence and diligence of the drivers.' But the junior officers in the artillery were poor, and on active service an officer of cavalry or infantry was frequently appointed to the command of batteries.

'The horse artillery', says Wilson, 'is no less well appointed, and the mounted detachments that accompany the guns ride excellent powerful horses. . . . The Cossaque artillery, worked by Cossaques, which is a late institution, consisted of 24 pieces, extremely light, and the carriages were fashioned with a care and nicety which did great credit to Russian workmanship.'

Earlier in this chapter there is mention of the division of artillery which Chef d'Escadrom Boulart was directed to raise for attachment to the Imperial Guard. This division went into action at Jena, and Boulart recounts his experiences as follows: 'The Guard marched to Jena. It was a long day and we only arrived there as night was falling; but it was necessary to cross the town, including a street where a fire was raging both to right and left of the crossing. To pass this obstacle took much time and demanded many precautions; guns and wagons had to be sent over one by one, after unloading the forage, which as usual they were carrying. I was lucky that there was no unfortunate incident. I had been ordered, as soon as I had passed through Jena, to go into camp on a high plateau, which dominated the town and the valley of the Saale, where the Guard had taken up a position. But my leading vehicles had hardly entered the steep and sunken road which led to the plateau, when they were brought to a halt because the road was too narrow. My anxiety was great because I knew we would be fighting the next day and my horses, worn out from their long march, were in great need of food and rest. There was no time to lose. At the foot of the height, I parked as well as I could all my vehicles which had not yet entered the sunken road; then, equipping my gunners with all the pick-axes that I had, I got them to hew at the rock to widen the road. It was difficult and heavy work and progress was slow. I was striving desperately to quicken the pace, and was everywhere— animating, pressing, and encouraging my men. I was worn out with fatigue and anxiety; I felt that the Guard could not fight without me, or at least that I would be dishonoured if my artillery did not appear in time to take part in the action. At last, at daybreak, at the very moment when the Guard left their fires to stand to arms, my last vehicles arrived on the plateau and I began to breathe in the happy relief that I had achieved my aim. The first musket shots were soon heard and a little later the action became general. The din gradually moved further away, but the Guard took no part; it remained in order of battle during the whole action, only changing position to move forward as the leading lines gained ground, and containing its impatience whilst awaiting an order to move into the attack. In fact an order arrived at midday, but it only concerned my artillery. The Emperor sent instructions that it was to move forward immediately and that I was to ride ahead and get his orders. In an instant my batteries were on the way, and whilst they advanced at a trot, I galloped off to report their arrival to His Majesty. I found him just finishing an address to a large body of cavalry. This cavalry had just returned from the brilliant charges which had decided the victory, and the Emperor was expressing his satisfaction. It was a stirring moment. I approached to take his orders. "Well done!" he said to me, "I do not need your artillery; return to my Guard."'

Shortly after the Battle of Jena, the artillery of the Guard arrived, and Boulart, with his artillery division, was transferred on attachment to Oudinot's special infantry division, composed of grenadier and light infantry battalions.

But Boulart had made his mark and before the 1809 campaign he was posted to the Horse Artillery of the Guard as a *Chef d'Escadron*. He was soon promoted to *Chef de Bataillon* in a new regiment of Foot Artillery of the Guard, discarding rather reluctantly the blue dolman and pelisse of the Guard's Horse Artillery.

When the French army entered Vienna in 1809, Boulart was commanding two batteries of the Foot Artillery of the Guard, equipped with a total of twelve pieces of ordnance. The Emperor inspected these two batteries at one of the daily parades at Schoenbrünn. As usual, he went into great detail, but found everything in order. One of the gunners, however, told the Emperor that one of the 12-pr. guns was 'mad'—that is, its fire was a little uncertain.

At daybreak on 22nd May Boulart, who had his two batteries on the north side of the island of Lobau and close to the river, was ordered to send one of his batteries forward with the Chasseurs of the Guard. Leaving one battery close to the bridge, Boulart followed the chasseurs with the other towards Essling. He brought his battery into action but was soon overwhelmed by the Austrian fire, his battery commander losing an arm and he himself being slightly wounded. The position was untenable, and he moved the battery closer to the chasseurs, establishing it in a tile factory by the village of Gross-Aspern. But he had to contend with the fire of at least twelve pieces against his six. Short of ammunition, he sent back for more, but all the ground to his rear was swept by the heavy enemy fire. Finally, when half his men and a third of his horses were out of action, lack of ammunition forced him to cease fire and give way to a fresh battery.

Marshal Masséna was now 300 to 400 yards in rear with the Chasseur Division of the Guard, and Boulart reported to him and remained with him until the end of the action. Masséna told him that the Austrians had cut the bridge over the Danube and thus their communications. That night the army withdrew to the island of Lobau.

Boulart writes that, 'On the 26th, as soon as the bridge was rebuilt, the Guard and my artillery crossed to the right bank, and moved to the village of Ebersdorf where Imperial Headquarters was. I had hardly been there an hour when the Emperor sent for me. I was taken into his office where he was standing by a table on which maps were spread out. "Have you brought back all your artillery?" he asked me. "Yes, Sire." "Have you any ammunition left?" "Some grape shot but no round shot." "And why have you not spat that out at the enemy's face?" "Sire, because I was not within range, and the position of my battery was subordinated to that of the troops to which I was attached. Marshal Masséna, who was there, could see that I was not able to do more." "How many men and horses have you lost?" "Sire (I gave him the figures)." "And your mad piece, did it fire well?" What a memory to recall such a minor detail! Nothing escaped him. "Yes, Sire, its fire has been better for I gave it my personal attention." "And your other pieces, are they in good condition?" "Sire, there is one of which the vent is greatly widened and which has need of a vent lining." "And why, Sir, has this lining not already been fitted?" He added in a high and angry tone, "In what regiment have you served?" This outburst, absolutely undeserved, disconcerted me a little. "Sire, I arrived on the Isle of Lobau where I had no resources with which to carry out this repair. There is only the arsenal at Vienna that might be able to do it, and already I have made arrangements to send the piece there." "Yes; expedite its departure; tomorrow I will inspect your artillery and you will show me the repaired piece." "Sire, your orders will be carried out." I knew the thing impossible, but it was no good saying so. The Emperor knew nothing of impossibilities.

'I was very worried when I left him, but I set about taking action immediately. I sent Captain Lefrancais to Vienna with the piece, telling him to expedite the repair if he could find at the arsenal a machine to install vent linings. But Captain Lefrancais would not be able to return in time for the Emperor's inspection; and it was necessary, therefore, to procure a gun to replace temporarily the missing one. It seemed to me that it should suffice if the Emperor could see that my batteries were complete and ready to move. I hurried to see General Songis, to tell him of my trouble and seek his help. "I would willingly do so," he said, "but in fact there are only Austrian 12-pr. guns in the general park, though these are of the same calibre as ours. If you wish I will put one at your disposal." For lack of anything better I accepted; but the thought of the inspection the next day depressed me. The Emperor would of course notice the absence of my piece; and what would he say if he was still in his present bad humour? At least I would not fare any better, and at the worst I should get another "broadside".

'The next day at 11 am I went to His Majesty's apartments; where I spent a long enough time in the antechamber with the Russian Colonel Czernischeff, a young and handsome man, beautifully turned out. At last I was summoned. He was not the same man as on the previous day; he had received excellent news of the Army of Italy and his face was cheerful and contented. I noticed this at once and was reassured. "Well, Commandant, your 12-pr., has it returned?" "Not yet, Sire. I am informed that I shall receive it during the day. Whilst waiting I have replaced it by a piece lent me by General Songis." "Have you replenished your ammunition?" "Yes,

Sire, I can now go into action." "Good. I will not inspect you." And this was all said in a kindly tone with considerable charm.'[21]

This account by Boulart tells us more about the personality of that remarkable man the Emperor Napoleon than do many books that have been written about him.

At the Battle of Wagram, which followed shortly after this incident, the French artillery fired 96,000 rounds. The day after the battle Boulart visited the ground which the Guard artillery had ploughed up with its projectiles and he did not find that the damage done was proportionate to the ammunition expended. Other parts of the field reinforced this impression. And yet never had such a mass of artillery been assembled, producing such a brisk, continuous and frightening noise; for those who heard the uproar from afar believed that the two armies were destroying themselves.[22]

After Wagram, Boulart was promoted Major in the Guard, which gave him the rank of Colonel in the Line and the title of 'Colonel-Major'.

1. Colonel R. W. Phipps, *The Armies of the First French Republic*, ed. Colonel C. F. Phipps and Elizabeth Sanders, 1926–1939 (5 vols.)
2. Count Yorck von Wartenburg, *Napoleon as a General*, ed. Major W. H. James, 1902
3. F. Loraine Petre, *Napoleon's Last Campaign in Germany 1813*, 1912
4. Edouard Detaille and Jules Richard, *L'Armée Française*, 1885–1889
5. ibid.
   Phipps, op. cit.
6. ibid.
7. Detaille, op. cit.
8. ibid.
   Henry Lachoque, adapted by Anne S. K. Brown, *The Anatomy of Glory*, 1961
9. Detaille, op. cit.
10. *Mémoires Militaires du Général Baron Boulart*
11. Detaille, op. cit.
12. Colonel H. C. B. Rogers, *Artillery through the Ages*, 1971
13. ibid.
14. ibid.
15. ibid.
16. ibid.
    Lachoque, op. cit.
17. Commandant Saski, *Campagne de 1809*, 1899
18. Phipps, op. cit.
19. ibid.
20. Sir Robert Wilson, *The Russian Army and the Campaigns in Poland 1806–7*, 1810
21. Boulart, op. cit.
22. ibid.

CHAPTER FIVE

ENGINEERS AND SIGNALS

Engineer Organization

Before the Revolution, engineers had no separate existence as a corps, though there was a staff of engineer officers. In 1789 there were six companies of miners which were attached to the artillery and six companies of sappers which actually formed part of the artillery. The artillery apparently thought this a gross waste of manpower for they transformed the sapper companies into companies of foot artillery.

On 23rd October 1793 the first step in creating a Corps of Engineers was made by an order directing the separation of the miner companies from the artillery. This separation became effective on 15th December when these companies were transferred to the Engineers, and on the same day a decree of the Convention ordered the formation of twelve battalions of sappers each of eight companies of 200 men, which should be attached to the Engineers. This date therefore is that of the creation of the Corps of Engineers.[1]

In 1791 there was set up the Central Committee on Fortifications. This body was re-organised on 3rd April 1795, and the decree effecting this also dealt with the whole organisation of the engineers. The establishment of the corps was laid down as 437 officers and six companies of miners. The officers were made up of 7 inspectors-general of fortification (3 generals of division and 4 generals of brigade), 30 directors (*chefs de brigade*, i.e. colonels), 60 assistant directors (*chefs de bataillon*) 260 engineer captains (of whom 12 were attached to the miners), and 80 engineer lieutenants (of whom 12 were attached to the miners). The Committee on Fortifications was composed of the inspectors-general and such officers as the Committee of Public Safety considered should attend. Finally, the decree mentioned nine regiments (obviously battalions) of sappers, but did not indicate why the establishment had been decreased from the twelve of two years earlier. These units were apparently considered as being only attached to the Corps of Engineers, and not an integral part of it as were the miner companies. On 24th January 1798 another decree reduced the number of sapper battalions to four.[2]

Under the Empire there were a number of notable changes in the engineer establishment. The six companies of miners were first reduced to five, then increased to nine, and in 1808 a tenth company was formed and the whole formed into two battalions. A little later the number of companies in each battalion was raised to six. The sapper battalions were increased in number once more until eventually there were eight—five French, one Dutch, one Italian, and one Spanish. But the losses in the campaign of 1812 led to the number being reduced to five. An Imperial innovation was an engineer train battalion, which was badly needed, and in 1806 each sapper battalion was directed to hold a park of tools. A number of pioneer companies were formed to provide unskilled labour for engineer work.[3]

Battalions of sappers and miners constituted 'magazines' of men from which armies and corps drew companies, and sometimes only detachments, according to their needs. Engineers took a major part in sieges, they were responsible for road works in the field, they advised the infantry in the construction of field fortifications, they laid out the works for protecting gun emplacements, and they were entirely responsible for the fortification of fixed defences. Except for field works, they were generally under the central control of the Chief Engineer. Pontoon bridges, as stated in the last chapter, were artillery equipment, but the engineers were required to build trestle and permanent bridges. The sole reason for this apparently illogical arrangement was that the artillery train was the most suitable organisation for the management and movement of the pontoons.[4] However, in the later campaigns of the Empire the engineers had their own train with the result that they, as well as the artillery, had pontoon bridging equipment. There was always great rivalry between these two corps and it is likely that Napoleon had conceded a claim by the engineers that they should gradually take over responsibility for all bridging.

In March 1809 Napoleon wrote to General Bertrand, Commandant of Engineers in the Army of Germany, laying down in some detail how the Engineers were to be organised for the coming campaign. The engineer war equipment was to be carried in 48 wagons with six-horse teams, and this train would amount to 30,000 engineer tools, about 300 horses, and from 180 to 200 men. Bertrand was to receive eight pontoon companies from the Army of the Rhine, one of which was to be attached to each of the three corps, one to the Guard (in addition to its own company), and one to the cavalry; whilst the remaining three were to be held in the general park. (It will be noted that these pontoon companies were under engineer and not artillery control.) The engineer establishment of each corps was to consist of one pontoon company, two sapper companies, and 6,000 engineer tools. The engineer park was to include the following units: a battalion of naval pioneers, 800 strong; a battalion of marines, 1,200 strong; 9 sapper companies with 900 men and 2 surgeons; 3 miner companies with 300 men and 1 surgeon; 3 pontoon companies with 300 men and 1 surgeon; 4 pioneer companies with 600 men and 1 surgeon; and 2 artillery companies with 6 pieces of ordnance. Two battalions were to be formed from the sapper and miner companies, one battalion from the pontoon companies, and one battalion from the pioneer companies. These four battalions were to be commanded by a major of the engineers. The naval pioneer battalion and the marine battalion were to be reformed into three battalions under the command of a colonel, *Capitaine de Vaisseau* (i.e. a naval officer holding rank as post captain). The whole of this engineer park was to form a reserve under the command of a general, and to it were to be attached a War Commissary, a regimental sergeant-major, and 4 ambulance wagons.[5]

On 30th January 1809 the engineer-geographers came into being as a new branch of the engineers, with the primary responsibility for ordnance survey and the production of maps of theatres of operations. The establishment comprised 4 colonels, 4 *chefs d'escadron*, 24 captains 1st class, 24 captains 2nd class, and 6 'pupils' who were second lieutenants or lower. The bottom ranks of the branch were to be filled from the *Ecole Polytechnique*.[6]

Fortifications

Probably the most important task of Napoleon's engineers was the construction of fortifications. Napoleon called fortification, 'a difficult science in which the least mistakes may have a great influence upon the success of a campaign and the fate of a nation.' The reason he placed so much value on it is shown by the following sentence: 'There are some military men who ask what is the use of fortresses, entrenched camps, and all the science of engineering? I in my turn should like to ask these men how is it possible to manœuvre with inferior or equal forces without the assistance of positions, fortifications, and all such accessories of our art?'

Napoleon himself wrote an *Essai sur la fortification de campagne* in which he distinguished between the various engineer tasks. There were works (generally entrenchments) which could be thrown up in between five and thirty minutes with the ordinary pioneer tools which every soldier should carry with him. There were other works which, although capable of affording some protection after an hour's work, had to be so planned that the labour of twenty hours or more would result in localities sufficiently strong to withstand attack by a force at least twice as powerful as that of the defenders. According to Napoleon: 'The natural positions usually available do not afford sufficient protection against a superior army without being supplemented by art.' Both these types of defence were field fortifications which the infantry and artillery were expected to do themselves, though perhaps with engineer advice on planning and layout.

In quite a different category were temporary works erected on the line of communications to protect important places. These were engineer tasks which might take several days and should be constructed, said Napoleon, of light masonry and wood. Nevertheless these temporary fortifications were no substitute for permanent fortifications because the latter needed much smaller garrisons.[7]

Napoleon placed particular value on fortified bridgeheads. In 1808 he said, 'No river, though it be as wide as the Vistula or as rapid as the Danube near its mouth, is an obstacle, provided one has free access to the opposite bank and is always ready to assume the offensive.' And in 1813, as regards the Elbe, he said, 'No river has ever yet been looked upon as an obstacle which could stop an advance for more than a few days; and its passage can only be defended by placing troops in large numbers in bridgeheads on the opposite bank, ready to assume the offensive as soon as the enemy begins crossing. Nothing is more dangerous than to try and defend a river seriously by occupying the near bank in force; for as soon as the enemy has forced a passage by surprise—and he always does force it—he finds the defending army in a very extended position and can prevent it concentrating.' He had strong views on the siting of fortified localities for the defence of bridgeheads. Those constructed on the Vistula did not meet with his approval because they were too close to the river and thus did not allow sufficient space for troops to shelter under their protection during the lengthy operation of crossing the river. At St. Helena he said that the engineers, 'ought to leave room between the works and the river, so that an army, without having to enter the works (a movement which might endanger its safety), can assemble between them and the bridge. . . . The bridgeheads which the engineers constructed in front of Marienwerder were quite close to the Vistula, and would have been of but little use to the army if it had been forced to cross that river in its retreat.'[8]

Balloons and Pigeons

The first balloon company was formed on 2nd April 1794 in the Army of the Sambre and Meuse, and remained with that army until it was transferred in 1797 to the Army of Egypt, where it was in due course disbanded.

A second balloon company was formed at Meudon on 23rd June 1794 and served in action first with the Army of the North and then with the Army of the Rhine. It was disbanded on 17th February 1799. A military balloon school was also formed in 1794 at Meudon, and this lasted till 1800.[9]

The *ci-devant* Marquis de Dampierre, who succeeded Dumouriez in command of the Army of the North on 4th April 1793, was a very keen balloonist. In 1788 he had become so absorbed in balloon ascents that he forgot that he was overstaying his leave, and on his eventual return to his regiment he was placed under arrest.

Balloons were much used by the French in the early campaigns, both for reconnaissance and communications; though as the balloon companies were eventually disbanded it would appear that Napoleon did not consider that the results justified the effort.

At the sieges of Valenciennes and Condé in 1793 the French garrisons made use of balloons to communicate with the headquarters of the neighbouring French field forces. At least one balloon from each of these towns fell into enemy hands. The Valenciennes balloon contained a carrier pigeon which was presumably intended to return with any messages for the garrison. However, its active service was terminated prematurely, for the Austrians cooked and ate it.[10]

Pigeons were probably used quite extensively for communications. Before the Allies laid siege to Le Quesnoy in 1793, General Gobert, commanding in that area, asked the *Conseil Général* to supply him with pigeons to provide communications between that fortress and Cambrai. The *Conseil* approved his request—as long as they did not have to pay for the pigeons.[11]

Perhaps the chief claim to fame of the Battle of Fleurus, on 26th June 1794, is that it was the first in which an aircraft took part. This aircraft was the famous French balloon *Entrepenant*, which was made by Guyton and Contille at Meudon. It was controlled by André-Jacques Garnerin, the inventor of parachutes, who had formed the balloon company at Meudon a few days before. The balloon was held by ropes and the car was occupied by General Morlot and an engineer officer, who were to reconnoitre the enemy and slide reports down the retaining ropes to the ground. Perhaps because they were to inexperienced or too high up, the reports they submitted contained little useful information, and some of this was incorrect.[12] The Austrians fired at it, and though they failed to hit it, this must have been the first anti-aircraft fire in history. Captain Charles François writes of the Battle of Fleurus: 'A balloon hovered over us, governed by means of ropes. Two officers occupied it and made known by signals the movements of the enemy. We took a battery of eight guns, and found some of them loaded and pointed at the balloon, which had contributed greatly in winning the battle.'[13] The balloon accompanied the army until 1796 when it was captured by the Austrians at Würzburg, and kept subsequently as a trophy in the Arsenal at Vienna.

Telegraph

Two brothers, Claude and Ignace Chappe, invented a form of semaphore for communicating over long distances by a chain of fixed stations. It was called the 'telegraph' or 'radiated telegraph' and was the first efficient signalling system to be devised. The Legislative Assembly was so impressed with it that they adopted it in 1792 to provide a national communications network. The apparatus consisted of an upright post with a crossbar at the top, at each end of which was a pivoted arm. At night lanterns were attached to the extremities of the pivoted arms. The semaphore stations were established on hilltops, never more than $7\frac{1}{2}$ miles apart, because this was the maximum distance at which lantern signals could be read at night. When the system was complete, telegraph 'lines' radiated from Paris in different directions.[14] The first line was established in 1793 between Paris and Lille. This was connected to Dunkirk in the same year and to Brussels in 1803. Other lines were constructed from Paris to Brest, Lyon, and Strasbourg. In 1805 the Lyon line was extended to Milan and the Strasbourg line to Huningen.

The earliest message over the system of which there is any record was sent to the Committee of Public Safety on 15th August 1794 reporting the surrender to the French of Quesnoy in the following acceptable phraseology of the period: 'Austrian garrison of 3,000 slaves has laid down its arms and surrendered at discretion.' It is said that this message reached Paris in one hour.[15]

The telegraph system played an important part during the preliminary stages of the 1809 campaign. Napoleon remained in Paris till the last moment, dealing with Government affairs; but on 30th March he sent Berthier, his Chief of Staff or *Major-Général*, to set up Imperial Headquarters at Strasbourg, where he would be in communication with Paris by telegraph line. Over this link Napoleon commanded his army at a distance and received reports on the situation. This telegraph chain had the disadvantage common to all visual signalling systems of being dependent on good visibility—a disadvantage which signal officers down the ages have found generals so reluctant to accept as a valid reason for the delay of messages! Almost inevitably (as all signal officers will agree!) there was a delay to a most important message with repercussions which endangered the course of operations. On 10th April Napoleon signalled operation orders to Berthier, but the message was so badly delayed by fog that the Major-General had left Strasbourg before it arrived and it did not reach him till 16th April at Augsburg. The message is of such importance in the history of signals that it is worth quoting in full. It ran as follows:

'The Emperor to the Major-General of the Army of Germany at Strasbourg.

'Paris 10th April 1890.

'Telegraphic despatch received at Strasbourg 13th at midday.

'I think that the Emperor of Austria will attack soon. Go to Augsburg and act in accordance with my instructions, and, if the enemy attacks before 15th, you must concentrate the troops at Augsburg and Donauworth, and make all ready to march.

'Send my Guard and my horses to Stuttgart.

'Napoleon.'

The message is endorsed in the margin in Berthier's hand: 'I have the honour to observe to H. M. that this despatch only reached me today at Augsburg, 16th April, at 6 am.'[16]

1. Edouard Detaille and Jules Richard, *L'Armée Française*, 1885–1889
2. ibid.
3. ibid.
4. ibid.
5. Commandant Saski, *Campagne de 1809*, 1899
6. ibid.
7. Count Yorck von Wartenburg, *Napoleon as a General*, ed. Major W. H. James, 1902
8. ibid.
9. Detaille, op. cit.
10. Colonel R. W. Phipps, *The Armies of the First French Republic*, ed. Colonel C. F. Phipps and Elizabeth Sanders, 1926–1939 (5 vols.)
11. ibid.
12. ibid.
13. Captain Charles Francois, *From Valmy to Waterloo*, ed. and transl. R. B. Douglas, 1906
14. Major-General R. F. H. Nalder, *The Royal Corps of Signals*, 1958
15. Phipps, op. cit.
    F. Loraine Petre, *Napoleon and the Archduke Charles*, 1909
16. ibid.
    Saski, op. cit.

CHAPTER SIX

ADMINISTRATION

Organisation

Under the old regime the King had at one time detailed, as commissariat officer for the army in the event of war, the *Intendant Civil* of the province which was nearest to the theatre of operations. The advantage of this arrangement was that the *Intendant Civil* had a knowledge of the frontier in his area. Under his orders there were a number of war commissaries. In later years the King allotted this task to a senior commissariat officer, who then took the title of '*Intendant*' of the King's armies, a title which he retained as an honour when the war was over. In 1788 there were 2 *intendants d'armée*, 23 chief commissaries, 127 commissaries, and 20 pupils. For a long time this administrative corps was recruited solely from civilians, though candidates for it had to receive military training by serving as army officers for five years. The Assembly abolished the corps on 20th September 1791, and replaced it by 23 commissaries and 134 war commissaries. As long as the tempo of the war was slow, these civilians managed to compete. But the Revolutionary armies did not function by the old methods, and as the rapidity of military operations increased difficulties arose. Money was not provided, and there were, in consequence, acute shortages in both munitions and supplies. To make matters worse, war ministers often accepted goods of lower quality. There was much mal-administration, and agreements for supplies made by generals-in-chief were often not ratified by the minister.[1]

On 10th July 1793 a more efficient administration was installed. Carnot was charged with responsibility for operations and personnel; Prieur with the manufacture of arms, munitions and equipment; and Robert Lindet and another Prieur with provisions, subsistence, and finance.

Carnot, in fact, directed the troops, Prieur clothed and equipped them, and Lindet fed and paid them. The administrative corps was reformed in personnel and its method of working was modified. It was now composed of 60 chief commissaries (*ordonnateurs*), 300 commissaries, and 240 2nd class commissaries. At the headquarters of each army there was a commissary-in-chief (*commissaire ordonnateur en chef*) who was head of all the army's administrative services. Theoretically he was not responsible to the army commander, but reported to and received his directions from his administrative superiors in Paris. In practice, however, he was regarded as subordinate to the general-in-chief commanding the army.[2]

When Napoleon, as First Consul, re-organised the French army, he separated the administrative functions from the direction of military operations, and on 8th March 1802 he established a Department of War Administration. The commissariat officers remained civilians, but the head of the department was a general of division. In 1804 there was a further reorganisation inside the new department. The duties of commissariat officers were confined to supply, and an inspectorate was set up with responsibility for administration of the troops and for the administrative inspection of units. The central inspectorate committee consisted of six inspectors-in-chief, of whom four were stationed in Paris, one in Italy, and one with the coastal army. There were 31 inspectors, of whom 24 were attached home districts and 7 were with the field army. Of these, Daru, the most famous and the one most trusted by Napoleon, went to the headquarters of camp staffs and soon afterwards became Intendant General of the Army, whilst the others were distributed between the camps at Montreuil, Saint-Omer, Bruges, and Utrecht, and the army in Hanover. There were also 15 1st class assistant inspectors, 26 2nd class, and 60 3rd class. On the commissariat side there were 38 chief commissaries, 100 1st class war commissaries, 100 2nd class war commissaries, and 50 assistants.[3] In the Department of War Administration each branch was headed by a director assisted by an administrative council. There was, for instance, a director of clothing, who was responsible for advising on markets and for inspecting cloth. There was also a director of remounts, and Napoleon, who scented a robber in every head contractor, suspected both these directorates.[4]

Transport

At the start of the Revolutionary Wars all transport was civilian. Ammunition moved in civil convoys and the artillery employed civilian waggoners to move their guns and other equipment. The army looked down on these civilian waggoners, and in the Army of the Sambre and Meuse the Hussars gave them the unflattering names of the Royal Cart Grease and the Four-Wheel Hussars. Under the Empire a large organisation, the Breidt Company, provided all the wagons, drivers, and teams of horses for the army; but it failed Napoleon so badly in the Eylau campaign that he was unable to manœuvre as he had intended. As a result he decided that transport should be taken over by the army and he instituted a Carriage Train Corps. Nine battalions, each of six companies, were authorised on 26th March 1807. A battalion was commanded by a captain, assisted by a lieutenant quartermaster, and each company was commanded by a senior non-commissioned officer. The new corps was such a success that the number of battalions was eventually increased to twenty three, including one for the Imperial Guard. The headquarters of the Carriage Train was at Evreux, where two companies of wheelwrights maintained the vehicles.[5]

The Carriage Train battalions figured prominently for the first time in the campaign of 1809. In March of that year the 2nd and 5th Battalions were already with the Army of the Rhine, whilst the 12th was forming at Commercy. From the depots in France of transport battalions serving with the Army of Spain, 200 wagons were being sent to Joigny where they were to be formed into two reserve battalions. It was reckoned that these units would provide five transport battalions for the coming campaign, with a total of 700 wagons.[6] In 1809 M. Daru was appointed to the civilian post of Intendant General of the force which was to become the Grand Army. His responsibilities included all military transport services, health, clothing, footwear, provisions, requisitions, and pay. Napoleon ordered him to report on the state of the army's transport, and this Daru did on 27th March 1809. He said that the two transport battalions already with the Army had 136 wagons each, excluding forge wagons and ammunition wagons. In addition there were 21 wagons in good condition but without horses. The 12th Battalion was completing formation at St. Mihiel with 136 wagons, and their horses were due to arrive between 28th March and 15th April. At Joigny a provisional battalion was being formed which would have 180 wagons. The men and horses for this battalion were due to join it between 18th and 20th April, and it would be organised in five companies. The total number of wagons would thus be 609. Half of these, however, would be drawn by unseasoned horses straight from the depots and driven by newly recruited driver. A large number of failures must therefore be expected on a long march. The wagons could together carry 600,000 rations of bread, or approximately the amount the army would eat in two days. To keep up a continual supply, therefore, the vehicle columns would have to be in constant movement and this was not practicable. In addition, some wagons would have to be detached for hospital service, and the Emperor had indeed ordered that four wagons in each transport company were to serve as ambulances. There would be 17 or 18 companies, so that 68 or 72 vehicles would have to be deducted from those available to carry supplies. As regards the organisation of the transport; it would be necessary to provide each unit with vehicles to fetch and carry their provisions. An infantry battalion should carry five days' supply, two days' in wagons and three days' on the man. The transport vehicles remaining under the control of Imperial Headquarters would be capable of carrying a reserve of 300,000 or 400,000 rations. Each infantry battalion would need two wagons and would be responsible for sending them back to the magazines to draw bread.[7]

Thus reported the great Intendant General, and it will be seen that his meticulous examination showed the original forecast to have been far too optimistic. His proposed organisation was undoubtedly the best way of making use of the limited number of vehicles, which were far too few to provide proper supply trains. The fighting strength of the Grand Army, including the troops supplied by the various German states, was about 200,000, and Daru's report suggests a total ration strength of about 300,000. By way of comparison, in the American Civil War the fighting strength of the Federal Army of the Potomac was about 140,000 men and the number of wagons for all purposes was about 5,000.

Most of the wagons of the transport battalions were lost in the Russian campaign of 1812, and much improvisation was therefore necessary for the operations in Germany during the following year. All kinds of civilian vehicles were impressed, and only in the Guard was the carriage train in reasonable order. An unexpected result of the 1812 campaign was that the movement of transport columns in 1813 was badly affected. In Russia, if trains dropped back behind the fighting troops, they fell into the hands of the Russians. Consequently, when there was any lagging, with inevitable intervals between units and vehicles, there was an order of, 'Serrez! Serrez!' (i.e. 'close up!), and horses pulling the rearmost carriages had to break into a trot. These perpetual accelerations were very tiring on the draught horses; and whenever the ground permitted, formations advanced on a wide front to keep the distances from front to rear short.[8]

It was probably during the Napoleonic campaigns that troops were first transported in road vehicles on a large scale. The Guard, particularly, was frequently transported long distances in this way. In 1805 the Paris column of the Guard was sent to Strasbourg by post—a very rapid means of travelling, with horses being changed at each posting stage (i.e. at about ten-mile intervals). The troops were packed four or five to a two-wheeled cart and twelve in a four-wheeled wagon, and covered an average of sixty miles a day, or, say, six post stages. This was very wearing on the men and the commissaries reported that it was very hard on the equipment. In 1806, in preparation for the campaign against Prussia, the Guard was moved in a long column of vehicles to Mayence. The commissaries went ahead to prepare the reliefs of horses, meals, and night stopping places.[9] This move was referred to in the following letter of 19th September 1806 from Napoleon to Marshal Bessieres, Colonel-General of the Guard:

'Cousin, order your chief of staff to leave on 23rd to reach Mayence as quickly as possible and there prepare for the organisation of the Guard as soon as it arrives. It is necessary to send off the bakers and all other workers of the Guard by the carriages established for the transport of the Guard, so that they may arrive at the same time as it does. Also order the chief commissary, surgeons, and clerks of the Guard to be at Mayence on 30th September.

'You, your ADCs, and the rest of your staff will leave on 24th to arrive at Mayence on 28th in order to accelerate the organisation of the units of my Guard and to prepare all that is necessary for your depot. You will send off the remainder of the mounted element of the Guard on 21st, so that by the evening of 21st no Guard personnel remain in Paris.

'The following units will compose my Guard:

Two regiments of *chasseurs à cheval*	1,200 men
Two regiments of *grenadiers à cheval*	1,200 men
One regiment of *gendarmerie d'élite*	400 men
The squadron of mamelukes	80 men
Two regiments of *chasseurs à pied*	2,000 men
Two regiments of *grenadiers à pied*	2,000 men
Four divisions of artillery of twenty-four pieces of ordnance, a park composed of twelve pieces of ordnance, and 1,000 artillerymen	1,000 men
Four battalions of foot dragoons, each battalion composed of four companies	2,400 men
Four battalions of grenadiers and light infantry composed of the 3rd and 4th battalions formed in the 5th, 25th, and 26th military divisions	2,400 men

All of these will make 12,000 men of infantry, cavalry, and artillery. As these battalions will need commanding officers, captains, and adjutants, leave only in the battalions of *velites* (apprentice guardsmen) one *chef de bataillon* each and take the other, with the four best captains, lieutenants, and second-lieutenants; all of whom will report at Mayence before 30th September and will be posted to the different battalions.'[10]

From the above, not only will the magnitude of the movement be apparent but also the detail into which Napoleon went. He had written to the King of Holland too on 19th September as follows: 'Circumstances

A Mounted 'Guide' 1800.

A Representative of the People, 1793.

A General of Division and Assistant Adjutant-Generals, 1799.

The Emperor's Staff 1804-1815.

An Assistant Adjutant-General 1804-1815.

A Grenadier of the Infantry of the Line 1789.

Soldiers of the Colonel-General Regiment and of the Paris National Guards, 1789.

Infantry of the Line, 1789.

An Officer of the Infantry of the Line, 1789.

Soldiers in the White and the Blue Uniforms, 1792.

*A Grenadier of the Infantry
of the Line, 1794.*

The 23rd Demi-Brigade, 1796.

Light Infantry,
1797.

Infantry of the Army of the Sambre and Meuse, 1795.

Infantry in Italy, 1796.

A Soldier of the Grenadier Company in the Infantry of the Line, 1806.

A Carbinier of the Light Infantry, 1806.

A Drummer of the Infantry of the Line, 1806.

Officer and Men of the Infantry of the Line, 1806.

A Sapper of the Infantry of the Line, 1806.

A Soldier of the Grenadier Company, Infantry of the Line, 1812.

A Regiment of the Infantry of the Line, 1813.

*Above:
A Trumpeter of th
Constitutional
Guard, 1791.*

A Colonel of the Infantry of the Line, 1812.

Infantry on the March, Army of the North, 1815.

*A Colonel of
Dragoons, 1789.*

Officer and Troopers of the Mestre de Camp General Regiment, 1789.

A Trumpeter of the Regiment of Saxon Hussars, 1789.

A Trooper of the 7th Regiment of Cavalry, 1789.

A Chasseur à Cheval, 1789.

*Uniform of the
Regiments of Cavalry,
1793.*

Chasseurs à Cheval, 1796.

Hussars in the Army of the Rhine, 1793.

A Camel Squadron of a Dragoon Regiment, Army of Egypt, 1798.

Hussars at a Review by the First Consul, 1800.

Dragoons in the Italian Campaign, 1800.

Officers of Chasseurs à Cheval and Hussars, 1805.

Carbiniers, 1806.

Cuirassiers, 1806.

Chasseurs à Cheval passing through Berlin, 1806.

Polish Light Horse, 1807.

Hussars Skirmishing, 1805-15.

Trumpeters of the 1st Cuirassiers, 1812.

General La Salle, Commander of a Light Cavalry Division and his staff, 1806.

Officers of Chasseurs à Cheval, 1812.

A Chasseur à Cheval of the Imperial Guard; Service Dress, 1805-15.

A Dragoon of the Imperial Guard, 1805-15.

Carbiniers in Russia, 1812.

The Emperor in the Field, 1812.

Dismounted Dragoons, 1806.

Elite Company of Dragoons, 1805-15.

A Colonel of the Light Horse Lancers, 1814.

1st Light Horse Lancers, Imperial Guard, 1807.

Lancers scouting ahead of a Regiment of Cuirassiers, 1815.

Horse Grenadiers of the Imperial Guard, 1815.

Soldiers of the Royal Corps of Artillery and Provincial Artillery Regiments, 1789.

Foot Artillery in Action, 1796.

Foot Artillery and the Artillery Train, 1806-12.

Horse Artillery, 1806-12.

Horse Artillery and the Artillery Train of the Imperial Guard, 1806-13.

Foot Artillery, Imperial Guard, 1808-15.

Engineer Corps, 1805-15.

*Sappers of the Engineers,
Imperial Guard, 1810-14.*

Engineer Corps – Completing a Breach, 1805-15.

Carriage train, 1805-15.

Chief Commissaries, 1796.

An Administrative Inspector.

Doctors and Wounded Soldiers, 1805-15.

Carriage Train and Administrative Personnel, 1804-15.

become more urgent every day. My Guard has left by post and will make the journey from Paris to Mayence in six days.' On 20th September he sent a follow-up directive to Bessieres: 'Cousin, have sent by stages, like the infantry of my Guard, a crew of sailors of my Guard, composed of 100 men, to report at Mayence.'[11]

The distance from Paris to Mayence is 345 miles, or say 35 stages. One may perhaps assume that the vehicles impressed for this march consisted of a mixture of two wheeled and four-wheeled varieties; and if about 10,000 dismounted men were lifted at an average of ten per vehicle, then there would have been about 1,000 vehicles. Some of these would have been drawn by two horses and others by four, so that an average of three horses per vehicle would require the provision at each stage of 3,000 fresh horses. One may perhaps calculate the time required for a ten-mile stage, including change of horses and short fall-outs for the men, at two hours. Twelve hours would thus be spent on the road each day before halting for the evening meal and camp. To arrange such a move smoothly, must have entailed very competent staff work.

Supply

By breaking away from the supply system of the eighteenth century, the armies of Revolutionary France gained immensely in mobility. In the early operations leading up to the Battle of Valmy, the Prussian Army, for instance, would halt until six days' rations of bread had been baked and loaded on to their enormous wagon train, and then march till the wagons were empty, when there would be a halt for a further six days' baking. Of course, the French soldiers were generally hungry and the Prussian soldiers were not. French units were expected to use their initiative in foraging; but this often resulted that in poor districts the men went without, whilst foraging in rich districts often degenerated into plunder, in place of orderly search and requisition.[12]

The difficulties of commanders over supply at this time are shown by Jourdan's campaign in Germany in 1796. He had practically no transport, and so was forced to live entirely on the country as he advanced; and this entailed moving on a much wider front than was tactically advisable. Marshal Soult said of these operations: 'General Jourdan doubtless made mistakes; but so did the Government, and for their mistakes, which were far worse, they tried to blame him. Jourdan's usual fault was that he deployed his army over so wide a front that it was impossible for the corps to support each other. The reason for this dispersion, however, was the difficulty of supply. We had no financial resources. . . . In Germany we had no administrative services to organise requisition; and so we had to make do with the resources of whatever locality we were in. Such resources were soon exhausted because the armies marched and counter-marched over the same country. Our army, therefore, could exist only by plunder, and this both raised the country against us and destroyed the discipline of the troops.'[13] The soldiers put the blame for lack of food on the commissaries. Bricard writes: 'The commissaries, who should have been feeding the troops, followed fifteen leagues behind and garnered what the poor soldier had harvested. They were as well off as the men in the ranks were wretched.'[14]

Unlike many of the Republic's generals, Napoleon paid particular attention to supply from his earliest days in high command. But although he often gave the most detailed orders regarding supply arrangements, he never allowed difficulties in supply to interfere with the course and direction of his operations. He was averse to long supply trains which would hamper his mobility and restrict his freedom of manœuvre, and so he expected his armies to live as far as possible off the countries in which they operated. In 1796 he said: 'We must separate to live but unite to fight.'[15]

He could be caustic about difficulties raised by his corps commanders. On 11th October 1805 Berthier wrote from Augsburg to Marmont: 'In all his letters General Marmont is always referring to the commissariat. I repeat that in a war of invasion and of rapid movements which the Emperor is waging there can be no depots, and the generals in command have themselves to see to it that they procure the necessary supplies from the countries which they traverse.' And on 24th October Napoleon said at Augsburg: 'We have marched without depots; circumstances have compelled us to do so. The season has been extraordinarily favourable for this; but though we were always victorious and could feed on the fruits of the earth, yet we suffered much. At a season when there were no potatoes in the fields, or if the army had been beaten, the want of depots would have been a most serious misfortune.'[16]

Some aspects of living on the country are described by Marbot, in relation to the advance into Prussia before the Battle of Jena. At Wurzburg the VII Corps marched past the Emperor, who, as usual, had notes about all the regiments and addressed appropriate remarks to each. 'To the 7th Light Regiment', Marbot relates, 'he said: "You are the best marchers in the Army; one never sees anyone left behind, particularly when approaching the enemy." Then he added, laughing, "But to render you complete justice I must tell you that you are the worst grumblers and the worst pilferers in the Army." "That's true, that's true," replied the soldiers, each of whom had a duck, a chicken, or a goose in his haversack. This was a corrupt practice which it was necessary to tolerate because . . . the armies of Napoleon, once they were in the field, only had ration issues rarely, and each man lived on the country as best as he could. This system doubtless had grave disadvantages; but it had the immense advantage of allowing us to push forward without being encumbered by convoys and magazines, thus giving us far more mobility than our enemies, whose movements were governed by cooking or the arrival of bread.'[17]

Before the start of the campaign in Poland, Napoleon said: 'Our greatest difficulty will be supplies.' This statement emphasised the logistic problems imposed by fighting in Poland as compared with the previous campaigns in Austria and Germany. In the latter countries Napoleon had never needed to bother much about provisions because the countryside was well stocked. But on 2nd February 1807 he wrote to Daru: 'Circumstances have forced me to return to the system of depots.'[18]

According to Von der Goltz in *The Nation in arms* (English translation of 1894): 'Napoleon evinced at all times extraordinary care for the measures to be taken to provide for the sustenance of his armies. Certainly he did not adhere to any fixed system, but took the means of nourishing his hosts just wherever he found them. He knew how, by promising high payments, by his dexterous treatment of authorities and communities, as well as by threats and brute force, to furnish himself with supplies, even in exhausted districts. . . . But, before all things, he was a master of organising his lines of rear communications; and purchases, requisition, and compulsory provisioning by the population, all contributed to fill his soldiers' bellies.'

Napoleon imposed an enormous war contribution on Prussia after his victories of 1806. Most of it he could not hope to realise in cash, but he levied supplies and charged their cost against the money that he was owed. He paid for manufactured articles in the same way; e.g. uniforms made at Hamburg, Magdeburg, Leipzig, and Berlin; saddles made at Berlin and other places; and boots made at a number of German towns.[19]

Napoleon regarded boots as particularly important, and he issued a written order in 1806 that, 'Every detachment coming from Paris and Boulogne should start with each man having two pairs of shoes in his knapsack, besides those he is wearing. At Mayence they will receive another pair to replace the shoes worn on the march. At Magdeburg they will receive a new pair to replace those worn on the march from Mayence to Magdeburg; so that every man should reach his unit with a pair of shoes on his feet and a pair in his knapsack.' Yet in spite of these detailed orders, soldiers were frequently in distress for lack of a pair of serviceable shoes.[20] The shocking Polish roads were probably largely responsible.

The Polish campaign is of particular interest in showing how Napoleon planned his supply in a country lacking resources. Davout's corps was due to reach Posen on 9th November 1806. Napoleon had selected this neighbourhood for his concentration area, and he ordered Davout to construct enormous bakeries to feed the whole army. In addition, supplies of all kinds were directed to Posen. Pushing on ahead, Davout captured the small fort of Linceya on 24th November. Linceya was about 70 miles due west of Warsaw and surrounded by marshes. There a great advanced magazine was established with immense quantities of stores and ammunition.[21]

By January 1807 the six French army corps were deployed over a line about 150 miles long, varying from about 10 to 100 miles east of the Vistula. A supply depot was established for each corps, and all but one of these were near or behind the Vistula. They were at Marienwerder for Bernadotte, at Thorn for Ney, at Plock for Soult, at Wyszogrod and Lowicz for Augereau, at Pultusk for Davout, and at Warsaw for Lannes. Their siting complied as far as possible with Napoleon's wish, 'not to have any encumbrances on the right bank of the Vistula, so that there might be no obstacle to the evacuation of that country should His Majesty see fit to order it'. Ney, Bernadotte, and Soult, whose corps were farthest from the Vistula, were allowed to have small intermediate depots. Each corps, except Bernadotte's, was given a concentration point in case the enemy should take the offensive. At each of these depots every sort of supply was collected and workshops were established for the repair of ordnance, clothes, and harness. Bakeries produced not only bread for current consumption, but also a large quantity of biscuit as a ration reserve.[22]

On 29th May 1807 Napoleon gave detailed instructions to Daru regarding supply for the summer campaign. He wished to provision his army for eight months and would require for current use and the provision of a reserve, 80,000 rations at Warsaw for the right wing, 100,000 rations at Thorn, Wroclavik, and Bromberg for the centre, and 80,000 for the left wing at Danzig, Marienburg, Elbing, and Marienwerder. The areas from which each point was to be supplied were to be marked on a map. To Warsaw would be assigned a breadth extending from Warsaw to Wroclavik, and a depth which included the districts of Warsaw and Kalisch; the centre was allotted the districts of Posen and Bromberg to a breadth represented by the line Wroclavik-Graudenz; and the left would draw from the country between Marienwerder and the sea, with a depth including the whole of Pomerania. Then followed the various sources of supply; instructions as to assessing the cheapest methods of obtaining supplies, based on the costs of purchase and carriage; and remarks as to the best way of starting markets and searching out the resources of a country.[23]

In preparation for his campaign against Austria in 1809, Napoleon arranged for depots to be so located that he could manœuvre by either bank of the Danube. Supply of the army during the advance to Vienna was comparatively easy, because the route of advance followed the Danube. The great river flows rapidly over this section, falling 930 feet over the 220 miles between Ulm and Vienna, and the influx of the River Iller at Ulm made the Danube navigable for flat-bottomed barges of 100 tons from that point. Even troops, therefore, could be transported more quickly by river than they could march. The river was not of the same value to the Austrians because its current was too strong for supplies to be brought upstream easily.[24]

The procedure by which units collected requisitioned supplies is described amusingly by Parquin. In the 1806 campaign he was *fourrier* (i.e. quartermaster-corporal) of his squadron in the 20th *Chasseurs à Cheval*. After the defeat of the Prussians, the regiment marched to the neighbourhood of Berlin. 'The day of our arrival,' writes Parquin, 'the trumpet sounded for *fourriers*: it was to go to Berlin and collect four days rations of which we were deficient. After having been supplied with carts we set off, *fourriers* and fatigue parties, all under the orders of Regimental Sergeant-Major Mozer, and taking the road to Berlin. When our regiment had marched through the town we had found it quiet and sad; we found it the following day entirely different; it was a small Paris. Everybody was going about his affairs, and the Sergeant-Major wanted to go about his pleasures. Consequently he approached me, and said, "*Fourrier* of the *élite* company, the issue will take about three hours; it is now mid-day; go with the detachment to the magazine. You will feed men and horses, then, when your turn comes, you will issue the rations. . . . As for me, I will dine at the hotel of the Black Eagle. You will take over from me during my absence." "With pleasure, Sergeant-Major," said I, taking the requisitions.

'I took my detachment to the magazine. I was there for an hour when an orderly arrived with a letter for Regimental Sergeant-Major Mozer. As I had replaced him I took the envelope: it was an order not to receive any rations but to tear up the orders and to rejoin the unit with the *fourriers* as quickly as possible because the regiment was on the way to Neustadt. Immediately, I gave the order to the detachment to mount and sent an orderly to the Black Eagle to inform Sergeant-Major Mozer that I was on the way with the *fourriers*.

'At the moment when I was about to tear up the requisitions, the Jew in charge of the ration issue said to me: "*Fourrier*, the Sergeant-Major who has the requisitions for the rations, is he here?" "No," I replied, "I have been detailed to act for him." "Have you got the requisitions?" "Yes, without doubt," I replied. "What are you going to do with them as you are not taking the rations?" "A good question," I said. "I will destroy them." Then the little Jew approached me. "*M. Fourrier*, you will probably copy the Sergeant-Major of the 7th. You can arrange things with me as he did." "Explain yourself," I said. "He exchanged the orders for a hundred gold Fredericks." "What proof can you give me?" As a reply the Jew, who was none other than the army contractor, showed me the orders which the 7th had given him. Having ascertained the truth, I did not hesitate. I concluded the bargain and the exchange was made; I receiving the hundred gold Fredericks. Each of these pieces was worth twenty-one francs. The detachment having mounted, we left at once and followed the route which the Colonel had given. We marched at the walk for about two hours when Sergeant-Major Mozer rejoined us. He took me apart and enquired eagerly as to what had happened to the requisitions, as the ration issue had not taken place. "You will grumble at me perhaps, Sergeant-Major, but here are fifty Fredericks which I got in exchange." "You have done badly," said the Sergeant-Major, putting them into his pocket, "they were worth more." '[25]

This basis of Napoleon's supply policy was to keep his army as well fed as he could without being hampered by the enormous trains of vehicles which would be necessary to ensure continuous and adequate supply. As a result the army was frequently hungry, but as long as the men were not so short of food as to impair their fitness for marching and fighting, he was not unduly concerned.

Officers and men of the Grand Army accepted hunger, like wounds, as one of the unpleasant hazards of a campaign. During the advance into Poland in January 1807, Marbot, who was on the staff of Marshal Augereau, had often to do without food. Before the Battle of Eylau the corps staff were at Zehan, a little hamlet near Eylau, where it had been hoped to find some food; but the Russians had pillaged everything, and an unfortunate regiment in the village, which had had no issue of rations for eight days, had to make do with potatoes and water. But, says Marbot, 'The equipment of the staff of VII Corps having been left at Landsberg, our supper was not as good as the soldiers because we were not able to procure any potatoes.' Of the approach march to Eylau, Marbot writes: 'At the head of the centre column, commanded by the Emperor in person, was Prince Murat's cavalry, then Marshal Soult's corps supported by that of Augereau, and finally came the Imperial Guard. Davout's corps marched on the right flank of this immense column, and that of Marshal Ney on the left. Such a large assembly of troops marching towards the same point soon exhausted the supplies which the country could afford; so we soon suffered much from hunger. Only the Guard, having wagons, carried rations with them; the other corps lived as well as they could, that is to say, did without practically everything.'[26]

The Guard were indeed privileged troops. In 1805 the wagon train accompanying the Guard consisted of 35 baggage wagons, 35 provision carts, 5 or 6 forage carts, 20 carts with medical supplies, and 25 ambulance wagons which transported the Guard's field hospital. As pack animals the Guard had a number of donkeys, and, with the typical humour of the French soldier, they were called 'mules' on the grounds that all personnel of the Guard were a rank higher than those of the Line! A soldier of the Guard carried a heavier pack than one of the Line. In it were two pairs of shoes and a spare pair of hob-nailed soles, cotton drill blouse and pantaloons, spare gaiters, a shirt, a sleeping bag, and four days rations of bread or biscuit. On top of the pack, or knapsack, was rolled his overcoat.[27]

Roads

Roads varied widely and their standard had a considerable affect on movement. There were a number of good roads in Prussia, and these facilitated the manœuvres and rapid advance of the French Army in the campaign of 1806. In fact, the existence of three good parallel roads with lateral communications almost dictated Napoleon's route of advance prior to the Jena–Auerstädt operations.[28] In the campaign in Poland during the following year things were very different; for throughout the area in which the army operated there was no metalled road at all. The best roads were mere banks of earth, without even revetment except where they crossed marshes and the banks would not hold without artificial support. In the dryness of summer or during the winter frosts, artillery and wagons could move along these roads with reasonable ease; but after heavy rain or during the spring thaws they became almost impassable. Napoleon said jokingly that in Poland he had discovered a new element—mud. In the worst places the depth of the mud could be measured in feet, rather than in inches. In December 1806 the wretched infantry sank down to their knees in it, whilst gun carriages were submerged to their axles and occasionally the guns completely disappeared. The infantry managed to cover about $1\frac{1}{4}$ miles in an hour, but even quadruple teams could not pull the guns as fast as that. And these were the best roads: the remainder were mere fair-weather tracks leading from one village to another.[29]

Comparing roads in Poland and Germany, Marbot wrote: 'Whilst we were in that horrible Poland, where there were no metalled roads, it was necessary to have twelve or as many as sixteen horses to pull a carriage in the bogs and swamps through which we marched. Even then it only went at a slow pace, and it was only when we got back into Germany that we at last found a civilised country with real roads.'[30]

In the campaign of 1809 in Austria the Grand Army encountered a mixture of good and very bad roads. The *chaussées* were suitable for all arms in all weather conditions, but there were not many of them. All the other roads were unmetalled earth tracks. Davout wrote to Berthier on 14th April 1809: 'The roads leading to Ratisbon are detestable. There is only one reaching the town and that is nothing but a defile for the last five miles.'[31]

Troop Reinforcements

The method of sending forward reinforcements to the army in the field is illustrated by the arrangements in force during the campaign in Poland of 1806–1807. (This was of course before the reorganisation of the infantry in 1808, described in Chapter 3.) A number of reinforcement depots had been established on the eastern frontier of France and in western Germany, and these came under Marshal Kellerman as commander of the Reserve Army. In the Grand Army there were 61 regiments, each normally of three battalions of which one was left in France to form the regimental depot. However, 18 regiments had four battalions—three with the Grand Army and one forming the depot.

On 2nd November 1806 Napoleon gave Kellerman the following orders:

1. He was to send to the front 8,000 or 10,000 conscripts, whom he would have collected by 15th November.
2. He was to form eight provisional battalions, the nucleus of each of which was to be a company sent back from each of eight 3rd battalions serving with the Grand Army. To this nucleus were to be added conscripts who had received eight to ten days' training, and who were to be sent to Magdeburg or Cassel to continue training with the provisional battalions.
3. As the training of the conscripts progressed, so they were to be formed first into companies, then into battalions, and finally into provisional regiments and despatched to join the Grand Army.
4. During this march the training was to be continued. Men left behind sick or footsore by one provisional battalion were to be collected by the following provisional battalion.
5. As these battalions passed through the principal area headquarters, such as Wurtemberg, Erfurt, Wittenburg, and Spandau, they were to be inspected by the local commander who was to submit reports on them to Imperial Headquarters.
6. On arrival at the Grand Army the provisional regiments were to be broken up and the men distributed as required to the various corps and regiments.[32] (A days' march, or stage, was generally about 15 miles, and there was a days rest every six or seven stages.)

Kellerman wrote a report on his activities as commander of the Reserve Army. At the start he had only enough officers and non-commissioned officers to carry on administration, and the rank and file were all sick, wounded, or convalescent. He was entirely dependent on the conscripts who began to reach him in October 1806. He considered that he could train a man into a reasonable soldier in one month, including instruction in musketry and target practice. During the whole campaign he despatched 20 provisional regiments of infantry and 11 of cavalry, numbering 50,683 men and 7,112 horses. He had many difficulties: troubles with clothing and transport contractors, sore backs amongst horses due to neglect, and so few officers that he had to promote (subject to the Emperor's confirmation) many non-commissioned officers. In addition to cavalry and infantry, Kellerman had to form several units of artillery and gendarmerie, which brought the total numbers despatched from his depots to 73,624 men and 9,559 horses. Apart from these, another 78,832 men and 9,747 horses from regimental depots in France crossed the Rhine at Mayence and Wesel. These figures did not include troops marching from Italy, Switzerland, and Holland or contingents from the German states.[33]

It will be noticed that Napoleon insisted on reinforcing existing units and would not allow the bad practice of forming entirely new units.

1. Edouard Detaille and Jules Richard, *L'Armée Française*, 1885–89
2. ibid.
3. ibid.
4. ibid.
5. ibid.
6. Commandant Saski, *Campagne de 1809*, 1899
7. ibid.
8. Baron von Odeleben, *A Circumstantial Narrative of the Campaign in Saxony*, French Edition, ed. Aubrey de Vitry, English transl., A. J. Kempe, 1820
9. Henry Lachoque, adapted by Anne S. K. Brown, *The Anatomy of Glory*, 1961
10. Docteur Lomier, *Le Bataillon des Marins de la Garde 1803–1815*, 1905
11. ibid.
12. Colonel R. W. Phipps, *The Armies of the First French Republic*, ed. Colonel C. F. Phipps and Elizabeth Sanders, 1926–1939 (5 vols.)
13. ibid.
14. *Journal du Cannonier Bricard*, Introduced by L. Larchey, 1894
15. Count Yorck von Wartenburg, *Napoleon as a General*, ed. Major W. H. James, 1902
16. ibid.
17. *Mémoires du Général Baron de Marbot*, 39th edition, 1891
18. Von Wartenburg, op. cit.
19. F. Loraine Petre, *Napoleon's Campaign in Poland*, 1901
20. ibid.
21. ibid.
22. ibid.
23. ibid.
24. F. Loarine Petre, *Napoleon and the Archduke Charles*, 1909
25. *Souvenirs de Capitaine Parquin* Introduction by F. Masson, 1892
26. Marbot, op. cit.
27. Lachoque, op. cit.
28. F. Loraine Petre, *Napoleon's Conquest of Prussia—1806*, 1907
29. Petre, *Napoleon's Campaign in Poland*

30. Marbot, op. cit.
31. Petre, *Napoleon and the Archduke Charles*
32. Petre, *Napoleon's Campaign in Poland*
33. ibid.

CHAPTER SEVEN

MEDICAL

As might perhaps be expected, the medical organisation for the armies of the Republic was deplorable. For example, Dugommier, when he took over command of the Army of the Eastern Pyrenees in 1794, found the hospitals in such a dreadful condition that he said that anyone entering them in the most robust health would be a sick man in a few days. He added that men were constantly trying to get out of them, whilst the very sick were carted off to the rear like so many spoilt goods.[1]

Percy, who was Surgeon-in-Chief of Jourdan's Army of the Rhine in 1799, shows in his memoirs how badly equipped was the medical department of that army. He singles out Saint-Cyr and Lefebvre, however, for their care of the medical staff. Lefebvre, in particular, was furious over a Government order which deprived surgeons of their horses, and wished he was in a position to confront the Medical Council and say to them: 'Come and see, you wretches, whether a surgeon, after covering eighteen miles on foot with a knapsack on his back, can succour the wounded with ease and adequacy.'[2]

However, in Napoleon's very select Army of Egypt medical affairs seem to have been arranged with greater efficiency. Berthier, the Chief of Staff, mentions the devotion to duty and the care exercised for the sick and wounded by Desquenettes, Chief Physician to the army, and Larrey, the Chief Surgeon. As regards casualties, Berthier says, 'The army engaged in the Syrian expedition lost, in the course of four months, seven hundred men by the plague and about five hundred killed in battle. The numbers of the wounded were certainly at least eighteen hundred, but of these not more than ninety suffered amputations; whilst almost all the others were likely to be cured soon, and in a condition to rejoin their respective corps.'

Plague excited particular terror, and, with the slightest fever, soldiers imagined they had it. Desguenettes, says Berthier, 'was constantly in the hospitals, visiting every patient himself and calming their apprehensions. He maintained that the glandular swellings, which were taken to be symptoms of the plague, came from a species of malignant fever, which could easily be cured by care and attention and keeping the patient's mind easy. He even went so far as to inoculate himself in the presence of the patients with the suppurated matter from these buboes, or boils, and then proceeded to cure himself by the same remedies which he ordered for them.'[3] One feels that Desguenettes has been insufficiently recognised as one of the heroes of the campaign.

Movement of sick and wounded was the responsibility of the commissaries; and J. M. Miot, a commissariat officer, writes that when Napoleon decided to abandon the siege of Acre, 'Immediately all the War Commissaries received orders to remove to Tentoura the wounded of their divisions, from which they were to take such means of transport as were required.'[4]

Hospitals of this period were marked by a black flag, and the anonymous historian of the siege of Genoa writes: 'The siege of Genoa is perhaps the only one in which the black flag, hoisted upon the hospitals, did not prevent the enemy from directing their fire upon these asylums of the unfortunate.'[5]

Although a vast improvement on those of Revolutionary France, the military hospitals were always the weakest part of the Imperial administration. This was probably due to the grave shortage of trained personnel, because Napoleon was very solicitous for his sick and wounded. This concern is reflected in his Bulletin of 5th December 1805, after the battle of Austerlitz, which says: 'During several hours of the night the Emperor went through the field of battle and had the wounded removed. . . . To every wounded soldier the Emperor left a person to take him to the wagons provided for the wounded. It is horrible to mention that 48 hours after the battle there were a great number of wounded Russians that could not be dressed. All the French were dressed before night.'[6]

The rear areas of a Napoleonic battlefield were not nice. As Jules Richard put it: 'All the baseness and all the shame are there, together with all the miseries and all the pain. The stragglers, the malingerers, all those who have fled from the battle or who have not dared to enter it, and who are ready to cry *sauve qui peut* or to pillage the baggage; all these jostle the brave doctors, who, scalpel in hand and apron at the waist, are attending to the wounded.'[7]

Two hours after the start of a battle the field hospitals might already be full, and by the evening other hospitals would have been opened and evacuation to base hospitals started. During a battle the Emperor placed no value on the life of a man, but as soon as it was over he would have liked as many surgeons on the battlefield as there were wounded. But with a large army, which was recruited by quantity rather than by quality, and which could be fighting several campaigns at the same time, there were never enough medical officers. Regiments, which had surgeon-majors and assistants on their establishments, required more than fifteen hundred; and nearly as many more were needed for field hospitals, base hospitals, and miscellaneous units and depots.[8]

The campaign in Poland of 1806–1807 presented especial problems, because the atrocious roads and the shortage of local transport made it increasingly difficult, as the army penetrated farther into the country, to bring up field hospital equipment and to provide ambulance vehicles to move the sick and wounded. To make matters worse, thousands of men fell sick because in this unhealthy countryside malarial mosquitoes bred in their myriads in the countless marshes and sluggish streams. This influx was greater than the number of doctors and attendants at the field hospitals could deal with. However, owing to a massive effort, probably with Daru's drive behind it, no less than 21 base hospitals had been opened in Warsaw alone by the end of January 1807. It was none too soon; for between them they had already more than 10,000 occupants. On top of these came the thousands of wounded from the battle of Eylau, the more seriously wounded arriving on carts or sledges, whilst those with slight wounds or minor ailments had walked.

Apart from Warsaw, base hospitals had been opened in each of the towns selected as supply depots for the various corps, and also at the intermediate depots allowed to Ney, Soult, and Bernadotte. Eylau exacted such a heavy toll of casualties that more hospitals were opened at Bromberg, Marienburg, Marienwerder, Elbing, and other places. Later, to relieve pressure on the hospitals in Poland, those sick and wounded who could stand the journey were transferred to Breslau and other places in Silesia where there were spacious barracks providing excellent accommodation. Indeed, such thorough preparations were made that, although on 30th June 1807 there were 27,376 men in hospital, there was room for another 30,000.

During the period 1st October 1806 to 31st October 1808, over 421,000 sick and wounded were admitted to hospital, of whom some 32,000 died. Nevertheless the average time spent in hospital was only 29 days, which suggests that the treatment was reasonably efficient. According to Daru's report, out of every 196 men in hospital during 1807, 47 were wounded and 105 had fever, leaving 44 suffering from other ailments. These figures refer only to French troops. In addition there were soldiers of the Allied forces and Russian prisoners of war, and these, during the period November 1806 to July 1807 varied between 1/12th and 1/7th of the number of French.[9]

At the battle of Eylau, with its heavy toll of casualties, the unfortunate wounded had the terrible cold added to the pain of their wounds. In Eylau itself the largest building had been turned into a hospital, but the town was no longer usable on the second day of the conflict. Temporary hospitals were then established in barns on the Landsberg road; but the accommodation they could offer was poor, because the straw and even the thatch from the roofs had been removed to feed the horses of the cavalry. The unfortunate wounded were exposed on all sides to the weather, and such straw as remained to form beds for them was sprinkled with snow. The cold was so intense that the operating instruments kept falling from the numbed hands of the men attending the surgeons. But compared to the sufferings of the French, those of the Russian wounded were far worse, because there were no medical arrangements for them at all.[10] The common Russian attitude at this period is shown by the reaction of Platow, the Attaman or General-in-Chief of the Cossacks, who, when asked by the Czar if he would like an increase in his medical staff (which consisted of a single officer), replied, 'God and your Majesty forbid; the fire of the enemy is not half as fatal as a drug.' Still, in Platow's defence it must be said that the Russian medical officers, uneducated and wretchedly paid, were frequently almost useless. Following the horrors of Eylau improvements were gradually made in the Russian medical department, and, aided by a zealous Surgeon-General, the Czar introduced new regulations with the result that at the battle of Friedland the wounded were dressed in the field for the first time. Nevertheless the Russians had insufficient qualified medical officers at their disposal to take up the new appointments, and the pay was too low to attract foreign doctors.[11]

Before the French Army could withdraw from the battlefield of Eylau, the thousands of French and Russian wounded had to be evacuated from the neighbouring villages and despatched to the base hospitals. Napoleon issued orders for their rapid removal, but this was a difficult task, owing to the shortage of transport and the appalling roads. Double, and even treble, teams of horses were needed on parts of the route to haul carriages through snow and sloughs of mud. The poor wounded suffered enormously from the jolting of these vehicles and from the bitter cold.[12]

Six years later casualties and hospitals were again a problem, but this time for quite a different reason. For the campaign of 1813 in Germany orders had been issued for the organisation of a field hospital battalion with 600 wagons and for base hospitals at Dresden, Leipzig, Torgau, Wittenberg, and Magdeburg, with a total capacity for 24,000 sick and wounded as well as 11,000 convalescents. But after the tremendous losses in the Russian campaign of the previous year there was not the administrative capacity to meet these requirements. The hospitals could not accommodate half these numbers and conditions in some of them were horrible.[13] When Napoleon abandoned the right bank of the Elbe in October 1813 there were no horses and vehicles to evacuate the wounded from the abandoned hospitals, and every day there might be seen more than a thousand wheelbarrows, arranged in regular files, and escorted by Saxon gendarmerie, being pushed towards Dresden laden with wounded.[14] Losses from sickness in this campaign gave Napoleon much concern and he issued instructions as to the caution to be exercised in the choice of camp sites. On 28th March 1813 he wrote to Eugène, 'Above all choose a very healthy soil. Consult the medical men and the natives on this point. Do not permit any exceptions. If you are close to marshes or inundated meadows, you may say what you like, but you are in an unhealthy spot and you must go higher up. You will understand that in such places I should lose my whole army in one spring month. I wish you to consult your common sense and the natives rather than the doctors.' On the same subject he had written previously to Davout on 16th August 1811, 'It is better to fight the most sanguinary battle than to encamp the troops in an unhealthy spot.'[15] Napoleon was only too well aware that his army suffered far greater losses from sickness than from battle.

What surgical treatment of the time was like is vividly described by Marbot, who was seriously wounded on two occasions. At the battle of Eylau his right foot was pierced by a sword thrust and became gangrenous, with the wound covered by a scab 'as large as a five-franc piece'. Marbot says: 'The doctor paled when he saw my wound; then getting four orderlies to hold me and arming himself with a scalpel, he took off the scab and excavated into my foot to remove the dead flesh, just as one cuts out the bad parts of an apple. I suffered much during this but without complaining; but it was not the same when the scalpel arrived at the live flesh and uncovered the muscles and bones which could be seen moving. The doctor, sitting on a chair, dipped a sponge into hot sugared wine which he let fall drop by drop into the hole that he had cut in my foot. The pain was excruciating. Nevertheless, for eight days I had to submit to this horrible torture, morning and evening, but my leg was saved.[16]

Marbot received another wound at the siege of Saragossa and was treated by Doctor Assalagny, one of the leading surgeons of the day. Marshal Lannes, on whose staff Marbot was, lent him a mattress and a blanket, and he used his own portmanteau as a pillow. But in the inn, which had been appropriated as a hospital, his room had neither a door nor covers to the windows, so that the wind blew right through it and even the rain came in. He writes: 'Added to that the ground floor was used as a field hospital and I had below me a great number of wounded, whose groaning contributed to my anguish, and the nauseating odour which filled the hospital penetrated into my room. More than 200 sutlers had established their stalls around the headquarters, and a camp was near to them; so that there were continual songs, cries, rolling of drums, and, completing the infernal music, a bass contributed by the great number of guns firing night and day against the town. I could not sleep. I spent fifteen days in this sad position; but at last my strong constitution took over and I was able to get up.'[17]

In 1813 Smithies, a soldier in the Royal Dragoons, noted at Vittoria on 21st June the care that the French took of their wounded in their retreat from the battlefield. In one case they dismounted a whole regiment of cavalry and placed the wounded on the backs of the horses to get them away. There was little animosity between British and French troops and much mutual respect. In 1813 and 1814, when the British Army advanced into France, Smithies mentions the increased fraternisation, particularly at the outposts, 'to mitigate', as he says, 'the miseries of warfare wherever it did not seem inconsistent with their duties.' There was, for example, a regular exchange of brandy and tea. Canteens with a sum of money would be left at agreed places by British soldiers and would soon be filled with brandy by the French. On one remarkable occasion Smithies says that French, Portuguese, and English soldiers were 'all plundering at the same time in one house. They all plundered in perfect harmony, no one disturbing the other on account of his nation or colour.'[18]

Fraternisation is perhaps hardly a suitable subject for inclusion in a chapter on medical affairs, but perhaps it can be excused on account of the frequent exchange of medical comforts which took place! Parquin, then a second lieutenant in the 20th *Chasseurs à Cheval*, has an interesting account of a meeting with the British in Spain. He first encountered the British Army during a reconnaissance some five or six miles from Cuidad Rodrigo. He says: 'Commandant de Vérigny, being in charge of the brigade line of patrols, wished to make the acquaintance of *Messieurs* the English officers and said to me: "Parquin, here is a bottle of excellent French brandy. Gallop towards the English line waving your white handkerchief, and when someone comes and asks what you want, say that you have come to suggest drinking toasts with those officers who are in line in front of us. If he accepts I will join you at the gallop with those officers who are with me." The Commandant had hardly finished talking to me when, having put the bottle of brandy in my sabretache, I left at a "flat-out" gallop, white handkerchief in hand. When I was within a reasonable distance of the English lines I waved it. An officer of the 10th English Dragoons approached me, also at a gallop, and asked me what I wanted. "I come to offer a bottle of brandy for your comrades and mine to drink before making your acquaintance in a different fashion." The English officer accepted and signalled his comrades. I did the same to Commandant de Vérigny, who joined me with some ten officers at the same time as an equivalent number of English officers arrived. The bottle was passed round and soon emptied. It was pronounced excellent, particularly by the English officers, who thanked us for our initiative, of which they appeared very appreciative. Conversation was then joined. They asked us how long we had been in Spain. "Not very long," I answered. "Two years ago at about this time we were engaged with the Austrians, and we came from France to make your acquaintance, *Messieurs*." "You are welcome," they all said. One of them added with a little pride: "Oh, we have made the acquaintance of the élite cavalry of the French Army; we had an affair with Napoleon's Regiment of Guides, of which we captured the commander, General Lefebvre-Desnouettes, at Benevente." Commandant de Vérigny replied: "An indiscretion by that General, in attacking twenty of your squadrons with four of his Guides, and a mistake of direction which prevented him finding the ford of the river, were the cause of that reverse. We will probably have an opportunity to take revenge for the Guides in the campaign which is about to open." An English officer asked if there was anyone amongst us from the town of Moulins en Bourbonnais who could take a letter to one of his countrymen who was a prisoner in that town. The Adjutant of the 13th *Chasseurs*, whose father was then Prefect at Moulins, accepted the charge with pleasure, and the letter was sent by an English flag of truce the following morning. It appeared that the conversation had lasted longer than the English General wished, because two or three round shot from the English lines fell not far from our group, and we were forced to separate, but not without accepting the drink of rum which the English officers offered us in exchange for our gesture.'[19]

1. Colonel R. W. Phipps, *The Armies of the First French Republic*, ed. Colonel C. F. Phipps and Elizabeth Sanders, 1926–1939 (5 vols.)
2. ibid.
3. Berthier, General de Division and Chef de L'Etat–Major-General of the Army of the East, *The Campaign in Egypt and Syria*, transl. 1817
4. L. M. Miot, *Narrative of the French Expedition to Egypt and Syria*, trans. 1817
5. Anonymous, *Journal during the Siege of Genoa*, transl. 1817
6. Napoleon, *Campaign in Germany, 1805, Thirty-First Bulletin, Austerlitz Dec. 5*, trans. 1817
7. Edouard Detaille and Jules Richard, *L'Armée Française*, 1885–1889
8. ibid.
9. F. Loraine Petre, *Napoleon's Campaign in Poland*, 1901
10. ibid.
11. Sir Robert Wilson, *The Russian Army and the Campaigns in Poland 1806 and 1807*, 1810
12. Petre, op. cit.
13. F. Loraine Petre, *Napoleon's Last Campaign in Germany, 1813*, 1912
14. Baron von Odeleben, *A Circumstantial Narrative of the Campaign in Saxony*, French edition, ed. Aubrey de Vitry; English transl. Alfred John Kempe, 1820

15. Count Yorck von Wartenburg, *Napoleon as a General*, ed. Major W. H. James, 1902
16. *Mémoires du Général Baron de Marbot*, 39th edition 1891
17. ibid.
18. 'James Smithies, 1st Royal Dragoons', Major E. Robson, *Journal of the Society for Army Historical Research*, Vol. XXXIV
19. *Souvenirs de Capitaine Parquin*, Introduction by F. Masson, 1892

IMPERIAL HEADQUARTERS

Background

If there was one thing that could be said of the organisation of Napoleon's Imperial Headquarters, it is that it resembled no command and staff system that preceded it or has succeeded it. It was the unique and highly centralised conception of a unique military genius; and had that genius been immortal, and also ageless and endowed with permanent good health, it would have been almost ideal. It follows that it was far better than any system existing in the armies which opposed the French.

But if the Imperial system of command and staff was unique, there was much continuity in the staff organisation as a whole during the transition through the eras of monarchy, republic, and empire; and this continuity is typified in the person of Berthier, Napoleon's famous Chief of Staff. In 1780 he was ADC to the Comte de Rochambeau, commanding the French army which was assisting the American colonists in their revolt against British rule. In 1786 he was appointed to the Staff Corps, and in 1789 he was a Lieutenant-Colonel and Chief of Staff to the Baron de Besenval, commanding the army in the neighbourhood of Paris. In December of the same year he was *Aide Maréchal General des Logis* (roughly equivalent to the British appointment of Assistant Quartermaster-General) on the staff of the new National Guard, commanded by the Marquis de Lafayette. On 1st April 1791 he was promoted Colonel, with the staff grade of Adjutant-General (later styled Adjutant-Commandant), and he subsequently served on the staffs of several divisions. He then became Chief of Staff to Rochambeau when the latter was appointed to command the Army of the North on its formation on 14th December 1791. After holding a further succession of staff appointments, he became Chief of Staff to

Napoleon in 1796, and so remained until the end of the campaign of 1814.[1]

In 1790 the National Assembly fixed a staff establishment for the army which included 4 Generals-in-Chief, 30 Lieutenant-Generals, 60 *Maréchaux de Camp* (Major-Generals), and 30 Adjutant-Generals (of whom 17 were Colonels and 13 Lieutenant-Colonels) as Chiefs of Staff to the Lieutenant-Generals. These numbers were soon insufficient for the rapidly expanding army, and there were considerable increases to the establishment in 1791 and 1792; after which further appointments were made without regard to the establishment. In 1792 the ranks of *Général de Division* and *Général de Brigade* replaced those of Lieutenant-General and *Maréchal de Camp* respectively.[2] (These two ranks gradually dropped in status and eventually became respectively equivalent to Major-General and Brigadier-General.)

In 1799 the establishment of staff officers of the army was promulgated by decree as 110 Adjutant-Generals holding rank as Colonel or Lieutenant-Colonel, 6 ADCs with the rank of Colonel, 30 ADCs with the rank of *Chef de Bataillon* (Major), and 484 *Adjoints* (Assistant Adjutant-Generals) who were Captains or Lieutenants. By 1801 this establishment had more than doubled, and by 1806 it had trebled. Under the Empire staff officers *houzardaient*, that is to say, they dressed themselves in hussar uniform, wearing dolmans and pelisses of striking colours and trimmed with precious furs. But most Generals retained the official, and comparatively plain, uniform of blue and gold.[3]

On 30th April 1793 the Convention decreed that *Représentants en Mission*, or *Représentants du Peuple aux Armées*, should accompany the armies in the field. Each of the eleven armies forthwith received these sinister additions to their staffs, generally four to each army. They had almost unlimited powers, and could arrest anyone in the army to which they were attached, from the Army Commander downwards. They were dressed in a gorgeous and flamboyant uniform, sporting plumes and tricolour scarves. A number of eminent soldiers, arrested by these generally unpleasant individuals, went to the guillotine. The 'Terror' ceased abruptly when Robespierre was executed on 27th July 1794. The diminished status of the Representatives is well illustrated by an incident on 5th September 1795. At 9 o'clock that night the gallant old soldier Lefebvre (who retained enough of his religion to make an *action de graces* every time he went into action) was leading his division across the Rhine, when a Representative objected to the operation because the moon was shining. Lefebvre, in language (says Phipps), impossible to quote, told him angrily to cover it and let his division pass. Some of the worst of the Representatives followed Robespierre to the scaffold, and the system was shortly abolished.[4]

In 1796 Jourdan, then commanding the Army of the Sambre and Meuse, was praised by a Prussian officer for his method of issuing orders and for the staff procedure at his headquarters. This officer, Colonel Lecoq, wrote to his King: 'General Jourdan arrived at 6 pm at Erlingen, where he placed his headquarters. Shutting himself up with some of his aides-de-camp, the Government Commissioner, the Intendant of Provisions, several officers, and heads of departments, he at once drew up the orders for the operations of the following morning, and all the correspondence, including the answer to my request. At nine o'clock all the business was finished, and the orderly officers were on their way to the different divisions. Each General of Division receives information on the general aim of the movements, and, in particular, on what concerns his division. It is for him afterwards to regulate the details of the work assigned to him. I could only admire the order which reigns on this point.'[5]

On the other hand, neither Jourdan nor his Chief of Staff, General of Division Ernouf, had much regimental experience and did not therefore appreciate how officers and men were worn out and made miserable by moves at short notice and continual changing of quarters.[6]

Jourdan had three Adjutant-Generals on his staff, whilst two more assisted Ernouf. Also on Jourdan's headquarters were a General of Division who commanded the artillery, a *Chef de Brigade* (Colonel) who commanded the engineers, and a General of Division commanding the left wing of the Army, who was himself assisted by two Adjutant-Generals. The Army consisted of four infantry divisions, an advanced guard of divisional strength, and the cavalry reserve; each of these being commanded by a General of Division. A division, or equivalent, consisted of from two to four brigades, each commanded by a General of Brigade. A divisional Staff included two Adjutant-Generals, except that only one was allotted to the cavalry reserve.[7]

Meanwhile, in the Army of Italy, Napoleon Bonaparte had already appreciated Berthier's ability as Chief of Staff. On 6th May 1796 he wrote to the Directory saying that since the start of the campaign Berthier had always spent the day with him in the field and the night at his office desk. He added that it was impossible to surpass him in activity, good will, courage and knowledge.[8] Under this invaluable man, Napoleon's command organisation developed from the comparatively small field headquarters of 1796 to the great Imperial Headquarters of the Austerlitz campaign and afterwards.

Imperial Headquarters—The Military Household or 'Maison'

Imperial Headquarters consisted of two separate organisations, the Emperor's *Maison*, or Military Household, and the Army Headquarters; the latter being itself divided into the General Staff and the department of the Intendant General, or General Commissariat of Army Stores.

The *Maison* comprised the Emperor's Court in the field and his personal military staff; and it included grand officers, generals, ADCs, orderly officers, secretaries, various dignitaries, and Court employees, together with attendants and servants. During the Jena–Auerstädt campaign it consisted of about 800 persons. Berthier had a place in it because he held the four offices of Vice-Constable, Master of the Hounds, Minister for War, and Chief of Staff of the Grand Army. Two other most important officers of the *Maison* were Duroc, Grand Marshal of the Palace, and Caulaincourt, Master of the Horse.

Duroc, Duc de Frioul, was primarily responsible for the management of the Emperor's Household, and was often entrusted by Napoleon with foreign missions. Caulaincourt, Duc de Vienne, superintended the stables, pages, messengers, and couriers. He had to accompany the Emperor everywhere he went; he held his reins and stirrup while he mounted, and handed him his whip; and he ensured that carriages were up to the required standard. Caulaincourt also supervised the training of horses, and of grooms, drivers, and postilions. When the Emperor travelled in his carriage, Caulaincourt rode in the vehicle which immediately preceded it. On horseback, he was responsible for handing to the Emperor the map of the area, when he wished to consult it.[9]

The *aides de camp* were almost all general officers and were entrusted with important missions and long distance reconnaissances; they also took verbal orders and information from the Emperor to the corps commanders. Sometimes Napoleon used them to take command of an improvised or composite force which had been detailed for a dangerous assault or to restore the situation. The orderly officers were really junior ADCs with the ranks of major or below, and they were employed on missions and with the carriage of written orders to corps commanders. Their number was fixed at twelve by a decree of 19th September 1806. The Emperor's orderly officers wore a dark green uniform and gold aiguillette on the left shoulder until 1810, when the dark green was replaced by sky blue with silver embroidery. Each of the Emperor's general *aides de camp* had themselves three *aides de camp* whom Napoleon also employed as orderly officers.

Other officials were the Marshal of the Palace who was in charge of the kitchen staff and who was assisted by the Prefect of the Palace; the Chamberlain; two equerries; four Court physicians and four or five surgeons; a Paymaster of the Crown; four pages, who were required to lead the Emperor's horse and prepare his horse relays; the Quartermasters of the Palace, who were responsible for cleaning, furnishing, and victualling; the under-staff of butler, *valets de chambre*, cooks, outriders and grooms; and the Emperor's personal domestic staff.[10]

The Imperial Cabinet

Finally, there was the Imperial Cabinet which was the inner sanctum of the *Maison* from which emanated all Napoleon's plans. It had only a small staff consisting of two cabinet secretaries, a private secretary, an archivist, the Topographical Office, and the Statistical Office. At the head of the Topographical Office was Bacler d'Albe, who had been a geographical draughtsman on Napoleon's headquarters in Italy in 1796. He soon became head of the Topographical Office and remained so until 1813. He was a Major in 1806, a Colonel in 1807, and a General in 1813. He was responsible for correcting maps, collating all information about the location of French and enemy troops, and for working out the length of marches and frontages and the distances between formations, etc. For seventeen years this remarkable man carried out the same duties, and Napoleon sent for him more often than anybody else and at any time of the day or night.[11]

As soon as the site for Imperial Headquarters had been reached, Bacler d'Albe set about the installation of the Emperor's study or command office. This was an operations room in which Napoleon did his planning and issued his orders. D'Albe had with him a number of portfolios, containing papers and maps, as well as two or three mahogany boxes with compartments containing a library of reference books, which were removed and laid out on tables. The centre of the room was always occupied by a very large table on which d'Albe spread out and oriented his map of the theatre of war. On it he had already emphasised the salient characteristics by colouring important rivers, contours, roads, frontiers, and other features. On it he now stuck pins with variously coloured heads to show the positions of units and formations of the French and enemy armies, according to the latest information received. Beside the map he laid a pair of dividers already set to a normal days march in accordance with the scale of the map. At night the map was illuminated by twenty candles placed around it. By the time the Emperor arrived, secretaries had established themselves in the corners of the room.[12]

On the arrival of any despatch which affected troop dispositions, it was sent to d'Albe, who made a summary of it and adjusted his coloured pins in accordance with the information that it contained. He then outlined the situation to the Emperor who, dividers in hand, followed his description on the map. In doing so, the large scale of the map often obliged Napoleon to lie on the table, d'Albe following suit. Baron de Fain, who was then the Archivist, says in his *Mémoires*: 'I have seen them more than once, stretched out on this large table, and interrupting each other by a sudden exclamation, right in the midst of their work, when their heads had come into collision.'[13]

The information from which d'Albe set up his pins on the map came principally from two sources. A detailed report on the positions of the Grand Army was prepared in the offices of the General Staff from returns submitted by the Chiefs of Staff of the various army corps, and this was sent daily by Berthier to the Emperor. Information about the enemy was compiled and presented to the Emperor by the head of the Statistical Office, Lelorgne d'Ideville. In peacetime d'Ideville was responsible for compiling the book on foreign armies from information supplied by French embassies and legations, who were particularly charged with finding out everything they could. This book always accompanied Napoleon in the field. D'Ideville was also secretary-interpreter and was employed by Napoleon to question prisoners and country people and to interpret documents.[14] D'Albe and d'Ideville, in fact, carried out those operational and intelligence staff functions which one would expect to have been co-ordinated by Berthier as Chief of Staff.

When Napoleon had reached a decision he dictated his orders. Baron de Méneval, who was his private secretary, has described the procedure in his *Mémoires* as follows: 'When his idea had reached maturity he began to walk slowly about the room and traverse its entire length. He then began to dictate in a serious and emphatic voice, without resting for a moment. As inspiration came to him, his voice assumed a more animated tone, and was accompanied by a sort of habit, which consisted in a movement of the right arm, which he twisted, at the same time pulling the cuff of the sleeve of his coat with his hand. In rendering his thought, expressions came without effort. They were sometimes incorrect, but their very incorrectness added to the energy of his language, and ever marvellously described what he wished to say.'

These orders were written down in very rough draft, for Napoleon dictated extremely rapidly. They were then written out neatly on the right-hand side of a piece of double elephant paper (i.e. 40 in. by 26¾ in.) divided into two. At the top was the address and in the margin was the place, date, and time, together with a summary of the subject. To this was added the name of the officer carrying the despatch (probably one of the Emperor's orderly officers) and the time he was to depart. The completed order was then cleared through Berthier's office. Urgent orders were written on little elephant size (28 in. by 23 in.) gilt-edged vellum paper without margin. The archivist kept a register of despatches sent out daily by the Emperor, including the names of officers carrying them and the times of their departure.[15]

But the above procedure was generally only used for orders sent to one addressee, such as a corps commander. General orders, dealing for instance with the movements of the whole army, were sent to Berthier. They contained the broad outlines of what was to be done, and from these

Berthier prepared the detailed orders, putting them into formal shape and including those staff matters which were required for their implementation. Even then they generally differed for each addressee; for each corps commander was normally only informed of the action he himself was to take, together with such information about neighbouring corps or cavalry activity as it was necessary for him to know. Napoleon's regard for secrecy was such that he imparted the details of a plan to as few people as possible. Even Berthier was often not told what aim an order was intended to achieve. As Baron Jomini (one-time Chief of Staff to Ney) says: 'The Emperor was really his own chief of staff. Holding in his hand a pair of dividers, opened for a distance by scale of seven to eight leagues in a straight line—a distance which, reckoning the turnings of the roads, was generally nine or ten leagues of march at the least [i.e. 22½ or 25 miles], bent, nay often lying over his map, on which the positions of the enemy were marked by pins of different colours, he arranged his own movements with a certainty of which we can scarcely form a just idea. Moving his dividers vigorously over his chart he judged in a moment of the number of marches for each of his corps, which would be necessary for it to reach any point he wished it to reach on a fixed day, and then, sticking his pins into those fresh positions, and calculating the speed at which each column could move, he dictated those orders which, if they had stood alone, would entitle him to glory.'[16]

Whilst on campaign Napoleon generally went to bed after dinner at about 8 o'clock. He was awakened as soon as reports from reconnaissances had come in, which would generally be about 1 or 2 o'clock in the morning. He would then set to work and would issue any necessary orders in time for them to enable corps commanders to take action by dawn. If an officer bearing important despatches arrived during the night, he reported first to Berthier, who always lived near the Emperor. Berthier then took the officer to see Napoleon who, if he was in bed, immediately got up, read the despatch, and dictated any necessary reply to Berthier. After having it copied into his order book, Berthier sent off this reply, probably by the officer who had brought the original despatch, and noted the latter's name and his time of departure. Before issuing any subsequent order to the corps concerned, Napoleon sent for Berthier's order book to read his previous instructions.

On the march, if necessary, Napoleon gave verbal orders to Berthier, who then dictated them to a secretary. But on reaching the fixed site of headquarters these orders were confirmed by fuller written ones.[17]

Army Headquarters

Army Headquarters, which were sited alongside the *Maison*, were Berthier's province. They comprised the private staff of the Chief of Staff, the Cabinet of the Chief of Staff, and the General Staff. The General Staff was itself divided into two categories—General Staff officers entrusted with army orders and the officers of the General Staff Cabinet.

The Cabinet of the Chief of Staff was manned by about a dozen civilian officials who dealt with administrative correspondence, movements, and personnel. The private staff of the Chief of Staff consisted of a number of ADCs, ranging in rank from Colonel to Lieutenant, the senior of whom was graded as an Assistant Chief of Staff, and also some senior officers who were entrusted with missions which required the authority of their rank. These latter came under the orders of the above mentioned Assistant Chief of Staff.

The General Staff were housed separately from Berthier and his Cabinet, who were close to the Emperor. The work of the General Staff was divided between three Assistant Chiefs of Staff. The first of these bore the title of Chief of the General Staff. He dealt directly with the Chiefs of Staff of the army corps, directed the work of the whole General Staff, and was responsible for the organisation of the line of communications. The second Assistant Chief of Staff was in charge of accommodation and marches and had the title of Quartermaster of the Army. He corresponded with the Adjutant-Commandants (Assistant Chiefs of Staff) on the corps staffs who were charged with this duty. The third Assistant Chief of Staff had the Survey Department under him. He was responsible for collecting topographical information and for drawing up daily a sketch map showing the positions occupied by French and Allied troops. Each of the Assistant Chiefs of Staff were served by a varying number of Staff officers.

The General Staff Cabinet consisted of three staff divisions comprising 31 officers, and the Survey Department of 30 officers. The first division dealt with the despatch of orders, movements, information, general correspondence, etc. The second was concerned with accommodation, police, hospitals, and subsistence distributions. Whilst the third was responsible for prisoners of war, deserters, conscripts, and discipline.

Also included in the Imperial Headquarters were the Intendant General of the Army with a staff of 43, the Commander of the Artillery with a staff of 18 officers, the Commander of the Engineers with 19 staff officers, and the Colonels General of the Guard.[18]

Movement of Imperial Headquarters

One of the Assistant Chiefs of Staff was appointed Camp Commandant, with responsibility for command of Imperial Headquarters, including its movement and setting up in a new location. This responsibility did not, however, extend to the *Maison*, which had its own organisation. The Baggage Master of the Army was responsible for the vehicles required by Imperial Headquarters. In movement the headquarters split into several echelons. There was a so-called 'Little Headquarters' which was the Emperor's tactical headquarters. While this moved the remainder, or main headquarters, might remain a distance of up to several days journey in rear, and the administrative part, under the Intendant General, might be separated again as a rear headquarters located at the centre for supplies.[19]

For the movement of the Imperial Cabinet, Napoleon had a campaign detachment which consisted of two sub-divisions, each able to lift and cater for the Cabinet, and each containing a light carriage for the Emperor, two light carriages for officers, one light carriage for Cabinet staff, a map wagon, a barouche for the Emperor, a mess barouche or 'britska' (a Polish carriage), two mess wagons, two wagons with spare saddlery and harness, a britska for the sick, a forge for two farriers, a britska carrying two artisans and a silversmith with their stores, a vehicle for a doctor's office, a vehicle for a harness maker, six mules (reserve for horses or mules), vehicles to carry tents and bedroom equipment, a baggage master in charge of the detachment, and sundry other ranks, such as the Emperor's servants, orderlies, mess servants, and drivers.[20]

Napoleon himself rode in the midst of his troops when close to the enemy. Otherwise he remained at Imperial Headquarters until the army corps were approaching the destinations he had given them. He then travelled in a carriage; either his large barouche if the distance was long or else in a light carriage on his short rapid trips between the headquarters of the various corps.[21]

Odeleben has given the following description of Napoleon in his barouche: 'Dressed in his uniform and with his head covered by a checkered handkerchief, the Emperor could sleep in his carriage as though in his bed. In the interior of the carriage were a number of drawers with locks and keys containing news from Paris, reports, and books. Opposite Napoleon was placed a list of the relays. A large lantern hung at the back of the carriage and lit up the interior, whilst four other lanterns illuminated the road. The mattresses which Roustam, Napoleon's Mameluke *valet de chambre*, arranged were skilfully packed into the carriage, and beneath the basket was stored a small reserve of torches. Roustam was alone on the box, and six powerful Limousine horses, driven by two coachmen, drew the coach, which was simple, green, supplied with two seats, and well suspended. There was a difference between the Emperor's seat and Berthier's, in as much as the one who accompanied Napoleon could not lie down.'[22]

Napoleon's saddle horses were divided into 'brigades' of nine each, and of these nine two were for the Emperor, one for the Grand Equerry (Caulaincourt), one for the secretary, and one each for the surgeon, the page, Roustam, a groom, and a servant. Spare horses were grouped round the brigade for Berthier, ADCs, and orderly officers. Where the roads were poor, Napoleon often covered great distances on horseback at a very fast pace. For instance, during a sharp frost, he rode the 86 miles from Valladolid to Burgos in $5\frac{1}{2}$ hours. The brigades of horses were placed at intervals in advance along the route he intended to follow, so that he found fresh horses every eight or ten miles. Similarly the carriage horses were divided into teams of three horses each. Fain, in his *Mémoires*, says that, 'The horses which the Emperor rode were Arabians; of small size, greyish-white coat, good-tempered, gentle gallopers, and easy amblers.'[23] Baron von Odeleben says that in the 1813 campaign the best and handsomest horse was a bay of Arabian breed with black mane and tail. The others were small but sure-footed, and almost all stallions with long tails. Besides the bay horse, Napoleon often had with him for his personal use two sorrel horses and one white.[24] Odeleben adds: 'Napoleon rode like a butcher. He held the bridle in his right hand with the left arm hanging. He looked as though he were suspended in his saddle. Whilst galloping his body rolled backwards and forwards and sideways, according to the speed of his horse. As soon as the animal stepped aside its rider lost his seat, and, as we know, Napoleon was thrown more than once.'[25]

When the Emperor left his headquarters on horseback he was accompanied by a large staff and escorted by four squadrons of cavalry selected from each of the four regiments of the Cavalry of the Old Guard: Grenadiers, *Chasseurs à Cheval*, Polish Light Horse, and Dragoons; all under the command of a General Aide de Camp.[26] Of these, the squadron of *Chasseurs à Cheval* were responsible for special duties. In March 1813 Parquin was transferred to the *Chasseurs à Cheval* of the Guard (dropping a rank in the process) and describes these duties. A troop of the squadron consisting of a lieutenant, a sergeant (*maréchal des logis*), 2 corporals (*brigadiers*), 22 *chasseurs*, and a trumpeter, rode before and behind the Emperor's group. In addition, immediately in front of the Emperor rode a corporal and 4 *chasseurs*, of whom one carried the Emperor's portfolio (containing maps, writing case, and dividers) and another his telescope. If [Napoleon stopped or dismounted, this detachment immediately did the same, fixing bayonets on their carbines and forming a square with the Emperor in the middle. The officer commanding the escort troop followed the Emperor continually, and only Berthier or Murat were allowed between him and Napoleon. In the field the *Chasseurs à Cheval* of the Guard were more usually referred to as the Guides, after the name of the unit to which they owed their origin. Napoleon, who knew the devotion of these Guides to his person, allowed them liberties which he would not have permitted from others. Parquin says that one day the horse of one of the *chasseurs* of the escort, who was galloping in front of Napoleon, fell, and while the guide was picking himself up, the Emperor passed him at a gallop and called him a bungler. This word had scarcely been uttered when Napoleon, who was thinking of other matters than of guiding his horse with reins and legs, rolled with his mount into the dust. Whilst, helped by a groom, the Emperor was mounting another horse, the *chasseur*, who had remounted, passed the Emperor at a gallop to resume his place with the advanced guard, and cried out sufficiently loud for Napoleon to hear: 'It appears that I am not the only bungler today.'[27]

The remainder of the cavalry of the escort rode about a mile behind the Emperor's group. In 1813 this group consisted of Napoleon, Berthier, Caulaincourt, the Marshal on duty, the two duty ADCs, two duty orderly officers, two officers who knew the language of the country, an official officer-interpreter, an officer connected with the stables, the duty page, and Roustam. Duroc used to belong to this group but by 1813 he was dead. Caulaincourt carried a map of the district suspended from a button of his coat and so folded that Napoleon could consult it at any moment. The other ADCs, orderly officers, generals, etc., rode immediately after the first squadron of the escort.[28]

When the Emperor had settled in his headquarters, the officer commanding the close escort troop was stationed in the apartment closest to him, while the other ranks of the troop stood holding the reins of their horses at the door of the house or tent occupied by the Emperor, who always had one of the horses of his stable saddled and bridled and held by two grooms. The troop charged with this duty was relieved every two hours. The first person who presented himself to the Emperor when he left his apartments was the officer commanding this troop.[29]

If the tactical headquarters did not settle down where there were houses, the soldiers of the Guard either built a shelter for the Emperor (as at Austerlitz and Jena), or they pitched, in the middle of the Guard camp, five tents of blue and white striped canvas. Two of these were attached together and were, respectively, Napoleon's study and bedroom. Of the others, one was allotted to Berthier, one to the senior officers as a sleeping and mess tent, and the remaining one to the junior officers. In this tented tactical headquarters, Napoleon would sometimes sit outside on a camp stool wearing his grey cloak, while two bands, belonging respectively to the Grenadiers and the *Chasseurs* of the Guard, played alternately at either end of the square.[30]

On campaign meals in the *Maison* were served at four tables. Napoleon and Berthier sat at one of these, one was for the officers of the Imperial Cabinet, one for the senior officers, and one for the junior officers. Dinner was served on a silver service engraved with the Imperial eagle, and there were from twelve to sixteen dishes to choose from. Napoleon himself ate sparingly and drank only a little of the brand of Burgundy (Chambertin) which he was never without on any of his campaigns. The meal only lasted about twenty minutes, and afterwards Napoleon liked to play whist or *vingt-et-un*—particularly the latter, for everyone joined in and Napoleon cheated openly and with tremendous enjoyment.[31]

Napoleon's Plans

Napoleon took considerable care over the preparation of his strategical plan before the start of a campaign. Having decided the broad method of achieving his strategical aim, he then selected on the map the most suitable area to concentrate his army. Only then did he consider the various actions which the enemy might take. He generally did this by posing a series of questions and supplying the answers. For instance, for the Ulm campaign of 1809 he selected Ratisbon as the concentration area. He then looked at the various courses open to the enemy and his own counters to them. These were included as follows in the orders he sent to Berthier from Paris on 30th March 1809;

'1. Will he move on Cham? We shall be able to assemble all our strength against him so as to hold him fast in the positions which we have reconnoitred in the Regen.

2. Will he move on Nuremberg? He will in that case be cut off from Bohemia.

3. Will he move on Bamberg? He will be cut off there too.

4. Will he resolve to march towards Dresden? In that case we shall enter Bohemia and pursue him into Germany.

5. Will he operate against the Tyrol and at the same time break out from Bohemia? In this case he will undoubtedly reach Innsbruck; but the ten or twelve regiments which he would have in Innsbruck could not take up a position near the issue from Bohemia, and these troops would only learn of the defeat of their army in Bohemia by our appearance at Salzburg.

6. Finally, if it should appear as if the enemy intended to take an extreme right or left wing as the goal of his operations, we shall have to choose the central line by a retreat to the Lech, while holding Augsburg occupied, so as to be certain of being able to make use of this town at any moment.'[32]

Officers of the British Army will recognise Napoleon's method as very much akin to the standard form of a military appreciation.

After the main movements had been initiated, Napoleon's next step was to direct a reconnaissance with the object of eliminating some of the questions he had posed and even, if possible, to ascertain the enemy's intention. This reconnaissance was conducted by spies in enemy territory, by officers sent on special missions, and by cavalry patrols; each of these categories being given particular places to visit and questions to answer.[33]

Once hostilities began, Napoleon directed the operations of his army in accordance with the following broad principles:

1. He adhered to one line of operations and kept his army massed on that line, so denying the enemy the opportunity of defeating any one column in detail. By massing his army, however, Napoleon did not mean or desire a close concentration, but that each of his corps should be within supporting distance of each other. This distance depended on circumstances, but might be a day's march.

2. He kept the enemy's main body as his principal objective, but not necessarily by striking directly at it. After the campaign of 1796–1797 he said: 'There are in Europe many good generals, but they see too many things at once; as for me I see only one thing, namely the enemy's main body. I try to crush it, confident that secondary matters will settle themselves.'

3. If possible, he chose a line of operations which would place him on one flank or even the rear of the enemy. This would be preferably the enemy's strategical wing; that is, the wing which if turned would most effectively drive him off his line of communications.

In conversation with Moreau in 1799, Napoleon replied to Moreau's statement that it is always the greater numbers that win, by saying: 'You are right, it is always the greater number that beats the lesser. When with inferior forces I had a larger army before me, I concentrated mine rapidly and fell like lightning upon one of the enemy's wings and routed it. Then I took advantage of the confusion, which this manœuvre never failed to produce in the opposing army, to attack it at another point, but always with my whole force. Thus I beat it in detail, and the victory which was the result was always, as you see, the triumph of the larger numbers over the lesser.[34]

In the conduct of the tactical battle, as compared with his strategical manœuvres, Napoleon told Saint-Cyr that he gave no preference to the attack in the centre over that on the wings. His principle, he said, was to attack the enemy with the greatest force possible. Once the corps nearest to the enemy became engaged, he left them to act without troubling himself as to their chances of success or reverse; but he took care not to yield too easily to calls from help from their commanders. He added that only towards the end of the day, when he saw that the enemy was worn out and had used up most of his reserves, did he unite what he had been able to keep as his own reserve, in order to launch into the attack a strong mass of all arms. Because the enemy was not in a position to meet this, he had almost always obtained a victory.[35]

Napoleon always chose his point of attack after a general consideration of the whole situation, and on strategical grounds, without taking any account of the tactical difficulties which his chosen point might present. The results of most of his battles were so very decisive just because he always attacked where the attack, if successful, would be most strategically effective.[36]

1. Colonel R. W. Phipps, *The Armies of the First French Republic*, ed. Colonel C. F. Phipps and Elizabeth Sanders, 1926–1939 (5 vols.)
2. Edouard Detaile and Jules Richard, *L'Armée Française*, 1885–1889
3. ibid.
4. ibid.
   Phipps, op. cit.
5. ibid.
6. ibid.
7. Detaille, op. cit.
8. Phipps, op. cit.
9. Colonel Vachée, *Napoleon at Work*, transl. G. F. Lees, 1914
10. ibid.
11. ibid.
12. Baron von Odeleben, *A Circumstantial Narrative of the Campaign in Saxony*, French edition, ed. Aubrey de Vitry; English transl. John Kempe, 1820
13. Vachée, op. cit.
14. ibid.
15. ibid.
16. Count Yorck von Wartenburg, *Napoleon as a General*, transl. Major W. H. James, 1902
17. Vachée, op. cit.
18. ibid.
    Von Wartenburg, op. cit.
19. Vachée, op. cit.
20. Docteur Lomier, *La Bataillon des Marins de la Garde 1803–1815*, 1905
21. Vachée, op. cit.
22. Odeleben, op. cit.
23. Vachée, op. cit.
    Von Wartenburg, op. cit.
24. Odeleben, op. cit.
25. ibid.
26. Vachée, op. cit.
27. *Souvenirs de Capitaine Parquin*, Introduction by F. Masson, 1892
28. Vachée, op. cit.
29. Parquin, op. cit.
30. Odeleben, op. cit.
31. Vachée, op cit.
32. Von Wartenburg, op. cit.

33. Major-General J. F. C. Fuller, *The Conduct of War*, 1961
34. Von Wartenburg, op. cit.
35. F. Loraine Petre, *Napoleon's Last Campaign in Germany, 1813*, 1912
36. Von Wartenburg, op. cit.

CHAPTER NINE

THE THIRD CORPS— AUERSTAEDT

The following two chapters are concerned with the operations of Marshal Davout's III Corps during the Prussian and Polish campaigns of 1806 and 1807. The intention is not so much to discuss these campaigns as to show (as stated in the Introduction) the working of the French Army in the field, at its prime, and the functioning of the unique Napoleonic staff and command system. For this reason, the movements and activities of other army corps of the Grand Army are only mentioned in so far as they affected the III Corps, and the movements and strengths of enemy forces are restricted as far as possible to what Davout knew at the time.

The Grand Army with which Napoleon engaged the Prussians consisted of the Imperial Guard and the following formations commanded by the Marshals as shown: I Corps, Bernadotte; III Corps, Davout; IV Corps, Soult; V Corps, Lannes; VI Corps, Ney; VII Corps, Augereau; and the Cavalry Reserve, Murat. The strengths of these formations were: Guard, 4,000 infantry and 5,000 cavalry; I Corps, 25,000; III Corps, 29,000; IV Corps, 35,000; V Corps, 23,000; VI Corps, 21,000; VII Corps, 16,000; and Cavalry Reserve, 20,000. In addition to these, there were 8,000 Departmental troops and the Bavarian Auxiliary Corps, also of 8,000. The Cavalry Reserve consisted of the Heavy Divisions of Nansouty and d'Hautpoul, the Dragoon Divisions of Klein, Beaumont, Grouchy, and Sahuc, and the Light Cavalry Brigades of Lasalle and Milhaud.

Napoleon's instructions for the opening of the offensive were that the Grand Army was to advance by three roads, one column on each road. The V Corps was to lead the left column, on the road Coburg–Saalfeld, followed a day's march behind by the VII Corps. The I Corps was at the

CAMPAIGN IN PRUSSIA 1806
Roads and Towns of Importance in the Operations

Magdeburg

R. Bode

R. Elbe

R. Saale

To Berlin 35 miles

Wittenberg

Dessau

R. Elbe

Bernburg

Düben

Halle

R. Elster

Leipzig

R. Mulde

R. Unstrutt

Merseburg

R. Saale

Nébra

Freiberg

R. Elster

Kösen

To Dresden

Naumburg

Apolda

Camburg

Dornburg

Zeitz

Erfurt

Jena

Gotha

Weimar

Gera

R. Ilm

Kahla

Roda

Neustadt

To Dresden 40 miles

Saalfeld

Possneck

Auma

Zwickau

Gräfenthal

Saalburg

Schleiz

Lobenstein

Tauna

Plauen

R. Saale

Nordhalben

Coburg

Hof

Kronach

Münchberg

Frontier of Austria

To Schweinfurt 15 miles

Lichtenfels

R. Main

R. Main

Scale/Miles

10 5 0   10   20   30

Bamberg

Bayreuth

To Amberg 30 miles

head of the centre column, marching along the road Kronach–Lobenstein–Schleiz, followed in turn by the III Corps, the Cavalry Reserve, and the Imperial Guard. The right column was to follow the road Hof–Plauen, and was composed, in order, of the IV Corps, the VI Corps, and the Bavarian Corps. The frontage of the whole army was about 38 miles and its depth about the same, or two days' march; so that Napoleon would be able to concentrate his entire strength within forty-eight hours. This was his standard balanced formation of the *bataillon carée*.

The III Corps, on orders from Berthier, had moved from its peacetime locations in Würtemberg and Baden, and had concentrated around Bamberg by the beginning of October. The Emperor arrived at Bamberg on 2nd October, and on 5th October, at his direction, Davout carried out an inspection of his army corps. Its order of battle and strengths was as follows:

Headquarters III Corps
Commander, Marshal Davout
Chief of Staff, General of Brigade Daultanne
Sub-Chiefs of Staff, Adjutants-Commandants Hervo and Romeuf
Attached to the Staff, Colonel Beaupré
Commander of the Artillery, General of Brigade Hanicque
Chief of Staff of the Artillery, Colonel Charbonnel
Commander of the Engineers, Colonel Touzard
Chief of Staff of the Engineers, Chef de Bataillon Breuille

1st Infantry Division
Commander, General of Division Morand
Generals of Brigade Debilly, d'Honnieres, and Brouard

13th Light Infantry Regiment, Colonel Guyardet	1,507
17th Line Regiment, Colonel Lanusse	2,080
30th Line Regiment, Colonel Valterre	2,059
51st Line Regiment, Colonel Baille	2,170
61st Line Regiment, Colonel Nicolas	2,140
One company Light Artillery, 6 pieces	100
One company Foot Artillery, 7 pieces	104
Two companies Artillery Train	130
Attached to Light Artillery from Artillery Train	49
Total strength 1st Division	10,339

2nd Infantry Division
Commander, General of Division Friant
Generals of Brigade Kister, Lochet, and Grandeau

33rd Line Regiment, Chef de Bataillon Cartier	2,048
48th Line Regiment, Colonel Barbanegre	1,616

108th Line Regiment, Colonel Higonet	1,625
111th Line Regiment, Colonel Gay	2,346
Half company Light Artillery, 2 pieces	40
One company Foot Artillery, 6 pieces	134
One company Artillery Train	85
Total strength 2nd Division	7,894

3rd Infantry Division
Commander, General of Division Gudin
Generals of Brigade Gauthier and Petit

12th Line Regiment, Colonel Vergès	2,059
21st Line Regiment, Colonel Decous	2,274
25th Line Regiment, Colonel Cassagne	1,849
85th Line Regiment, Colonel Viala	2,170
Half company Light Artillery, 2 pieces	40
One company Foot Artillery, 6 pieces	83
One company Artillery Train	120
Total strength 3rd Division	8,595

Divisional Cavalry
Commander, General of Brigade Vialannes

1st Chasseurs à Cheval, Colonel Exelmans	420
2nd Chasseurs à Cheval, Colonel Bousson	530
12th Chasseurs à Cheval, Colonel Guyon	470
Total strength cavalry	1,420

Corps Troops

Park of Reserve Artillery	500
Detachment Gendarmes and 6th Sapper Company	130
Total strength III Corps	28,878

The infantry of a division was frequently, indeed normally, organised into two brigades each of two regiments; and such a brigade was commanded by one of the Generals of Brigade. But these Generals of Brigade constituted a pool of senior officers at the disposal of the Divisional, or even the Corps, Commander, and they were often used to take command of one of the special task forces, which were so frequently formed in the Napoleonic Army. The extreme flexibility of the French organisation will become apparent as the operations are followed.

Napoleon's Orders to the III Corps 7th October
At 4 am 7th October Davout received the following orders from Berthier:

'The Emperor orders, Marshal, that you move your headquarters during 7th October to Lichtenfels. Your 1st Division will camp around that town; your two others between Bamberg and Lichtenfels in such a way that tomorrow, 8th, your army corps can be concentrated in order of battle in front of Kronach in a position to support Marshal Bernadotte, who should during 9th reach the Saale.

'I inform you that the right of the army, leaving Amberg, will occupy Bayreuth on 7th and will be at Hof on 9th. It is composed of the corps of Marshals Soult and Ney.

'The centre will occupy Kronach. It will move via Lobenstein. It is composed of your corps, of that of Marshal Bernadotte, of the greater part of the reserve, and of the Imperial Guard (of which Marshal Lefebvre is about to take over command, transferring the V Corps to Marshal Lannes).

'The left, leaving Schweinfurth, is directed on Coburg, and from there by Gräfenthal; it is composed of Marshals Lannes and Augereau.

'Headquarters is at Bamberg. It will be on 8th at Lichtenfels, and on 9th at Kronach.'

This is a typically concise and very clear Napoleonic order, and its layout and sequence are of considerable interest. It starts off by telling Davout what he is to do; it includes the location of his headquarters, because Napoleon must know where he can be contacted, and it specifies the disposition of his divisions so that Napoleon can be sure that this strategically important corps can be used as required. Next comes the information; first about Bernadotte whom Davout must be ready to support, secondly about the movements of the army as a whole, and lastly about the successive locations of Imperial Headquarters. There is no mention of Napoleon's intention or any information about the locations, strengths, or movements of the enemy. This latter information was normally communicated separately, but Napoleon rarely disclosed his own intentions.

The March of the III Corps

The 1st Division led the III Corps column, with the Corps cavalry forming a screen in front. The leading corps in each column were covered, not only by their own light cavalry, but also by the light brigades from the Cavalry Reserve; the whole being co-ordinated by Murat. On 9th October, ahead of the III Corps, Murat's light cavalry and the I Corps encountered the enemy at Schleiz and drove them back with difficulty.

On 10th October the III Corps reached Schleiz, the 1st and 2nd Divisions bivouacking on the heights north of it. On the same day Imperial Headquarters was established at Saalberg, some six miles to the south. A restless, and perhaps anxious, Napoleon arrived at Headquarters III Corps, and then personally selected positions for the 1st and 2nd

Divisions, whilst, at his instructions, Duroc of his staff selected a position for the 3rd Division south of Schleiz. The Emperor then sent the two light companies of the 108th Regiment (belonging to the 2nd Division) on a reconnaissance towards Saalfeld, on the road being followed by the left column. Nothing had as yet been heard from the V Corps, and Napoleon feared an attack from the left. In his official report, of course, Davout says nothing of what he may have felt at this Imperial interference! He may well have accepted it as part of the system, for, as will be seen, he did much the same thing himself. Later in the day heavy gunfire was heard in the direction of Saalfeld, and in the evening Davout heard that Lannes had encountered and routed the Prussian advanced guard under Prince Hohenlohe.

On 11th October the III Corps, preceded by its light cavalry, marched via Auma and took up a position five miles beyond that town at Mitt-Pöllnitz. Imperial Headquarters on that day was at Auma. As Napoleon had come to the conclusion that no considerable enemy forces faced his right wing, he began a switch to the left. On 10th October Ney's VI Corps was ordered to move west towards Tauna, and Soult, who had reached Plauen with the IV Corps, was directed due north to Gera.

Late on 11th October the information available to Napoleon led him to believe that the Prussians intended to concentrate about Erfurt, and he issued orders that would swing his whole army into a wheel to the left, roughly on to the line of the Saale. Davout with the III Corps was to march to Naumburg. Murat, with the light cavalry of the Reserve, was to advance on Zeitz and then, if the Prussian concentration at Erfurt was confirmed, turn west to Naumburg. The I Corps was to pass through Gera ahead of the IV Corps and Bernadotte was then to follow Murat. The IV Corps under Soult was to continue its march to Gera, but was then to halt and await further orders. Ney's VI Corps was directed on Auma, moving across the rear of the III Corps. Lannes with the V Corps was to advance to Jena, and Augereau's VII Corps was to follow him as far as Kahla. By the time these moves had been completed the army would be ranged on a front from Kahla on the left to Naumburg on the right, with a reserve line from Auma through Gera to Zeitz, so that the army was still in a *bataillon carrée* and able to move in any direction required.

Following the receipt of the Emperor's orders, Davout wrote out a proclamation to his troops, telling them that the Emperor by his able manoeuvres intended to put the Prussians into the same position as the Austrian Army had found itself in the previous year. This was read out by unit commanders before the start of the march on 12th and was received with enthusiastic cries of '*Vive l'Empereur*'.

The three regiments of *chasseurs à cheval*, under Vialannes, headed the march of the III Corps, with one squadron as an advanced guard. Just beyond Naumburg, and some 30 miles from the starting point, the cavalry encountered three Prussian squadrons escorting twenty-one pontoons. Vialannes charged them and captured the pontoons as well as forty baggage wagons with their teams and large magazines of supplies which the Prussians had established at Naumburg. It was apparent that Naumburg was an important centre on the Prussian lines of communications. The main road from Erfurt and Weimar crossed the Saale at Kösen, some five miles to the west, before coming into Naumburg. From Naumburg the main road to Merseburg, Halle, and Magdeburg crossed the Saale again just north-west of the town, and three miles further on it crossed the River Unstrutt at Freiburg. These various bridges were of considerable importance, and the pontoons were obviously intended to supplement them, or replace them if necessary.

Late in the day the 1st Division marched into Naumburg and took up a position on the heights around it. The 2nd Division followed and halted near a village short of the town. The 3rd Division was overtaken by the Emperor on his way from Auma to Gera, and halted to pay him military honours. Continuing its march, it was unable to reach Naumburg that day and halted some miles to the south.

The III Corps cavalry, in the meantime, reconnoitred forward as far as the River Unstrutt. The 1st Chasseurs then took up a position by the Freiburg bridge, whilst the 2nd and 12th watched the Saale below Naumburg. General Vialannes, therefore, had all his cavalry watching the northern approaches to Naumburg. Davout established his headquarters in the town. The I Corps by this time had reached Zeitz, and was therefore some fifteen miles south-east of the III Corps.

Late on 12th Napoleon directed that the army was to rest on the following day, except that the VI Corps was to march to Roda from Auma, and the I Corps was to join the III at Naumburg. The *bataillon carrée* was thus being abandoned and the army committed firmly to the line of the Saale. A central magazine was to be established at Auma and all corps, except the two which were moving, were to replenish with provisions and ammunition.

However, the day of rest was not to materialise. At 9 am on 13th Napoleon received information which led him to inform Murat that the enemy had started to retreat towards Magdeburg. Murat, with the light cavalry, and Bernadotte were ordered to march to Dornburg to fill the gap between Davout and Lannes, and to support the latter if he should be attacked. Soult was ordered to move one division and his cavalry to Roda, and the other two divisions to Kostritz. From the Cavalry Reserve, the Heavy Divisions of Nansouty and d'Hautpoul were ordered to Roda. The III Corps was now becoming the right of the line.

Meanwhile, in the III Corps, Davout's attention was still turned to the north, from whence he thought that enemy reinforcements might arrive with a threat to the army's right flank. He rode out to the Chateau of Freiburg, commanding the bridge over the Unstrutt, and put a detachment of the 13th Light Infantry, of the 1st Infantry Division, into the Chateau, with orders to burn the bridge if the enemy should appear. The rest of the regiment he posted on the left bank of the Saale to guard the bridge on the Naumburg–Freiburg road. The other regiments of the 1st Division bivouacked along this road, whilst, early on 13th the 2nd Division moved into the positions vacated by the 1st Division.

The 3rd Division marched at 4 am on 13th, and arrived early in the Naumburg area, taking up a position about the hamlet of Neu Flemingen on the Naumburg-Camburg road.

Napoleon arrived within five or six miles of Jena early in the afternoon of 13th. He now knew that Lannes was facing some 40,000 or 50,000 Prussians and expected the enemy to attack that evening or the next day. He immediately ordered the Guard, Soult, and Ney to advance rapidly to Jena, and sent orders to Davout and Bernadotte that if they heard an attack developing on Lannes that evening they were to move to their left to his support. This put an entirely different complexion on affairs and Davout ordered a cavalry patrol to be sent out on the Weimar road, beyond the Kösen bridge. Later he rode out himself along this road and towards 4 pm on the heights bordering the Saale beyond Kösen he encountered a party of some 30 troopers of the 1st *Chasseurs* in disorderly flight. This was a patrol which had been attacked and dispersed by several squadrons of Prussian cavalry. Davout rallied them and sent them off to establish a line of vedettes about 600 yards ahead. It was apparent to him from this incident that a large body of enemy troops was advancing, either towards the bridge over the Saale at Kösen or to that over the Unstrutt at Freiburg. Davout rode back and ordered the first regiment he found, the 25th of the 3rd Division, to send its two light companies (one from each battalion) to take up a position in front of the Kösen bridge. He then probably rode on to see Gudin, Commander of the 3rd Division, with the result that the 2nd Battalion of the 25th Regiment was sent to reinforce the bridge guard.

At 3 am on the 14th October Davout received orders from the Emperor, timed 10 pm on 13th October and written from his bivouac on the heights north of Jena. Berthier wrote that the Emperor had identified a Prussian army deployed about two and half miles away, and extending from the heights of Jena to his front as far as Weimar. He intended to attack in the morning. He directed Davout to march via Auerstaedt to Apolda and fall on the rear of the enemy, but left him to choose his own route, provided he took part in the battle. Berthier added, 'If Marshal Bernadotte is with you, you will be able to march together, but the Emperor hopes that he will be in the position indicated to him, that is, Dornburg.'

Davout immediately summoned his divisional and cavalry commanders and issued orders for the advance of the III Corps. He then went off to see Bernadotte, whose I Corps had marched into Naumburg the previous evening. Davout gave Bernadotte a copy of the Emperor's orders and asked him what he proposed to do. Bernadotte, who had no wish to be associated with Davout, chose to assume that the Emperor wished him to go to Dornburg, and said he would march to Camburg, which was on the way to that town.

The Battle of Auerstaedt, 14th October

Though he did not know it, Marshal Davout, with a fighting strength of 26,000, was about to engage in battle with the main enemy army under the King of Prussia and the Duke of Brunswick, consisting of 54,000 infantry and more than 12,000 cavalry; whereas some fifteen miles away Napoleon at Jena with 96,000 men (of whom, however, only about 54,000 took part in the battle) was confronting 53,000 Prussians under Hohenlohe and Ruchel.

The country beyond the Saale, over which the III Corps was to fight, was largely high plateau, intersected by streams, small ravines, and sunken roads, and covered with a number of villages. Towards the north the plateau was crowned with hillocks and many copses. The River Saale was nowhere fordable, and its left bank was wooded and very steep. After crossing the river at Kösen, the Weimar road climbed by a long steep slope to the plateau of Hassenhausen; bridge and road presenting a defile which the troops of the III Corps would have to traverse before being able to deploy on the plateau. As there was no other road which would enable Davout to comply with the Emperor's order to move through Auerstaedt to Apolda, it was important to seize the head of this defile.

Because the 3rd Division was nearest to the Kösen bridge, Marshal Davout directed that the Corps would advance by the left, that is, with the 3rd Division leading, followed by the 2nd Division, and then by the 1st, of which the units were strung out along the Freiburg road, ready to continue the march in that direction.

The 25th Regiment, preceded by a squadron of the 1st *Chasseurs à Cheval*, moved forward from the bridge before dawn and took up a position on the plateau to cover the defile. At 6.30 am General of Division Gudin, commander of the 3rd Division, crossed the bridge at the head of his main body. Half an hour before dawn there had been a fog which was so thick that there was only about ten yards' visibility, but this was now slowly lifting. Davout knew that the enemy were not too far away, but he did not know where they were or in what strength. Accordingly he ordered Colonel Burcke, his senior ADC, to take a fighting patrol from the 1st *Chasseurs*, under the command of a captain, and get information. This was a normal use of senior ADCs; officers who were selected for their ability and determination and who knew the mind of their commander.

Burcke rode forward without encountering any vedettes or outposts until he discovered a body of Prussian cavalry in and about the village of Hassenhausen. He was not spotted in the fog, and Burcke ordered his detachment to stir the Prussians up by firing at them with their pistols. After recovering from their surprise, some two enemy squadrons made a somewhat disorderly charge. Burcke succeeded in taking a few prisoners; but now, as he had fulfilled his mission and the enemy in much superior strength was mounting better organised attacks, he withdrew rapidly. Galloping back, he encountered the 25th Regiment advancing in column on the right of the main road, and rallied his detachment behind them. Away to the left of the road the 85th Regiment was also advancing in column. These two regiments formed a brigade under the command of General of Brigade Gauthier, and to him Burcke reported the approach of the enemy cavalry. Gauthier ordered the 25th Regiment to form battalion squares, and these repulsed the two enemy squadrons. Behind them, however, coming along the road from Hassenhausen was the remainder of the Prussian advanced guard of some 600 cavalry, a battalion of grenadiers, and a light battery, all under the command of General Blücher. Gauthier had deployed the artillery allotted to his brigade across the road, and as the enemy came out of the fog these guns opened a rapid and devastating fire with grape shot. The Prussians were taken by surprise in close order, and both cavalry and grenadiers broke in confusion and the artillery drivers fled. Gauthier placed his ADC, Captain Lagoublaye, in command of a force of the two grenadier companies and one light company of the 25th Regiment, supported by the *chasseur* detachment; and with these troops Lagoublaye attacked the immobilised Prussian battery, capturing its six guns. This is another instance of the use of an ADC, at a lower command level, to command a special task force, rather than entrusting the attack to the regimental commander.

After this success Gauthier continued his advance, sending the 25th Regiment forward in column directly along the road to Hassenhausen and the 85th towards the height to the left of the village. The Prussians tried to halt the progress of the 25th by opening artillery fire to stop them forming square, and then charging with the re-formed cavalry. But the 25th repulsed this attack and swept on to capture the battery and its guns.

Gauthier was now running into trouble because a mass of Prussian infantry was forming beyond Hassenhausen (in fact the whole of the Prussian 3rd Division) and behind it was a very strong body of cavalry.

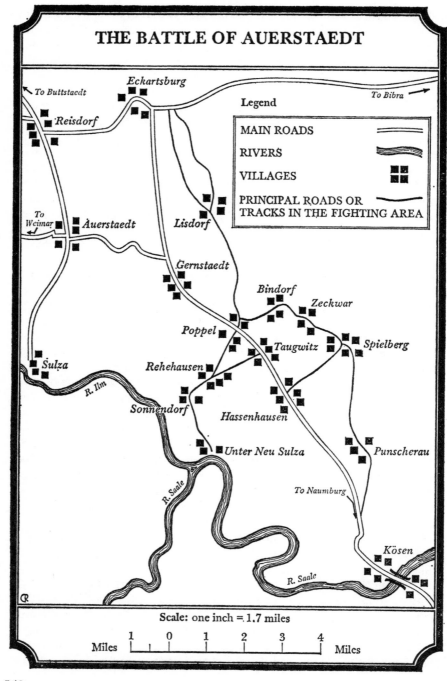

THE BATTLE OF AUERSTAEDT

To Buttstaedt

Eckartsburg

Reisdorf

To Bibra

Legend

MAIN ROADS	
RIVERS	
VILLAGES	
PRINCIPAL ROADS OR TRACKS IN THE FIGHTING AREA	

To Weimar

Auerstaedt

Lisdorf

Gernstaedt

Bindorf

Zeckwar

Poppel

Taugwitz

Spielberg

Rehehausen

Sulza

R. Ilm

Sonnendorf

Hassenhausen

Unter Neu Sulza

Punscherau

R. Saale

To Naumburg

Kösen

R. Saale

Scale: one inch = 1.7 miles

Miles   1   0   1   2   3   4   Miles

The 25th, moving slightly to the right of the village, beat off another attack.

Davout came forward to see the situation for himself. It was clear that Gauthier was in danger of being outflanked from his right by Prussian cavalry. Behind Gauthier was General of Brigade Petit commanding a brigade of the other two regiments of the 3rd Division, the 21st and the 12th. The 21st was leading and Davout ordered Petit to send it up to the support of the 25th, with the 12th following it, echeloned to the right rear. Davout also ordered six guns of the divisional artillery to support this movement. The Corps Commander, it will be noted, was taking direct control of the situation rather than issuing his orders through General Gudin. The Prussians opposed the deployment and advance of Petit's brigade with heavy fire; whilst Blücher moved through the fog with twenty-five squadrons, feeling for the French right flank. Suddenly the fog lifted and he found himself in the rear of the French infantry. Blücher charged; but the French regiments had already formed squares by battalions, and around these the Prussian cavalry surged without being able to make any impression. Davout, Gudin, and Petit moved from square to square to hearten by their presence the morale of the troops. The Prussians in their repeated charges suffered heavy casualties. Blücher's horse was killed under him, and eventually the remnants fell back to Eckartsberg, five miles away.

Meanwhile, on the left of Hassenhausen the 85th Regiment, supported only by the remaining two guns (8-prs.) of the 3rd Division's artillery saw deploying before them ever-increasing masses of Prussians. Immediately in front was part of the enemy's 1st Division, whilst the whole of their 2nd Division was beginning to threaten the left of the 85th's position.

At 8.30 am, doubtless to Davout's relief, General of Division Friant, at the head of the 2nd Division in close battalion columns, rode on to the plateau with his 111th Regiment leading. Davout immediately sent Colonel Touzard, Commander of the Engineers, to lead the 111th Regiment up on to the right of the 3rd Division. Moving into position the 111th came under heavy fire from an enemy six-gun battery. Davout ordered Friant's next regiment, the 108th, to capture it. This was done by the 2nd Battalion while the 1st Battalion chased the enemy out of the village of Spielberg. This was part of a detached brigade of the Prussian 1st Division advancing from Poppel, which was trying to turn the French right. Davout directed Friant to prevent this outflanking movement, and the latter sent his 33rd and 48th Regiments, under General of Brigade Kister, to the right of Spielberg, and detached four infantry companies under an Engineer captain to search the wood on the extreme right and drive any enemy out of it. This use of Engineer officers, by both the Corps and a Divisional Commander, in an infantry role is of interest.

Davout now further protected his right by placing all his three cavalry regiments there, and Vialannes led them in a charge against the Prussian battalions which had already been shaken by the French infantry. The threat to the right had at the moment been defeated, but on the left the 85th Regiment had been fighting a desperate and isolated battle on the height to the left of Hassenhausen. After a long struggle against very superior enemy forces, it had nearly been overrun when Davout was at last able to switch the 12th Regiment to reinforce it; and at the same time he moved the 21st Regiment into the village of Hassenhausen. The situation, however, was still very dangerous, for the 12th Regiment had hardly crossed the main road behind Hassenhausen when it was attacked by superior enemy forces sweeping round the left flank of the 85th. For the moment it looked as if the 3rd Division, its left flank turned, was about to be overwhelmed, when, in the nick of time, the 1st Division, under General of Division Morand, arrived on the battlefield. Davout immediately ordered it to take up a position on the left of the 3rd Division, and rode with Morand to place himself at its head.

In accordance with Davout's orders, Morand had left the 2nd Battalion 17th Regiment to guard the Kösen bridge. The rest of the division marched to the left of Hassenhausen plateau in columns of double companies at company distance. The 13th Light Infantry Regiment led the columns with two 4-pr. guns. As the 1st Division approached the enemy, General of Brigade d'Honnieres, who was leading the 13th Light Infantry, was ordered to deploy one of its battalions to form a line of skirmishers, to keep the other in close column, and to move towards the Hassenhausen bell tower, because the 3rd Division was going to close in its left a little and abandon the village.

The 13th Light Infantry found the enemy already established in front of Hassenhausen with a battery and a strong body of infantry. The 13th attacked, driving the Prussians back through the village and beyond it; but they advanced too far and, isolated from the remainder of the division and assailed by much superior forces, the regiment was obliged to retire and give up the village again to the enemy. It was now about 10.30 am.

Whilst the 13th Light Infantry had been diverted towards Hassenhausen, the remainder of the 1st Division continued its advance on its original axis. Leading were the 61st Regiment on the right and the 51st on the left, both with their two battalions in line each in column of double companies. The two regiments formed a brigade under General of Brigade Debilly. Behind came General of Brigade Brouard with on the right the 30th Regiment and on the left the 17th Regiment (less its 2nd Battalion); both regiments being so disposed that their battalions covered the intervals between those of the leading brigade. The 1st Battalion 17th Regiment moved close to the Saale, with its left flank near to the slope which formed the bank of the river.

The 1st Division was now charged by strong forces of Prussian cavalry, trying to roll up the French left flank. All these charges were beaten off by the steady battalion squares; Davout again moving from square to square to hearten the infantry.

On the III Corps right Friant with the 2nd Division was pressing forward from Spielberg towards Zeckwar against the Prussian left and harrassing their flank with well placed and well direct artillery.

The right of the 1st Division began to gain ground. General Debilly advanced with the 61st Regiment to the head of a ravine which led to Rehehausen and which was defended by a strong body of Prussian infantry supported by mortars. After a fierce struggle the Prussians were driven back, abandoning their mortars to the French. On the left of the 61st, the 51st was subjected to a heavy artillery fire, followed by cavalry charges and an infantry attack. Although suffering heavy casualties, the regiment held its ground.

The Prussians had noted that there were no cavalry units on the French left, and the King of Prussia decided to try again to turn the left of the 1st Division and stop the French advance on Rehehausen. A strong Prussian force moved via Sonnendorf to the heights bordering the left bank of the River Ilm, and three companies of infantry descended to the river bottom. To stop this turning movement there were only the 30th Regiment and the 1st Battalion 17th Regiment. Davout, however, had spotted the enemy threat and informed Morand, who moved all the seven guns of his Foot Artillery to the support of the 30th Regiment. The enemy attack carried out by the greater part of their 1st Reserve Division, including the regiments of the Prussian Guards, ran into a storm of grape and was completely shattered. Morand now swung his left forward, cleared the Ilm heights, and placed his artillery on a dominating spur from which it could take the Prussian army in the flank. At about the same time Friant, on the right of the III Corps had got forward to Poppel and had put his guns on a height to the right of it from which they could command the enemy's left wing.

Friant had had a long hard fight at Zeckwar, but after driving the Prussians out of the village, he had ordered General of Brigade Lochet to advance on Poppel with the 108th Regiment. The 6th Sapper Company (corps troops) was also placed under Lochet's command. The 108th made rapid progress towards Poppel, capturing an enemy colour, several pieces of artillery, and a number of prisoners. Meanwhile the 6th Sapper Company, after moving along the main road from Zeckwar, turned the defenders' left flank and charged with the bayonet into the village. The

Prussians in Poppel had been organising a counter-attack to assist their forward companies cut off by the Poppel stream; but this bold attack by the small company of sappers so shook them that they remained on the defensive, and the troops who had been cut off, numbering about 1,000 men, laid down their arms. This surprising use of engineer troops in an infantry role shows that Davout had been forced to throw everything he had into the battle, because he could ill afford casualties amongst his few sappers. It also shows, however, the flexibility of the French Army, and that sappers must have been trained as shock troops.

The Prussian cavalry made a last attempt to turn Friant's right, but were thrown back by the 48th Regiment.

Following the successes gained by his right and left wings, Davout now advanced his centre. Gudin's 3rd Division attacked and captured the village of Taugwitz and its forward elements moved up level with the 1st and 2nd Divisions. At 12.30 pm the leading Prussian divisions began to give way and by 1 pm the enemy had evacuated all the high ground about Hassenhausen. The Prussians were only saved from complete defeat at this juncture by the intervention of their reserve divisions. Since the beginning of the battle, these two divisions had been deployed in order of battle on the high ground between the villages of Auerstaedt and Gernstadt, but a large part of one of them had already been badly mauled in the attack on Morand's left wing. This reserve now moved forward on to the high ground between Taugwitz and Rehehausen with its front behind the stream running from Poppel to Rehehausen. There it displayed a firm front, while the three Prussian divisions which had borne the brunt of the fighting fell back in disorder, abandoning a large part of their artillery.

The Prussian reserve was reasonably secure from a frontal attack, but its flanks were hammered from the same two artillery positions which had been established by Morand and Friant on the right and left respectively. The Prussians could not stand it, and gave way, retiring to their original positions. However, here they were attacked vigorously by the now victorious French. The 2nd Division marched on Lissdorff and menaced their left, whilst the 3rd Division drove ahead from Poppel. The Prussian reserve was forced to retire again and took up a third position on the high ground in front of Eckartsburg.

Arriving at the headquarters of the 3rd Division, Davout directed Gudin to move his division towards the foot of the left side of the plateau and form in order of battle. He then ordered General Petit to assault the plateau with the four grenadier companies of the 12th and 21st Regiments. Petit attacked without replying to the Prussian fire, and his troops climbed rapidly up the hill with their bayonets fixed. At the same time General of Brigade Grandeau of the 2nd Division stormed up the right of the hill with the greater part of the 111th Regiment. These assaulting troops were followed by the remainder of the 2nd and 3rd Divisions. The Prussians broke in front of this well planned attack, abandoning their excellent and final position with such haste that they left twenty pieces of ordnance in Petit's hands. The French followed up the enemy as far as the Chateau of Eckartsburg, and here at about 4.30 pm the main operation came to a halt. General Vialannes continued the pursuit with his three regiments of *Chasseurs*, pressing the Prussian left to drive the fleeing enemy towards the Saale and Apolda, the line of advance indicated by the Emperor. Finally, after collecting many prisoners and guns, he went into bivouac at Buttstädt, some ten miles from the battle-field. The 2nd Battalion 17th Regiment, which had been guarding the Kösen bridge, was deployed in an outpost position beyond the battlefield; and it too collected a large number of prisoners, as wounded and straggling enemy soldiers wandered into the French lines.

Perhaps the most striking aspect of this amazing encounter battle, is the very effective use that the French made of their excellent artillery. Gauthier defeated the Prussian advanced guard with his brigade guns; Morand used the bulk of his divisional artillery to smash the enemy attempt to turn his left flank; and it was the flanking bombardment from the guns of the 1st and 2nd Divisions which forced the retreat of the Prussian reserve divisions from their forward position.

The victory was in large part due, however, to the tactical ability of Davout and his senior commanders. Davout fought a magnificent en-counter battle against heavy odds. He was everywhere that danger threatened, sizing up the situation and taking immediate and improvised action, as one by one his divisions struggled up to the plateau. He had no information as to enemy strength or intentions, and the lack of intelligence was intensified by the thick fog which obscured the initial moves of both his own troops and those of the enemy. The threat to Gauthier's right he countered by throwing in Petit, and as the first of Friant's troops arrived he seized them to stem the Prussian attempts to roll up his right flank; when the 1st Division reached the battlefield he led them personally to stem the sudden threat to his left; and finally he swung his whole corps into a co-ordinated attack which routed an army about two and half times as strong as his own.

Davout must have been an excellent trainer of men, for his subordinate commanders were not only of marked ability, but they all seemed to be inside their Corps Commander's mind, in that they not only knew what to do but what each other would do in a given set of circumstances. Morand, Friant, and Gudin exploited every opportunity that came their way, and by dash and tactical ability threw the numerically superior but rigid Prussian formations back on the defensive. And in the Generals of

Brigade, such as Petit, Gauthier, d'Honnieres, Debilly, and Lochet, the III Corps had men who were quite happy in leading complete brigades, or small improvised forces of a few companies, in dashing attacks on the enemy. Davout had merely to give them some men and tell them to do something. Nothing else was necessary because they knew exactly how to do it. The III Corps was probably unique in Napoleon's Army; it is unlikely that any of the others could have won at Auerstaedt. In fact, during the years 1806 and 1807 Marshal Davout probably commanded the finest fighting formation for its size in the world.

Casualties in the III Corps had been heavy. In the 1st Division Morand had been wounded, Debilly killed, and d'Honnieres wounded; and of other senior officers, Adjutant-Commandant Coehorn, Colonel Guyardet, and Colonel Nicolas were wounded. In the 2nd Division Colonel Higonet had been killed. In the 3rd Division Adjutant-Commandant Delotz died of his wounds, Generals Gauthier and Petit were wounded, Colonel Vergès was thought to be mortally wounded, and Colonel Viala was wounded. Colonel Bousson of the 2nd *Chasseurs à Cheval* was badly wounded as was also Colonel Burcke, ADC to Davout. Most generals, senior officers, and staff officers had either been grazed by bullets or had had horses killed under them—some as many as three horses. The total casualties in the three divisions were 252 officers and 6,581 other ranks. With the addition of the losses in the cavalry, engineers, and staff, about one-third of the III Corps were casualties.

On the same day that Davout had gained his victory at Auerstaedt, Napoleon had defeated the remainder of the Prussian Army at Jena. If Bernadotte had assisted Davout, instead of remaining inactive some ten miles away at Dornburg, the Prussian Army would have been entirely destroyed. Napoleon was furious with Bernadotte and, it appears, actually contemplated having him court-martialled. At St. Helena Napoleon said that Bernadotte had told Davout at Naumburg that if he marched with him his Corps, being No. I, must lead the way because Davout only commanded No. III. To this Davout objected that this would cause confusion because Bernadotte's Corps would have to pass through his to get in front.[1] General Rapp says[2] that the day after the battle Napoleon said to him: 'Bernadotte has behaved badly. He would have been enchanted to see Devout fail in that affair, which does him the greatest honour, all the more so because Bernadotte had rendered his position difficult.'

On 15th October, at 2 am, Davout sent General of Brigade Lochet with his brigade of the 2nd Division to reinforce the detachment of the 13th Light Infantry which he had posted on the morning of 13th October to guard the Freiburg bridge. He told Lochet to destroy all the bridges over the Unstrutt to stop the remnants of the Prussian Army from using them to escape to the north. Later that day the whole of the 2nd Division concentrated at Freiburg and was joined by the 2nd *Chasseurs à Cheval*. The 3rd Division remained in position beyond the battlefield to await the Prussians, who, surrounded on all sides, might try and cross the Saale and retreat through Naumburg. The 1st Division, preceded by the 1st and 12th *Chasseurs à Cheval*, crossed the Saale by the Kösen bridge at midday and marched through Naumburg to bivouac seven miles beyond it on the road to Leipzig.

On 16th October the III Corps made preparatory moves for an advance on Leipzig. The 1st Division marched to Weissenfels and halted with its left on the Saale, whilst its advanced guard of the 13th Light Infantry and the 1st *Chasseurs à Cheval* seized the bridge over the Rippach at Porsten, about four miles ahead. On the left the 2nd *Chasseurs à Cheval* carried out a reconnaissance as far as Merseburg, and the 108th Regiment of the 2nd Division marched to Markröhlitz; the remainder of the division remaining at Freiburg. The 3rd Division crossed the Saale at Kösen and marched to Schönburg on the Leipzig road, leaving the 85th Regiment to garrison Naumburg until the arrival there of Imperial Headquarters. On 17th information was received that there were no enemy in Leipzig and all divisions rested.

Immediately after the defeat of the Prussians Napoleon began making arrangements for a rapid pursuit. The III Corps became the right of a great sweep forward of all the French corps over a front of about fifty miles; though fifty miles farther to the right the Bavarian Corps was making for Dresden and beyond. Bernadotte marched to the left of Davout as far as Halle, but he then turned west and was replaced as Davout's neighbour by Lannes, with V Corps, who had followed Davout through Naumburg. Behind Lannes came the Emperor and the Guard, followed by Augereau with the VII Corps.

On 16th Napoleon had ordered Bernadotte to make for Nebra on the Unstrutt. From there Bernadotte had notified Davout of his intention of marching against Halle and requesting Davout's co-operation by moving cavalry to Merseburg; and this was the reason for the reconnaissance by the 2nd *Chasseurs*.

On 18th October Davout entered Leipzig at the head of the advanced guard of the 1st Division. General Macon was appointed governor of the town, and his first act was to set up a hospital to receive 2,000 wounded.

On 19th October the III Corps marched to Düben on the River Mulde. Just after midnight Davout left with an advanced guard of 1,000 picked men under the command of Colonel Lanusse (17th Regiment) and 100 troopers of the 1st *Chasseurs à Cheval* on a dash to seize the bridge over the Elbe at Wittenberg. The troops had already marched about twenty miles from Leipzig to Düben, and it was another twenty on to Wittenberg. But the matter was urgent for it had become known that a Prussian officer had been sent to Wittenberg to have the bridge burnt on the approach of the French. By the time that Devout's detachment arrived this officer had already covered the bridge with pitch, and as soon as he saw the French he set fire to it and to a large quantity of fascines which had been placed along it. But the *chasseurs* and Lanusse's picked men rushed on to the bridge and, with the willing help of the Saxon inhabitants, prevented the Prussian soldiers from defending it long enough for it to burn. In less than two hours the bridge was entirely repaired. The seizure of this bridge intact was essential to the advance of the III Corps. The Corps' objective was now Berlin, for the Emperor, as a reward for its brilliant conduct at Auerstaedt, had promised it that it should have the honour of being the first to enter the enemy's capital city.

In accordance with the Emperor's orders, Davout ordered Colonel of Engineers Touzard to construct defences on both banks of the Elbe at Wittenberg to prevent the bridge being captured by a *coup de main*.

On 22nd October Napoleon established Imperial Headquarters at Wittenberg and the Guard marched into the town. As soon as he arrived the Emperor issued the orders for the march to Berlin of the III Corps. They included the following: Berlin was to be entered at midday on 25th October, General Hulin was to be installed as commandant, and one regiment was to be left in the city; light cavalry posts were to be established on the roads leading to Landsberg, Kustrin, and Frankfurt-on-Oder; the III Corps was to take up a position 2½ miles beyond Berlin with its right on the River Spree and its left on the road to Landsberg; Davout's headquarters was to be located in a house in the country on the Kustrin road and behind his troops; huts of wood and straw were to be built because it was the Emperor's intention to give the troops some days rest; when the troops had formed their camp, one third of them could visit Berlin whilst the other two thirds remained in camp; the formal entry of the III Corps into Berlin was to be made by the Dresden road, each division was to have its artillery with it, and there was to be an interval of one hour's march between each division; and, finally, the Emperor would probably stay at the Charlottenburg Palace.

The March to Berlin and Frankfurt-on-Oder

At 5 pm on 22nd October the III Corps started its march, the 1st Division leading. On 23rd October Davout sent on ahead to Berlin Adjutant-Commandant Romoeuf, accompanied by the Colonels of Artillery and Engineers and the Chief Commissary, and escorted by 100 troopers of the 2nd *Chasseurs à Cheval*. Romoeuf was to announce the arrival of the III Corps and was to co-ordinate with the city authorities measures to ensure supplies for the French troops and for the maintenance of public order.

He was also to take note of the various public establishments, academies, palaces, libraries, etc., in order to see what force the General Commandant of Berlin would need to ensure their protection. The other three officers of the party were to note arsenals, armouries, barracks, clothing stores, provisions of all kinds, hospitals, etc.

The above party entered Berlin at midday on 24th, whilst on the evening of that day the 1st Division marched into Templehof. Davout despatched his Assistant Chief of Staff, Adjutant-Commandant Hervo to reconnoitre the area in which the III Corps was to camp. He was accompanied by the Engineer officers attached to each of the divisions to trace out the camp. He was to arrange for the provision of wood and straw for the huts and forage for the horses. The allotment of administrative duties between various officers of the Corps staff will be noted, and also the tasks which they were expected to be able to undertake.

On 25th October at 10 am Davout with all his staff was at the head of the III Corps on the road into Berlin. As he entered the city, the magistrates, followed by the principal citizens, brought him the keys. These he handed back, saying that they must only pay homage to the Emperor. He then rode through the town, followed by the III Corps, amidst an immense crowd of people who had gathered to watch the French army march in. The Corps went on to its camping ground, where provisions, forage, and the building materials for the huts had already been delivered. (Hervo and Romoeuf must have had their own methods of persuading the Prussian authorities that any delay would be inadvisable!) Vialannes now took 400 *chasseurs* on a forty-mile ride to Frankfurt-on-Oder to surprise the town and prevent the enemy from burning the bridge.

The next day the Emperor entered Berlin. He told Davout that he would review the III Corps on 28th October. In accordance with his normal custom, this was a very detailed inspection of every unit, and during it he made a number of promotions. Afterwards he had all officers and non-commissioned officers gathered round him and he gave them a very appreciative address on their conduct at the Battle of Auerstaedt. For gallantry in the battle he granted 500 decorations of the Legion of Honour to Officers, NCOs and men.

Apart from their achievements in battle, the marches of the III Corps soldiers had been no mean feat. The distance as the crow flies between Schleiz, where the Corps was on 10th October, and Berlin, which it entered on 25th October, is 166 miles.[3] The distance by road, of course, was very much greater, and a battle had been fought as well.

On 29th October Davout issued orders for the III Corps to march the following day at 6 am to Frankfurt-on-Oder. On the way, Gudin was ordered to take the 3rd Division to Kustrin on the Oder, about fifteen miles north of Frankfurt, and to capture the bridge and the fortress which lay on the far bank. The 2nd *Chasseurs à Cheval* and a battery of six extra pieces were attached to him.

On 31st October Davout with the 1st and 2nd Divisions arrived at Frankfurt at 8 am. Gudin was too late at Kustrin. His advanced guard attacked and overpowered a Prussian covering force of 500 men on the left bank of the river, but the governor of the fortress had burnt the bridge. Gudin captured some large and useful magazines of food and summoned the fortress without success. However, the Emperor did not wish Gudin's division to be delayed in besieging a fortress, and, despatching other troops to relieve it, ordered Gudin to rejoin the III Corps. Davout had been ordered to cross the Oder and deploy his Corps in observation.

On 1st November at daybreak Gudin's division marched towards Frankfurt leaving Gauthier with one regiment to watch the fortress until the relieving troops arrived. Petit remained behind to relieve the posts of the 21st Regiment, and was about to follow Gudin when he was approached by a Prussian officer with a flag of truce. There followed the most astounding capitulation. Gauthier had one regiment and two field guns, and to this small force the Governor surrendered a fortress which had a garrison of 4,000 men, was well supplied, and had ninety guns mounted on the ramparts.

On receiving the news of the surrender, Davout rode to Kustrin accompanied by his Engineer Colonel Touzard. He ordered the latter to have the bridge repaired as quickly as possible.

It was just one month since the III Corps had arrived at Bamberg. The war against Prussia had ended; that against Russia was about to start.

Most of the information in this chapter is derived from Marshal Davout's own official report, entitled *Opérations du 3ᵉ Corps 1806–1807*, and published in 1896 by his nephew, General Davout, Duke of Auerstaedt.

Other works consulted are:

Count Yorck von Wartenberg, *Napoleon as a General*, transl. Major W. H. James, 1902
F. Loraine Petre, *Napoleon's Conquest of Prussia—1806*, 1907
Brigadier General V. J. Esposito and Colonel J. R. Elting, *A Military History and Atlas of the Napoleonic Wars*, 1964

Specific references are:

1. *Mémoires pour Servir a l'Histoire de France sous le Regne de Napoleon I, Ecrits sous la Dictee, a Ste. Helene, par Montholon et Gourgaud*, 1823–1825
2. General Rapp, *Mémoires Ecrit par Lui-Meme*, 1823
3. Wartenberg, op. cit.

CHAPTER TEN

THE THIRD CORPS— POLAND

On 2nd November 1806 Napoleon ordered Davout to move the III Corps into Poland and to be prepared to encounter the Russian army, which, by virtue of a treaty signed in October between the Prussian and Russian Governments, was about to enter the part of Poland allotted to the King of Prussia at the last partition. The 1st *Chasseurs à Cheval* had actually marched for Posen the previous day and reached it on 4th November, to receive a tremendous welcome from the Poles.

Berthier informed Davout that Prince Jerome, commanding the auxiliary corps of Bavarian and Würtemberg troops, should arrive at Frankfurt on 2nd November, and that from there he would march to Krossen, with instructions to invest Glogau and to despatch a reconnaissance detachment to Breslau. Davout was to keep in touch with Jerome. On 6th November a further instruction from the Emperor to Davout directed him to march to Posen and informed him that Augereau had been ordered to establish Headquarters VII Corps at Küstrin on 7th November.

On 9th November Davout rode into Posen and was welcomed outside the town gates by the magistrates and most of the inhabitants. The 2nd Division marched in later the same day, and by 12th November the whole of the Corps was concentrated in and around the town. The Emperor had placed under Davout's command a large force of cavalry consisting of General Milhaud's Light Cavalry Brigade, General Beaumont's Dragoon Division, and General Namsouty's Heavy Cavalry Division.

Davout's principal task at Posen was to arrange supplies for the Grand Army, the major portion of which would have to pass through Posen on its way to the Vistula. It was no easy task because the country between the

Rivers Warta, on which Posen lay, and Vistula was one of the least fertile parts of Poland. Magazines of all kinds of food and stores had to be established along the roads leading to Thorn and Warsaw; and the movement of all these commodities was difficult because the unmetalled roads were at their worst on account of the wet season and very few vehicles were obtainable. There was only one bridge over the Warta and this was in such bad state of repair that it was quite unsuitable for heavy traffic. Davout gave Touzard the job of repairing it and also of building a second bridge. However, the local inhabitants assisted with material and labour, and under the direction of Touzard and his Engineer officers the work was carried out promptly and efficiently.

On 15th November Davout had finished his preparations at Posen and was about to continue his march. The situation of the Grand Army was then as follows: Ney (VI Corps), having captured Magdeburg, was *en route* for Berlin; Soult (IV Corps) and Bernadotte (I Corps), and also part of the cavalry under Murat, were also marching to Berlin; Lannes (V Corps) was approaching Thorn, followed by the Dragoon Division commanded by General Becker; and Augereau (VII Corps) had been ordered to leave Driesen for Bromberg. During the approach to the Vistula the V and VII Corps were to form the left wing; the III Corps, reinforced by the Cavalry of Nansouty, Milhaud, and Beaumont, was to be the centre; and the Bavarian and Würtemburg Corps were to be on the right at Kalisz. Murat was ordered by Napoleon to go to Posen and take command of these four corps.

On 16th November Davout started, taking the road to Warsaw. Vialanne's and Milhaud's Light Cavalry Brigades formed a wide screen across the front of the advance, whilst Nansouty's Division moved on the right flank and Beaumont's on the left. The light cavalry had several engagements with Russian Cossacks.

On 28th November Murat rode into Warsaw at the head of the cavalry, the city having been evacuated by the Russians. On 29th he wrote to Davout: 'I am leaving the Corps of Marshal Lannes on the Bzura, occupying Lowicz and Sochaczew. You will leave one division at Blonie with your reserve park; you will establish yourself in Warsaw with one division; the other will be billeted in the outskirts of Warsaw, where its headquarters will be. Your cavalry should watch the Vistula from the Bzura to Warsaw . . . . I order that provisioning should be carried out at Blonie, Lowicz, and Sochaczew.' In compliance with these orders, Davout put the 1st Division in Warsaw, the 2nd Division about Blonie, and the 3rd Division in the outskirts of Warsaw.

Augereau had now reached the Vistula and was on Lannes's left; whilst Napoleon and the Imperial Guard were at Posen. On the opposite bank of the Vistula the Russians occupied the Warsaw suburb of Praga. On

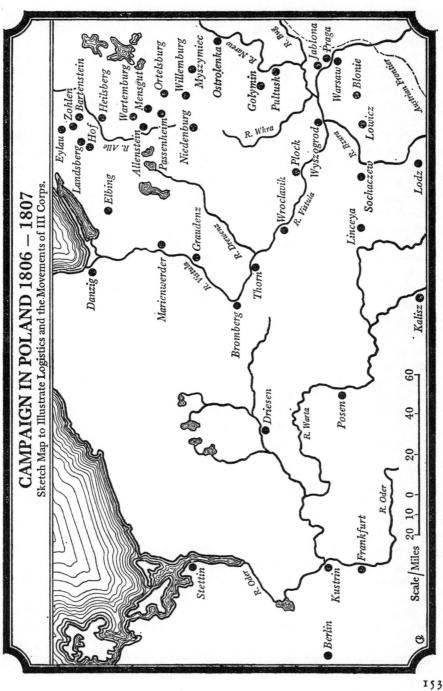

CAMPAIGN IN POLAND 1806 – 1807

Sketch Map to Illustrate Logistics and the Movements of III Corps.

Eylau
Zohlen
Bartenstein
Heilsberg
Landsberg
Hof
Wartemburg
Mensgut
Allenstein
Ortelsburg
Willemburg
Myszyniec
Passenheim
Ostrolenka
Niedenburg
Golymin
Pultusk
Jablona
Praga
Warsaw
Blonie
Elbing
R. Bug
R. Narew
Lowicz
R. Wkra
Austrian Frontier
Danzig
Marienwerder
Graudenz
Wrocławik
Plock
Wyszogrod
R. Bzura
Sochaczew
Lodz
R. Vistula
R. Drewenz
R. Vistula
Thorn
Linceya
Bromberg
Driesen
Posen
R. Warta
Stettin
R. Oder
Kustrin
Frankfurt
R. Oder
Berlin
Kalisz

Scale / Miles
20 10 0 20 40 60

153

2nd December, however, they evacuated it and the 17th Regiment of the 1st Division, with two 4-pr. guns, crossed the Vistula and took possession of Praga.

On 3rd December the Russians retired behind the River Bug, and on the same day Milhaud crossed over to the right bank with the 2nd and 13th *Chasseurs à Cheval*, the 30th Regiment of the 1st Division, and a detachment of light artillery. On 4th and 5th December the remainder of the 1st Division crossed the Vistula.

The French were now faced with the problem of crossing the Bug. Davout decided to entrust the task to General Gauthier of the 3rd Division. The right bank of the Bug was high, but the left bank was low, flat, and marshy. This gave the Russians a marked advantage in the defence. On 6th December General Brouard of the 1st Division was established with the 17th Regiment and two 4-pr. guns on the bank of the Bug with a line of posts stretching westwards from its junction with the Narew. The 30th Regiment and General d'Honnieres' Brigade were formed in two echelons in rear of the 17th between the Bug and Praga, with their right flank on the Austrian frontier (which at this time ran northwards to the Bug from a point about eight miles east of Warsaw) and their left in contact with Gauthier's Brigade. Gauthier had pushed an advanced guard up to Okunin near the junction of the Wkra with the Bug.

Late on 6th Gauthier tried a surprise crossing of the Bug to seize a foothold on the right bank. But the large ferry boat in which the attempt was made was pushed off course by slabs of floating ice and it stranded in the middle of the river.

On 8th December Davout established an advanced headquarters at Jablona on the Vistula about eight miles north of Praga, and conveniently placed for him to visit all parts of the Bug where a passage could be attempted.

The Crossing of the Bug

After a reconnaissance on 9th December, Davout ordered Gauthier to try and cross the river by the village of Okunin, where the conditions appeared to be most favourable. The curve of the Bug, just after it was joined by the Wkra, formed a peninsula, opposite the village, which appeared easy to fortify and to support by artillery fire from the left bank. In preparation for his crossing Gauthier arranged for a feint attack on his right at Gora, which was to be carried out by General Milhaud with three companies of the 1st Battalion of the 85th Regiment of the 3rd Division and a detachment of the 13th *Chasseurs à Cheval*, supported by a howitzer. Milhaud was allotted a river ferry and two small skiffs, and into the ferry he put a hundred of the best skirmishers of the battalion of the 85th

Regiment, with orders not to attempt the crossing until the first troops from Okunin were over.

For his crossing at Okunin, Gauthier had three light infantry companies from the 25th and 85th Regiments, a battalion of the 25th, six companies of the 2nd Battalion 85th Regiment and one 8-pr. gun. The 1st Battalion 85th Regiment (less detached companies) was in reserve behind Gora. At 5.30 am on 10th December Gauthier embarked a light infantry company of the 85th Regiment in twelve skiffs with orders to land on the right bank, to seize a position a hundred yards from the river, and not to fire, but await the troops who would follow. This operation was carried out successfully, and before daybreak the remainder of Gauthier's assault force crossed at the same place without any engagement with the Russians. Gauthier then ordered Colonel Duplin (who had succeeded Colonel Viala in command of the 85th Regiment) to take the battalion of the 25th Regiment on a reconnaissance towards Pomichowo. Milhaud's feint attack at Gora started at 7 am, but it was limited to fire action as an actual crossing was clearly unnecessary.

As soon as Gauthier's force was established, Touzard arrived to lay out a defended bridgehead, and both troops and local peasants were employed on the construction of the works, which presented an effective obstacle within twenty-four hours. At the same time a pontoon bridge across the Bug to the bridgehead was built rapidly under the direction of General Hanicque, commanding the Corps Artillery. Davout directed Gauthier to construct, about 150 yards in rear of his first line of entrenchments, a breastwork of sufficient length to provide cover for a third of his force, formed in column of attack, and to build in rear of this again a redoubt to hold another third as a reserve.

The crossing of the Bug provides another interesting use of a General of Brigade; that is, the conduct of a river crossing, for which Davout allotted him such troops as he thought he would need, and even put the General commanding the light cavalry under his orders. The building of the bridge, it will be noted, was made an artillery and not an engineer responsibility.

On 11th December the Russians launched the attack on the bridgehead which Davout had expected. During the night they had pushed forward to assault positions, and at daybreak they opened a heavy artillery fire, followed by the infantry attack. After heavy fighting they were driven off.

Other corps were now moving up. The V Corps crossed the Vistula at Praga and the VII Corps crossed it a little below its junction with the Bug.

To the right of the peninsula, on which the bridgehead was established, was a triangular island, formed by the Wkra splitting into two arms to flow into the Bug. The island was partly covered by woods and was crossed by a marshy canal. The French had only occupied a third of it, and, as fire from enemy troops who occupied the remainder was a nuisance, Davout on 20th December ordered Petit to capture the rest of the island. This was done without difficulty.

On 22nd December Friant's 2nd Division crossed the Bug at Okunin and moved north to the vicinity of Pomichowo, where it bivouacked. At dusk on the same day the 1st Division pulled out from its riverside positions, from which it had been threatening attack, and moved downstream to Okunin, leaving one battalion to light the usual fires and mount the customary picquets and patrols. The division then crossed over the bridge and bivouacked in the bridgehead area. The bulk of the III Corps was now across the Bug, though the heavy equipment and artillery reserve remained on the left bank.

The Crossing of the Wkra and the Action at Czarnowo

On 23rd December the Emperor arrived in the Okunin entrenched camp and during the morning carried out a reconnaissance of the area. East of Czarnowo the right bank of the Bug is bordered by a fairly steep hill. At Czarnowo the Bug turns south but the slight escarpment continues due east to the Wkra at Pornichowo, and it dominates the low lying ground to the south between the Bug and the Wkra. North of this escarpment was the main Russian position, in which were about fifteen thousand man and twenty guns, mostly behind breastworks. The Russian right flank rested on the Wkra, protected by entrenchments, whilst the left flank was on the Bug. The enemy outposts were sited along the banks on their side of the two rivers. On their withdrawal the Russians had burnt the bridge over the Wkra at Pornichowo, and had also destroyed an old and half ruined bridge further upstream. In addition, when Petit drove them off the island, they destroyed the bridge which they had used over the eastern arm of the Wkra. The ground between the two rivers and the main Russian position was largely covered by marshy fields and woods, and in these the enemy had constructed numerous abatis, which were defended by the outposts, so that the area was nearly as difficult to force as the main position.

Napoleon examined the whole terrain from several points. He even climbed a ladder on top of a house on the island in order to see what was happening on the far bank. He then gave, on the ground, the following order for a night attack to Davout, written at his dictation by Colonel (Adjutant-Commandant) Hervo, Assistant Chief of Staff III Corps:

'The 1st Division will move to the island and form up as far away as possible from the enemy.

'The whole of the 3rd Division will remain in the bridgehead, will not take part at all in the attack, and will remain as a reserve.

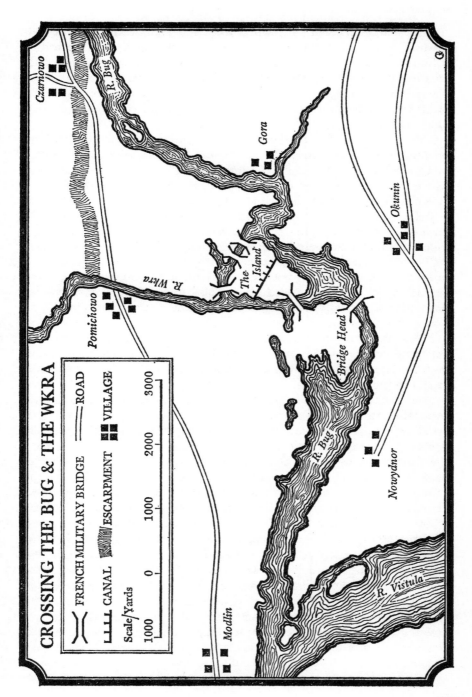

CROSSING THE BUG & THE WKRA

FRENCH MILITARY BRIDGE ══ ROAD
├┴┤ CANAL ▓▓ ESCARPMENT ▦ VILLAGE

Scale/Yards
1000   0   1000   2000   3000

Czarnowo

R. Bug

Gora

Okunin

R. Wkra

The Island

Pomichowo

Bridge Head

R. Bug

Nowydnor

Modlin

R. Vistula

'Two battalions will be formed from the eight companies of light infantry, which, with the 13th Light Infantry Regiment, will form three columns. These three columns will move in complete silence to the crossing points of the canal and will halt in the middle of the island beyond musket range. They will each be accompanied by three pieces of ordnance, as detailed by column commanders, escorted by a company of light infantry.

'The action will start by the escorting companies moving forward and opening fire on the enemy from behind hedges; whilst the artillery officers will deploy their guns and open fire with grapeshot on the troops which the enemy will not fail to move up to oppose the crossing.

'Under the cover of the artillery fire the boats and bridges will be launched and the three columns will cross the river. As soon as they are on the far bank, three piquets of *chasseurs à cheval*, each of sixty men, will follow them and charge the enemy, pursuing them and taking prisoners.

'The 17th Regiment will cross immediately afterwards, forming in order of battle and leaving between each battalion an interval of 150 yards behind which will be placed three squadrons of light cavalry. The remainder of the 1st Division will cross next and form up behind.'

This is an interesting example of the Napoleonic method when so much depended on the success of a divisional attack. The Emperor by-passed both the Corps and the Divisional Commanders, to give his own detailed orders to the 1st Division.

Napoleon followed this attack order with instructions as to how a successful crossing was to be exploited. After the passage of the Wkra the 1st Division was to advance on Czarnowo to attack the left of the Russian main position; whilst Petit of the 3rd Division was to cross the river at the same points as the 1st Division, and then go upstream along the left bank of the Wkra and seize the Russian trenches facing Ponichowo. To support this second operation, the Emperor placed six 12-pr. guns on the heights in front of Ponichowo to batter the flank of the enemy position whilst Petit attacked its front. Napoleon also ordered that a large quantity of damp straw was to be lit near Pomichowo along the river bank for about 1,800 to 2,400 yards so as to make a lot of smoke. Each light infantryman was to be supplied with a truss of hay to which he was to set fire as soon as the artillery bombardment started. The object was to cause a diversion by making the enemy expect a crossing of the river about Pomichowo on their right whilst Morand's division was making the real crossing from the island. Petit was to carry out his operation with his own brigade, and the rest of the light cavalry under General Marulaz were ordered to follow Petit's Brigade and to try and cut off the enemy artillery as soon as it began to retire from the emplacements opposite Pomichowo.

General Hanicque, Commander of the Artillery, was ordered to bring up all available boats to throw a bridge over the western arm of the Wkra to the island, whilst Touzard was made responsible for the assault boats and bridges to be launched over the eastern arm, and also for the repair of the Pomichowo bridge.

To all these arrangements, Napoleon added another, which contributed much to the French success. Captain Perrin, one of Davout's ADCs, was ordered to lead a detachment up the right bank of the Wkra, level with Petit on the left bank, so that he could take in the flank any Russian troops who opposed Petit's advance. The detachment consisted of thirty of the best skirmishers in the 3rd Division, fifty other infantry, and two guns.

In accordance with Napoleon's orders, Morand, Commander of the 1st Division, composed his three columns of attack as follows: first column, 2nd Battalion 13th Light Infantry; second column, the light infantry companies of the 17th and 30th Regiments; third column, the light infantry companies of the 51st and 61st Regiments. The columns crossed the first arm of the Wkra by Hanicque's new bridge and halted on the canal line. As soon as the guns arrived, they, preceded by the skirmishers, advanced to the second arm of the river, under cover of the gathering dusk. The fire of the skirmishers was followed soon by the grapeshot from the guns, and under cover of this the three columns crossed the river; one by a ferry, one by a boat brought up by the engineers, and the third by two boats brought by the sailors of the Guard. Almost immediately engineer officers began the construction of a bridge which was quickly completed, and over it went the cavalry and artillery. Colonel Guyardet of the 13th Light Infantry used his regimental sappers to open up a wide ride through the forest as far as the east–west road running from Czarnowo to Pomichowo. Behind the sappers the light infantry columns exploited towards the Russian main position. It was about 7 pm and of course quite dark, so that the troops were probably moving in a dense column along the ride. The 17th Regiment was ordered to reconnoitre the approaches to Czarnowo. It took the Russians by surprise and captured the batteries defending the approaches to the village. However, the Russians mounted an immediate and strong counter-attack and forced the right of the 17th to fall back. At the same time the light infantry columns were fiercely attacked.

The 17th Regiment rallied in good order under cover of the woods, where the enemy did not dare pursue in the dark. However, as the regiment had used up all its ammunition, Morand decided to relieve it by the 30th Regiment. General Brouard led it forward, but as he reached the foot of the entrenchments he was wounded in the face by grape-shot.

The whole of the 1st Division was now across the Wkra, as well as General Marulaz's Light Cavalry Brigade and General Latour-Maubourg's dragoon Brigade. Davout now ordered Morand to advance on Czarnowo with his whole division and capture the village. Probably, however, the crossing of the Wkra was behind schedule, for Davout ordered Petit to move against the Russian right with 400 men of the 12th Regiment instead of waiting for his whole brigade.

The Russians were now pouring down a heavy fire of bullets and grape-shot on all the ground over which the French were trying to advance. They had the advantage of a very complete knowledge of the whole terrain. The 1st Division advanced echeloned back from the right, with from right to left the 30th Regiment, the 1st Battalion 17th Regiment, and the 1st Battalion 13th Light Infantry. In the darkness the French were guided only by the flash from the enemy guns and muskets. The 1st Battalion 30th penetrated into the ravine which protected the village and turned it on the river flank, whilst the 2nd 30th attacked the village in front, and the 1st 17th advanced through a fir wood and attacked the left of the village. The 1st 13th and 2nd 17th formed up in support on a plateau in front of the wood, with behind them squadrons of *chasseurs à cheval* and dragoons. Meanwhile the light infantry columns were pushing forward on the left and clearing enemy posts out of the woods. Coming slowly behind this advance were the 51st and 61st Regiments in divisional reserve.

On the other flank of the battlefield Petit, with his 400 men, advanced towards the entrenchments on the height opposite Pomichowo, supported by Perrin's detachment on the right bank of the Wkra. Petit's advance was led by a light infantry company deployed as skirmishers. Behind these were two companies in line, and following these a grenadier company in reserve. The troops were close to the enemy position when the Russians spotted them and opened a very heavy fire. Immediately the six 12-prs., detailed to support Petit, opened a bombardment from the heights on the right bank in front of Pomichowo, and they were joined by two other pieces farther upstream. At the same time the trusses of hay were lit so that to the enemy it appeared in the moonlight as if a massive concentration of infantry were preparing to cross the river behind a smoke screen. Under cover of all this Petit's men rushed the enemy redoubts with such dash that the Russian guns had only time for one discharge, before they were rapidly withdrawn on the road to Czarnowo.

Petit put a party into the enemy's abandoned works and formed the rest of his command into a square, to await the counter-attack that he knew must come. The troops were hardly ready before the Russians attacked from every direction, supported by some guns on the Czarnowo road. With the assistance of heavy fire from the 12-prs on the right bank, this attack was beaten off, and the enemy retired. A few minutes later they attacked again, with similar lack of success. There was no further enemy activity for about half an hour.

Davout now reinforced Petit with a light infantry company from the 85th Regiment and the two grenadier companies of the 21st Regiment; but before they reached him the Russians made another, but also unsuccessful, attack. A little later Davout sent Petit five companies of the 2nd Battalion 12th Regiment, but decided to retain the remainder of this regiment as a bridge guard.

Towards 2 am the Russians attacked Petit again; advancing against his front with skirmishers thrown out on the flanks, whilst a body of cavalry came down the Czarnowo road to try and turn his flank. The grenadier companies of the 21st Regiment were on this road with a light infantry company deployed as skirmishers in front. These let the cavalry get as close as possible before firing a volley which routed them. The infantry attack was better sustained and it was half an hour before it was repulsed.

Petit reported to Davout that the enemy had withdrawn on his front, and the latter sent Colonel Exelmans, commanding the 1st *Chasseurs à Cheval*, with one squadron to support him. As soon as they arrived Petit sent forward some companies of the 21st Regiment towards Czarnowo. Exelmans, with his squadron and preceded by a company of light infantry as skirmishers, moved on the right flank and soon gained contact with the 1st Division, which had driven the enemy out of Czarnowo. The Russians were falling back in disorder, but, rallied in the shelter of the woods and staged another furious counter-attack. This was beaten off by heavy French fire from guns and muskets at a range of 30 yards. The Russian retreat was now final, and General Marulaz moved rapidly towards their rear and charged, but the darkness and marshes prevented any success.

The Russians retreated towards Nasielsk, some miles to the north, followed by the 1st Battalion 17th Regiment and the 51st Regiment, supported by General Latour-Maubourg with his dragoons and flanked by Marulaz's light cavalry.

In his report on this battle, Davout says that the manœuvres of the troops were performed as well as if it had been daylight and with just as much order and precision. To have driven a superior enemy out of such a strong position at night was an astounding feat and testifies to the high morale and standard of training of the troops of the III Corps.

The crossing of the Wkra provides a most interesting example of relatively minor tactics in a Napoleonic campaign, as compared with the great set battles which are more usually studied.

In his reconnaissance of the Russian position, Napoleon discovered that its very strength was a source of weakness against a well mounted night attack. The greatest difficulty in moving troops at night is to keep

F

direction and alignment. But in this operation there were two excellent aids to direction; the right bank of the Bug led to the left flank of the Russian position, whilst the left bank of the Wkra led to the Russian right flank. Napoleon decided to attack both these flanks, using the island as a jumping off place. The enemy's left flank was the more important because Czarnowo was the key to the position; with that village taken the Russian line of retreat would be threatened and their position would no longer be tenable. The attack on the Russian right flank could be supported by artillery in position on the right bank of the Wkra; the attack on the left flank would have to rely on its own resources. For these reasons the operation against Czarnowo would need the most troops and Napoleon allotted it the whole of the 1st Division with cavalry support.

The canal across the island provided a convenient start line along which the troops could form, and the left bank of the eastern arm of the Wkra was an unmistakable first objective. In the subsequent advance, the light infantry on the left had no direction line to follow, so that the sappers, probably with an officer keeping them on a compass bearing, cleared a wide swathe through the undergrowth by which the following troops could keep their direction and alignment and any reinforcements could follow up the left of this attack. For the strike northwards up the Wkra, Davout had doubtless appreciated that it was better to send Petit ahead with a small force rather than wait for his complete brigade. Results justified this decision, because the artillery fire across the Wkra was so effective that a comparatively small force of infantry sufficed.

The whole operation was brilliant in both conception and execution and is undoubtedly one of the classic night attacks in the history of war.

Friant, with his 2nd Division, left the bivouac west of Pomichowo at 4 am and, marching via the island, reached Czarnowo at daybreak. Napoleon, who wished the 1st Division to have some rest, directed Friant to pursue the enemy towards Nasielsk. When he was close to that place, Friant placed all the light infantry companies of the Division under Chef de Bataillon Thoulouse, 33rd Regiment, and sent them on a turning movement to the left to try and cut off the enemy's retreat. Though Thoulouse did not quite succeed, he surprised the Russians and captured three guns and a number of prisoners.

The 2nd Division now reached heavily wooded country. The 1st Brigade led the advance into the forest, leaving the 2nd Battalion 48th Regiment behind as a reserve, and soon ran into stubborn resistance which the intervention of its reserve failed to overcome. Owing to the bad roads the divisional artillery had not yet come up, but Friant, throwing all his infantry into the attack, drove the enemy back in such disorder that only the early winter night saved them from disaster. As it was the

French captured a great quantity of artillery which had stuck in the mud and had been abandoned.

After this action the 2nd Division bivouacked along the roads beyond Nasielsk. The 1st Division, following the 2nd, moved into Nasielsk; and the 3rd, following a different route, bivouacked short of that town.

Gudin, commander of the 3rd Division, had put his wrist out of joint on 3rd November and took no further part in the operations until 20th January. Davout had effectively commanded the 3rd Division directly himself. At 11 am he directed Petit to take temporary command of the division, but attached to him his Chief of Staff, General of Brigade Daultanne. The effect of this was that Petit, although commander of the 3rd Division, was bound to take the operational advice of Daultanne. This was a common and well understood practice when an officer in temporary command was considered to lack experience.

At daybreak on 25th December, the III Corps continued its march and towards the end of the day drove enemy rearguards from the town of Stregoczyn.

The Battles of Pultusk and Golymin

On the morning of 26th the 1st Division, preceded by the 1st and 2nd *Chasseurs à Cheval* under General Marulaz, marched to make contact with the VII Corps and Murat's cavalry, which were advancing towards Golymin. It was followed by the 2nd Division and by the Dragoon Division commanded by General Rapp. The 3rd Division marched at 6 am, but was directed towards Pultusk in pursuit of Russian troops who had retired in that direction, and with orders to place itself between that enemy column and the V Corps, which Davout knew was marching to Pultusk. There was a danger, otherwise, that the Russian column might move round the rear of the V Corps.

There had been a complete thaw for two days, which is rare at this season in Poland. The ground over which the division had to march was a mixture of marsh and clay and the roads were frightful. Mounted troops, artillery, and infantry could only drag themselves along with difficulty and it took two hours to march about two miles.

The 3rd Division had hardly left Stregoczyn when it was informed by its skirmishers that there was a considerable body of enemy cavalry in front, covering a column of artillery and vehicles which were apparently stuck in the mud. The enemy cavalry were Cossacks, and they retired in front of the French advance, abandoning a large quantity of ordnance, ammunition wagons, ambulances, and many other vehicles.

After acquiring this booty, and not wishing to become engaged with the very superior forces which it appeared from prisoners were in front of him, Daultanne prepared to take up a position for the night. At this juncture, however, the noise of an artillery bombardment was heard from the direction of Pultusk. Daultanne presumed that the V Corps was engaged with the enemy and therefore continued his advance with the object of making contact with the V Corps and supporting its attacks.

The 3rd Division was advancing with its battalions in close column, probably of double companies, and in four parallel regimental columns with its left on the Prshavodovo stream and its front covered by a cloud of skirmishers. The enemy were found in position on the plateau west of Pultusk with their left in front of the town and their right refused at a right angle on the heights of Moshina. The extreme right was covered by a large body of Cossacks in the formation of a badly proportioned 'Z'.

To make the enemy disclose the strength of their defence of the village of Moshina, in front of which skirmished a number of Cossacks, Daultanne had double teams attached to an 8-pr. gun, which was dragged forward sufficiently close to fire some shots into the village. But all that came out were some hundreds of Cossacks who retired to rally on the right of the Russian main position.

The 3rd Division continued its advance while Daultanne rode out to the right to see where Lannes's troops were. He found the V Corps in a similar formation, with a cloud of skirmishers in front engaged with the enemy. Daultanne reported his arrival to Lannes and told him of the attack he was mounting. There was no time, however, to co-ordinate arrangements.

As he approached the angle on the right of the enemy's line, Daultanne deployed his infantry into a line of half battalions at fifty yards interval. The attack went in with considerable dash and the leading Russian infantry were driven back from the plateau towards the Bialovizna ravine. Further progress was halted by the Russian reserves, posted in the copses lining the Novo Miesto road. Here the French pushed forward slowly against a fierce resistance. As dusk was falling the 34th Regiment of the V Corps, on the right of the 3rd Division, gave way and fell back. Thus uncovered, the right of the 3rd Division was charged by Russian cavalry. Hastily forming square, the steady 85th Regiment repulsed this and subsequent attacks. The last and heaviest of these occured at 8 pm, and amidst a violent wind and heavy snow.

A short time before this an ADC arrived from Headquarters V Corps with a request to Daultanne not to retire because Lannes was about to renew his attack. An hour later, however, there was still no sign of any activity on the V Corps front, and Daultanne sent an officer to find out what was happening. He returned to report that the V Corps had fallen back to the positions it had occupied before the action started. Daultanne, therefore, withdrew his front line, taking up a defensive position about a hundred yards back. Here he rested as many of his tired troops as he

The following three maps are contemporary Plans of the Battle of Pultusk, compiled by Sir Robert Wilson from Russian sources, and reproduced in his book *The Russian Army and the Campaigns in Poland*, published in 1810

Plan 1 shows the disposition of the Russian forces, probably with fair accuracy, and the movements of the French troops as they appeared to the Russians. The top of the plan points to the West, and North is therefore to the right.

The main Russian position is held by two lines of infantry and guns at 'A', with a strong refused right flank at 'B' and 'C'. The right and centre of this position is covered by a cloud of Cossacks at 'G', supported by regular cavalry at 'F' and 'I'. The left was covered by cavalry at 'K', but these are shown as withdrawing to 'D', in face of the French advance, behind a regiment of sharpshooters deployed at 'N'.

The French troops are shown advancing in columns, preceded by long lines of skirmishers.

The second plan shows the French attack developing, and Daultanne's strong pressure against the Russian right flank. It also shows the lines of fire of the Russian guns.

Plan 3 gives the position at the close of the action. The main Russian position still holds, though the French have occupied most of the plateau. On the Russian right wing the French, after initial success, have been driven back by a Russian counter-attack, supported by enfilade fire from a battery. The French troops are depicted as retiring in disorder. This is a perhaps pardonable exaggeration of the rout of the 34th Regiment of the V Corps, on Daultanne's right, and Daultanne's subsequent withdrawal of the 3rd Division to conform.

165

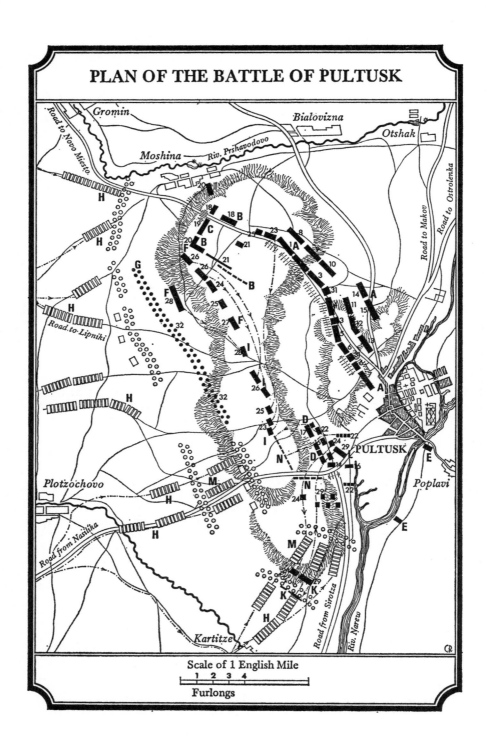

PLAN OF THE BATTLE OF PULTUSK

Scale of 1 English Mile

1 2 3 4

Furlongs

BATTLE OF PULTUSK

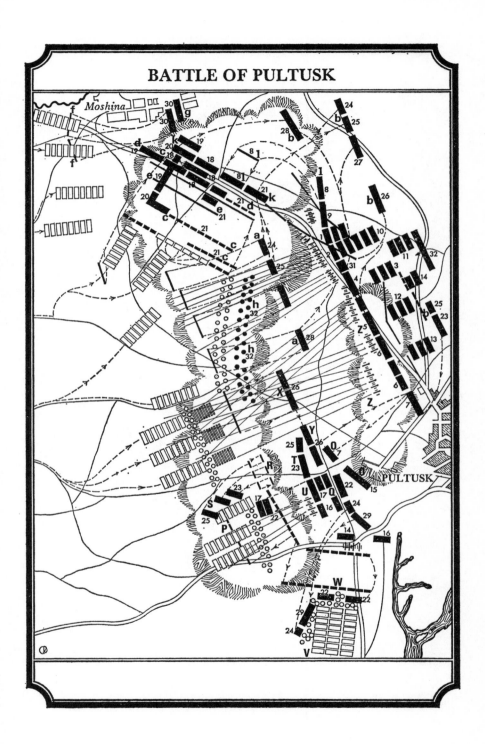

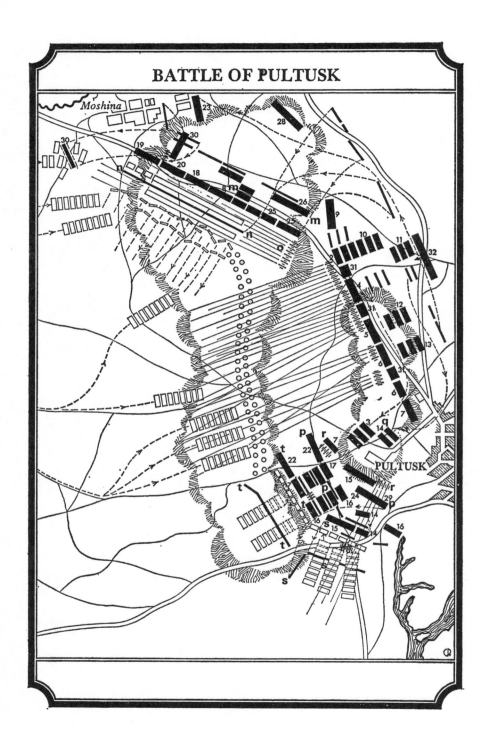

BATTLE OF PULTUSK

could in the shelter of the wood. The soldiers had been marching and fighting all day, often in mud which came half way up the leg. Adjutant-Commandant Allin was despatched to inform Lannes of the position taken up to cover the left flank of the V Corps.

The night of 26/27th December was very quiet. Information reached Daultanne that the Russians had vacated their positions during the night and had withdrawn across the Narew. It was apparent that Lannes would have no difficulty in entering Pultusk. At 3 am Daultanne received orders to rejoin the III Corps at Garnowo if his presence was no longer necessary to the V Corps. At 8 am, therefore, Daultanne and the 3rd Division marched away from Pultusk.

The task given to Daultanne was interesting and difficult. He had to prevent a Russian force from moving round Lannes's left flank to his rear, but how he acted seems to have been left to his own initiative. It is clear that Davout considered it an operation beyond the capacity of the gallant Petit. Daultanne took part in Lannes's battle, but he was not put under the latter's orders and retained his independence of action. Daultanne played a very important role with considerable skill. Without the assistance of the 3rd Division, the V Corps would probably have been defeated, and quite conceivably destroyed, by the very superior numbers of the enemy.

In the meantime, Marulaz, who with the light cavalry was acting as advanced guard to the 1st Division, had seized 26 guns, 80 ammunition wagons, and 200 other vehicles that the Russians had abandoned, and had then made contact with the advanced guard of Murat's cavalry on the road to Golymin. In front of them Russian cavalry were retreating towards Golymin and enemy infantry were preparing to defend the woods in front of the village.

The cavalry were closely followed by the 1st Brigade of Morand's 1st Division, consisting of the 2nd Battalion 13th Regiment, the 17th Regiment, and the 30th Regiment. Behind the 1st Brigade came the 2nd Brigade under General d'Honnieres. At about 3.30 pm the 1st Brigade formed into battalion columns, each battalion in column of companies. Morand directed the brigade to attack the Golymin Wood. The skirmishers took post ahead of the columns which were now formed of double companies to follow the skirmishers through the wood. The enemy made a strong resistance, and finally discarded their knapsacks (a Russian habit) to charge with the bayonet. But the fire of the French columns and the activities of the skirmishers forced them to abandon the wood, leaving their 4,000 knapsacks behind. The left of the enemy position was then turned by the 2nd Brigade, covered on the right by Rapp's Dragoons. Having driven the enemy out of their positions, Davout stopped the attack at nightfall and awaited the arrival of the remainder of his Corps. The 1st Division, fighting without artillery (which had been unable to keep up on account of the bad roads) had defeated an enemy in very much greater strength supported by from twelve to fifteen pieces of ordnance.

About an hour after dark Augereau's VII Corps was engaged with the enemy about three miles away to the left of the III Corps, but Davout was too uncertain about Augereau's point of attack to co-operate. The 2nd Division arrived during the evening and would have been ready to join in the battle the following morning; but during the night the Russians retired.

This was the virtual end of active operations for the time being. On 28th Napoleon halted the further advance of his troops and on 29th the III Corps went into billets in the area Pultusk–Nasielsk–Golymin.

Napoleon now allotted sectors to the various corps. Davout was ordered to occupy the peninsula between the Bug and the Narew as far east as Ostrow and to establish his headquarters in Pultusk, and this move was completed on 3rd January. Marulaz's light cavalry was posted along the Narew as far as the outskirts of Ostrolenka, which was still occupied by the Russians. On 17th January Davout reinforced Marulaz with the 13th Light Infantry Regiment. On 18th January General of Brigade Ricard joined the 1st Division to replace Brouard who had been wounded at Czarnowo. General Becker's dragoon division was put under Davout's orders and billeted in the peninsula.

On 15th January Napoleon ordered the 3rd Division to march to Warsaw to have some days rest. It arrived there on 21st and was rejoined by General Gudin, who took over command again from Petit. On 26th the Division was reviewed by Napoleon.

The III Corps outposts were harried constantly by Cossacks, but with little success except when a body of about a thousand surprised the 2nd Squadron of the 1st *Chasseurs à Cheval* and inflicted heavy casualties, principally because the *chasseurs* had failed to comply with the Corps Commander's instructions. Davout had laid down that all cavalry posts were to include detachments of infantry and that alarm posts were to be surrounded by properly constructed defence works.

Napoleon's plans for keeping his army in winter quarters were brought to naught when on 27th January he was informed of a Russian movement towards Thorn on the Vistula with the aim of attacking his left. From Imperial Headquarters in Warsaw he issued instructions to all corps to vacate their winter quarters and to concentrate, ready to take the offensive. As regards the III Corps, Davout was to move to Pultusk all the troops he had on the right bank of the Narew and as many as he could of those on the left bank without giving warning to the Russians. As a deception, the more distant posts on the Narew were to remain. Napoleon told

Davout that he would be at Pultusk, personally, on 28th, that Murat would be at Willemberg on the same day, and that Soult had been ordered to concentrate his corps at Willemberg.

Davout ordered Morand to assemble the 1st Division between Pultusk and Makow and to march to Myszyniec, passing through Ostrolenka. The 1st Division arrived at Myszyniec on 31st January at 4 pm, and here it was rejoined by the 13th Light Infantry from its detached duty with the light cavalry. It was put under Ricard's orders. The 2nd Division arrived at Ostrolenka on 30th January and marched for Myszienic the following day. The 3rd Division left Warsaw on 29th January, after a march of over 30 miles. The next day it marched another 20 miles to Przasznic.

On 2nd February the 1st and 2nd Divisions were near Ortelsburg. Here Friant was ordered to leave the 111th Regiment which, with the 2nd *Chasseurs à Cheval* and two 8-pr. guns, formed a flank guard to cover the move from interference by a Russian force on the upper Narew, until the arrival of the V Corps in that area.

On 3rd February the 1st Division marched at daybreak on the Passenheim road. The 2nd Division was ordered directly by the Emperor to go to Wartemburg. As the division was reduced to three regiments, Davout attached to it the 51st Regiment (less a half battalion) from the 1st Division to form a reserve. The 3rd Division was ordered by the Emperor to march to Mensgut.

On 4th February parties of *chasseurs à cheval* were sent out in various directions on reconnaissance to try and find news of the enemy. They were followed by the rest of Marulaz's *Chasseurs* Brigade, now reduced to two regiments, the 1st and 12th. On the same day the 1st Division marched into Wartemburg.

On 5th February Marulaz, with eighty *chasseurs*, rode into Heilsberg, having heard that the enemy had abandoned the town. He seized the keys of a considerable magazine that the enemy had established; but the Russians, informed of what a small force he had with him, re-entered the town, and Marulaz had only just time to retreat by a side road and cross the Alle by the half-burnt girder which remained of the bridge. Here he assembled his brigade, but half an hour later the Russians opened a heavy artillery fire and he had to retire.

The III Corps arrived at Gutstadt on 5th February, driving back Russian rearguards. Here the 2nd Division made contact with Saint-Hilaire's Division of the IV Corps. The following day Davout was ordered to direct the movements of the IV Corps as well as his own III Corps. The 1st Division, preceded by the *chasseurs* as advanced guard, led the advance towards Heilsberg. The information was that the enemy occupied the left bank of the Alle and had burnt all the bridges. Davout, accompanied by Morand, rode forward on a personal reconnaissance, and was fired at by Russian light batteries. Morand threw his leading brigade into the attack. The half battalion of the 51st Regiment crossed the river by a partly burnt bridge and advanced towards the town gate. It was followed by the 13th, which formed a bridgehead, whilst the 17th occupied a suburb on the near side of the river. In the face of this vigorous attack the Russians retreated, just as the 2nd Division came into sight on the left bank of the Alle. Marulaz, followed by the two divisions, set off in pursuit. The 3rd Division did not arrive till the action was over.

On 7th February the III Corps started at 4 am towards Landsberg, with Marulaz covering the right flank. At Hof, Davout, having ridden forward, reported to the Emperor. The day before at this place the enemy rear guard had been destroyed by the Cuirassier Division. Napoleon told him that the Russians were in retreat by the Heilsburg-Eylau road and directed him to advance on Eylau by this road.

Marulaz was sent ahead to cover the III Corps movement, and three miles from Eylau he ran into the Russian outposts. From then until nightfall he protected the infantry marching up behind him by stopping repeated charges by Russian Hussars in greatly superior strength.

At 2 pm, whilst Davout was marching towards Eylau, he received an order from Berthier telling him to form in columns on the road from Bartenstein to Eylau, and to halt with the heads of his columns four miles from Eylau. The 2nd Division, in the lead accordingly turned right for Zohlen and took up a position on the road between Beisleiden and Persuschen. The 1st Division followed and formed at Zohlen. The 3rd Division was sufficiently far in rear to wheel right at a junction where a road led to Bartenstein, entering that town at 10 pm, and driving parties of Russian cavalry out of it. The division then bivouacked beyond Bartenstein on the Eylau road. Marulaz, who had been on the outskirts of Eylau, left it when the IV Corps had moved into position and rejoined the III Corps. Davout established his headquarters at Beisleiden.

The Battle of Eylau

The main Russian army had taken up a position near Eylau, and as Murat's cavalry, followed by Soult's Corps reached the area early on the afternoon of 7th, an encounter battle had developed which grew into a desperate struggle for the village of Eylau, lasting until nightfall.

During the night 7/8th Davout received an order to move before daybreak to join the IV Corps and attack the enemy's left flank. He was informed that the Russian army was holding a position with its left at the village of Serpallen and its right near Althof, and that it was formed in several lines.

The III Corps contained the same regiments with which it had fought the Battle of Auerstaedt, but they were much reduced in strength because

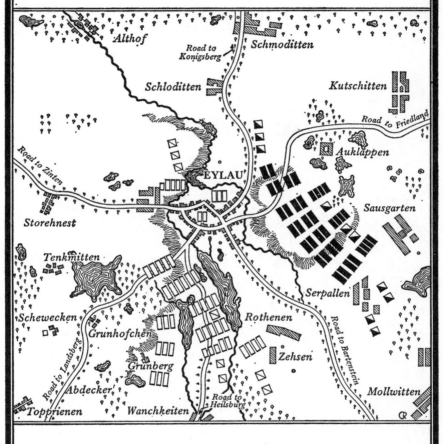

SKETCH OF THE POSITION OF EYLAU
on the Morning of the 8th February, 1807

Althof

Road to
Konigsberg

Schmoditten

Schloditten

Kutschitten

Road to Friedland

Road to Zinten

EYLAU

Auklappen

Sausgarten

Storehnest

Tenkmitten

Serpallen

Schewecken

Rothenen

Grunhofchen

Road to Landsberg

Zehsen

Road to Bartenstein

Grunberg

Abdecker

Road to
Heilsburg

Mollwitten

Topprienen

Wanchkeiten

Two contemporary Plans of the Battle of Eylau, compiled by Sir
Robert Wilson from Russian sources, and reproduced in his afore-
mentioned book
*The first plan shows the position at Eylau on the morning of 8th February
1807 before the approach of Davout's III Corps had been spotted by the
Russians.*

Position of the Combined Army on the Night of the 8th. of February after the **BATTLE** and of the points to which the Enemy were repelled.

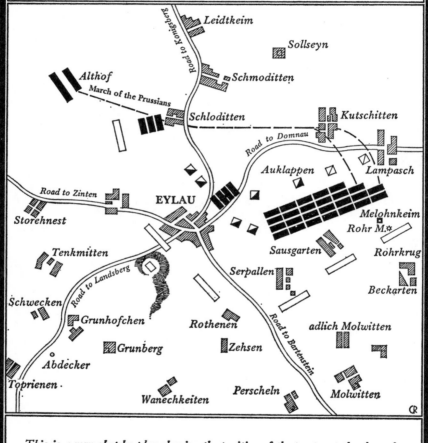

This is a very sketchy plan showing the position of the troops at the close of the battle and the route of advance of the Prussian Corps. This plan is obviously largely guess-work, for the Russians were in such a state of confusion that it is most unlikely that anyone knew the exact position of their own troops, let alone that of the French.

of the losses in that battle and in the marches and actions in which it had been subsequently engaged. The fighting strengths were now:

1st Division	6,000
2nd Division (less the 111th Regiment left at Myszyniec)	4,000
3rd Division (less the 2nd Battalion 85th Regiment at Ortelsburg)	4,400
1st and 12th *Chasseurs* (2nd *Chasseurs* were at Myszniec)	600
Total	15,000

The three divisions were ordered to march two hours before dawn. Marulax, with the 2nd Division following, headed straight for Serpallen. The 1st Division marched next, joining the Eylau road at Perguschen. Last came the 3rd Division, which started at 3 am.

It was not yet daylight when the light cavalry and leading infantry encountered Cossacks in front of Serpallen. These retired after exchanging a few shots. As dawn broke the 2nd Division was already deployed and in action on the high ground in front of Serpallen and had pushed forward some companies of the 48th Regiment to occupy the village. The light cavalry was on the right whilst the 1st Division was forming in rear of the 2nd.

Battle was now engaged along the whole French line, which included the III Corps, the IV Corps, the VII Corps, Murat's cavalry, and the Imperial Guard. Davout sent out an officer and escort to try and locate Saint-Hilaire's division of IV Corps in order to contact it with his left wing.

A large body of enemy cavalry appeared from the direction of Sausgarten. Friant ordered General of Brigade Lochet to lead the 33rd Regiment in the direction of Sausgarten. Lochet, assisted by Marulaz operating on his right flank, repulsed an attack by the enemy cavalry, but the latter were soon supported by a force of some 8,000 to 10,000 Russian infantry advancing from the right of Sausgarten, whilst the same body of cavalry, which had re-formed, threatened to turn Davout's right. Davout ordered the whole of the 2nd Division to move to the right against the Russian attack, whilst the 1st Division took its place in front of Serpallen. The three regiments available to Friant, the 33rd, 48th, and 108th, advanced against the considerably stronger body of enemy infantry and drove the Russians back after a long and sanguinary struggle. But the Russian retirement was covered by a numerous artillery which dismounted two of the French 4-prs. and caused heavy casualties in the regiments of the 2nd Division. Friant then sent skirmishers against the Russian right flank, and they soon threw the retreating enemy infantry into complete disorder.

Morand, now in the Serpallen position, was ordered by Davout to attack. At the same time Davout retained Morand's 2nd Brigade, consisting of the 51st and 61st Regiments under d'Honnieres, in Corps reserve until the arrival of the 3rd Division. The attack, therefore was carried out by Ricard's 1st Brigade of the 13th, 17th, and 30th Regiments. The 30th Regiment marched to the left of Serpallen, whilst the 13th Light Infantry and the 2nd Battalion 17th Regiment passed through the middle and to the right of the same village; the whole of the brigade reforming beyond it. Morand retained the 1st Battalion 17th Regiment in divisional reserve on the right. The brigade now moved forward supported by a company of light artillery, but under heavy fire from a strong force of artillery which the Russians had established on the high ground about 400 yards in front.

Gudin soon appeared at the head of the 3rd Division, so Davout sent the 51st Regiment to support the hard-pressed Friant and let Morand have back d'Honnieres with the 61st. Morand, in the meantime, had made contact with Saint-Hilaire's Division on his left.

Friant was suffering much from artillery fire from the direction of Sausgarten. He ordered Lochet to attack the village with a battalion of the 33rd Regiment. This attack was at first successful, but Lochet could not maintain his position for more than half an hour, because he was obliged to fall back before the advance of some 4,000 enemy infantry. As he retired Russian cavalry charged the squares of both the 33rd and 48th Regiments, but were unable to break them. The 51st Regiment arrived in time to help stem this attack.

The enemy cavalry were thus repulsed and retired in disorder, but the Russian infantry which had driven Lochet out of Sausgarten, were reinforced by another 2,000 men, and resumed their advance. The attack fell on the 33rd and 48th Regiments, but they were supported by a terrific fire from the 2nd Division's artillery, and the Russian infantry withered away in face of this storm of grape shot. Friant was able to re-occupy Sausgarten but Lochet had been killed.

Whilst the 2nd Division was engaged in this heavy fighting, the 1st Division was facing repeated attacks about Serpallen. The Russians had massed considerable strength in this sector and their infantry advanced against the adjacent divisions of Morand and Saint-Hilaire. The 13th Light Infantry suffered heavy casualties, and Morand replaced it in the line by the 1st Battalion 17th Regiment and withdrew it into reserve.

Morand now prepared to mount a counter-attack and ordered d'Honnieres to move the 61st Regiment, formed in two lines, up on to the right flank of the Division. On the left of the 30th and 17th Regiments was a battalion of the 10th Light Infantry Regiment of Saint-Hilaire's Division. The Russians, no more than 200 yards away, moved forward to meet the French advance, heads lowered, bayonets forward, and supported by thirty guns. They approached to within about twenty yards but then, shaken by the fire from the French battalions, they turned and fled in the greatest disorder. Their artillery, left without infantry support, carried on firing and the gunners were killed beside their pieces.

Morand had gained a notable success and had captured all the thirty guns which had been in action against him. But he had hardly reformed his lines to hold his new position, when the Russians mounted a counter-attack. A body of cavalry and infantry which had been held in reserve and which had been concealed by the folds in the ground and by eddies of snow, surprised the 10th Light Infantry Regiment, and drove it back in disorder for two or three hundred yards. Its retirement carried it into the right of the 1st Division and caused some confusion. The situation was restored by a charge of dragoons of Klein's division, and Morand was able to consolidate and to retain his hold on Serpallen.

The 1st Division had matters in hand, but Davout was anxious about his right, which the enemy was again endeavouring to turn. He accordingly despatched Petit with the 12th Regiment and the greater part of the 3rd Division's artillery to reinforce Friant's right. However Friant had already taken the offensive. He had held Sausgarten against renewed attacks and had forced the Russians to retire in such disorder that he had followed them up as far as Anklappen. This threat to their rear forced the Russians holding the hillocks north of Serpallen to fall back and enabled Morand to occupy them. The 1st Division now formed a pivot on which Davout manœuvred his centre and right.

To fill the gap between Friant and Morand, Davout sent Gudin with the 1st Battalion 85th Regiment and the 25th to occupy a position on a height between Sausgarten and Anklappen, facing the latter village. However, this was only a preliminary move to a re-grouping of his Corps. This entailed drawing up his formations in preparation for a decisive attack and was carried out under covering fire from six 12-pr. guns. He sent the 30th Regiment to his extreme right to hold a defensive position on the flank. This regiment had suffered heavy casualties but was still displaying a remarkably high morale.

The 48th Regiment was now ordered to attack Anklappen, and captured the village with considerable gallantry; but an enemy counter-attack forced it to retreat. Part of the 51st Regiment and four companies of the 108th Regiment now attacked and drove the enemy from the woods to the right of Anklappen, half way between Sausgarten and Kutschitten. They were supported by Milhaud's 1st Dragoon Division, which had been put under Davout's orders, and Marulaz with the 1st and 12th *Chasseurs à Cheval* stopped Cossack attempts to get behind the attacking French. The pursuit reached the outskirts of Kutschitten; and to exploit this success Gauthier was ordered to attack Anklappen with the 2nd

Battalion 25th Regiment, supported by the 1st Battalion, whilst Colonel Duplin with the 1st Battalion 85th attacked the little wood to the left of it, held by several Russian battalions. These attacks were successful, both wood and village being captured. They were followed by the capture of Kutschitten by elements of the 51st and 108th Regiments.

It was at this junction that the Prussian Corps under General Lestocq arrived in the nick of time to save the Russian Army from complete destruction from Davout's enveloping attack. The Prussians attacked Kutschitten and drove out the companies of the 51st and 108th, which suffered heavy casualties during their withdrawal to the wood from which they had debouched. The ground being unsuitable for cavalry, Milhaud's dragoons could not help.

The Russians rallied behind the Prussians, and after the loss of Kutschitten a heavy attack developed against the French right. The brunt of this was borne by the 12th Regiment, which had to give way. To plug this dangerous gap which was opening in the right of his line, Davout sent Gudin with the 1st Battalion 25th Regiment to take command of the various units of the 2nd Division which were falling back in disorder through the wood north of Sausgarten. The moment was critical, and Davout rode round the ranks of the rallied but gravely weakened regiments exhorting them to die with honour. 'Brave men', he said, 'will find here a glorious death; only the cowards will visit the deserts of Siberia.' One has a suspicion that the gallant Davout was even more rattled than his troops.

There remained only half an hour of daylight. Davout placed all his artillery on the hillocks round Anklappen, which was still held by Gauthier with the 2nd Battalion 25th Regiment. From there the French guns inflicted enormous losses on Prussians and Russians, as they threw in three further attacks to try and break the French line. After 7 pm the French troops were ordered to light their camp fires; and if the light they gave helped the enemy attacks, it gave confidence to the soldiers of the III Corps and helped them to make good defensive positions. About 10 pm the fighting suddenly stopped; both Prussians and Russians were retreating from the battlefield.

The battle had been fought under most difficult conditions. A violent wind had raged all day, driving the flakes and eddies of the snow into the eyes of the French so that commanders could hardly see the movements of the troops and the soldiers had difficulty in hearing the commands of their officers. Units were ordered to close up, particularly during those periods when the snow fell in such thick flakes that objects ten paces away could hardly be seen. The Russians had the wind at their backs, and so were fighting under considerably easier conditions, but certainly on the French side the conditions were almost similar to a night action.

The losses in the III Corps were appalling, amounting to over 5,000 in killed, wounded, and prisoners of all ranks; or one third of the strength with which Davout had entered the battle.

During the night the Corps Artillery Park arrived on the battlefield and replenished all the artillery and infantry ammunition that had been consumed during the day, and so put the III Corps in a position to renew the battle.

Unlike the previous engagements described, at Eylau the III Corps was only a part, and a minor part, of an army fighting under the direct command of the Emperor. By its magnificent fighting ability it had, however, contributed considerably more than its share to an indecisive victory.

The flexibility of the French organisation is again a notable feature. Regiments were switched between divisions as required, or taken by the Corps Commander for his reserve; the invaluable generals of brigade were used for exploits involving the command of a battalion and upwards; and the mobile and devastating use of the artillery reminds one of Rommel's anti-tank guns in the Western Desert.

One takes leave of the III Corps with reluctance. The history of war affords all too few examples of such an attractive team of commanders as Davout, Morand, Friant, Gudin, Petit, Gauthier, and the others.

As in the previous chapter, most of the information in this one comes from Marshal Davout's *Operations du 3e Corps 1806–1807*

The following other works have been consulted:

Count Yorck von Wartenberg, *Napoleon as a General*; transl. Major W. H. James, 1902
F. Loraine Petre, *Napoleon's Campaign in Poland*, 1901
Brigadier General V. J. Esposito and Colonel J. R. Elting, *A Military History and Atlas of the Napoleonic Wars*, 1964
Sir Robert Wilson, *The Russian Army and the Campaigns in Poland 1806–1807*, 1810

CHAPTER ELEVEN

EPILOGUE

Just west of the little town of Montmirail, on the north side of the main road between Paris and Chalons-sur-Marne, stands a tall column, topped by the same guilded eagle that led the Imperial regiments to battle. The pedestal at the foot of the column has inscriptions on each of its four sides. That facing the road reads: '*1866. 13 Aout. Ce monument a été élèvé par les ordres de l'Empereur Napoleon III. C'est de cette place que l'Empereur Napoleon I commanda son Armée le 11 Fevrier 1814*' (i.e. '1866. 13th August. This monument has been erected by the orders of the Emperor Napoleon III. It was on this site that the Emperor Napoleon I commanded his Army on 11th February 1814.') The other three sides are inscribed, respectively: '*1814, 11 Fevrier, Montmirail, Marchais; 1814, 12 Fevrier, Nesle, Chateauthierry; 1814, 10 Fevrier, Champaubert, 14 Fevrier, Vauchamps.*' The inscriptions infer, of course to the series of brilliant victories over the Russian and Prussian troops commanded by General Blücher during these five days in the country which stretches between the Rivers Marne and Petit Morin.

The last two chapters have dealt with the events during the campaigns of 1806 and 1807 which concerned the commander of an army corps, with main emphasis on the tactics of infantry and artillery. This one, in contrast, relates incidents in the campaign of 1814 as they were seen by the commander of a squadron of cavalry in the service of the Emperor he worshipped. The officer is the 26-year-old Captain Parquin of the 2nd *Chasseurs à Cheval* of the Guard, Member of the Legion of Honour. The events are related from memory, and like the memories of every soldier who ever fought they are not historically accurate in every detail.

Denis Charles Parquin, on the recommendation of Marshal Marmont was posted to the 1st *Chasseurs à Cheval* of the Guard in March 1813, dropping, as was customary, a rank in the process. How he obtained the Cross of the Legion of Honour is related in his own words as follows:

'On 6th April 1813 I was in the full dress of my corps at the head of my troop with two squadrons of the Regiment at one of the reviews which the Emperor held frequently in the court of the Tuileries, after his return from the campaign in Russia. I wished to speak to His Majesty, but I was afraid I might miss the opportunity because the Emperor did not bother about his Guides and often passed at the gallop without stopping near them; so I dismounted at a moment when our squadrons were at ease and went and placed myself on the left of a regiment of infantry of the Young Guard which the Emperor was reviewing.

'"Who are you?" asked the Emperor when he arrived at the place where I was standing. "An officer of your Old Guard, Sire; I have dropped a rank to serve Your Majesty." "What do you want?" "A decoration." "What have you done to deserve it?" "I am a Parisian who enrolled as a volunteer at the age of sixteen. I have been through eight campaigns. I won my commission on the battlefield and received ten wounds, though I would not change them for the number I inflicted on the enemy. I have captured a colour in Portugal, and on this occasion the commander-in-chief recommended me for a decoration; but it is far from Portugal to Moscow and the reply has not yet come." "Very well! I will bring it myself! Berthier, write out the award of the cross for this officer and see that his diploma is sent to him tomorrow. I do not wish that I should be in debt to this gallant young man any longer." And so I was decorated.'[1]

On 21st December 1813, whilst in camp in Champagne, Parquin was promoted Captain and posted to the 2nd *Chasseurs à Cheval* of the Guard. On the same day he was ordered to go to Paris and take command of the 11th Company of his new unit. At the beginning of December Napoleon had reorganised the Cavalry of the Guard into a heavy division consisting of the 1st (or Old Guard) *Chasseurs à Cheval*, the Horse Grenadiers, and the Dragoons; and a light division of the 2nd (or Young Guard) *Chasseurs à Cheval*, and the 1st and 2nd Lancers.[2] Parquin's 11th Company was a new one which was just being formed round a nucleus, or cadre, of NCOs of the Old Guard. (It is likely that at this stage there were only six companies, making three squadrons, in each regiment and that they were numbered right through the 1st and 2nd *Chasseurs*; so that the latter would consist when complete of the 7th to 12th Companies.)

Before he left for Paris, the Regimental Paymaster had given Parquin twenty bags, each containing a thousand francs. These were being sent by the Administrative Council of the *Chasseurs à Cheval* of the Guard (acting for the Colonel of the Regiment) to the tailor Rabusson, who had the regimental tailoring contract. Parquin was very worried over his responsibility for all this money. Arriving at Saint Dizier with his treasure, he met General Cambronne commanding the 2nd *Chasseurs à Pied* of the Guard with whom he was acquainted. In conversation it transpired that Cambronne was anxious as to how he was to change Imperial Treasury bonds into cash to pay his regiment, because the bonds were not presentable for another ten days. Parquin saw a way out of his own difficulty and offered the twenty thousand francs which he had in exchange for an equivalent sum in Treasury bonds. Cambronne was so relieved and delighted that he stood Parquin an excellent dinner that evening in Saint Dizier.

Parquin reached Paris on 23rd December, having travelled post from Saint Dizier in company with a cavalry colonel and a captain in the Horse Grenadiers of the Guard. All three were making the journey on account of their promotion. At the end of the campaign of 1814 Parquin was the only one left alive. The Colonel was killed at the Battle of Montmirail and the Captain at the Battle of Craonne.

On arriving in Paris Parquin assumed command of the 11th Company, which was still being formed. Though he does not say so, the men were probably a mixture of selected volunteers, old soldiers recalled to the colours, and men drafted from various units of the cavalry of the line. The 2nd *Chassuers à Cheval* of the Guard (with a strength, probably, of only four companies) were then outside Antwerp, in the Army of the North. But when on 6th February Parquin received orders for his company to march from Paris, it was to join the Old Guard in Champagne. He was pleased, but never found out why he was to have the privilege of serving beside the Old Guard rather than with his own unit. The 11th Company formed part of a detachment of six hundred cavalrymen of the Guard under the command of *Chef d'Escadron* Kirmann, who had previously been Parquin's Captain in the 20th *Chasseurs à Cheval.* The detachment included a company of Mamelukes under the command of a remarkable character. Captain Ibrahim Bey was an old soldier who had been one of the original body of Mamelukes of the French Army formed in the time of the Consulate, and who had been living in retirement in Marseilles during the past fourteen years. The squadron, as formed in 1801, consisted of four companies, one of which was commanded by Captain Ibrahim Bey. Few Frenchmen had seen the exotic uniform of these soldiers, and when Ibrahim Bey arrived in Paris his dress attracted a crowd. By chance he wandered into the corn market, where some people hooted and whistled at him and others threw mud, jeering that it was not carnival time to justify his dressing up as a Turk. Ibrahim Bey, who did not understand the French, and much less their jesting, took out his pistols and shot two of his tormentors dead. He then prepared to continue the fight with his sword, but a military patrol arrived, and he surrendered to them without offering any resistance. News of this incident reached

Napoleon, the First Consul, and he had Ibrahim Bey brought before him for interrogation. The Mameluke explained that he had only acted as was customary in his own country to punish people who interfered with members of this martial organisation. Napoleon told him that he was not to undertake police duties in France, and that he was to leave Paris immediately and live in Marseilles. He added that he was not to carry arms, and that he would be given a rate of pay from which would be deducted a sum to pay pensions to the widows of the men he had killed. And so Ibrahim Bey had lived in Marseilles until, in response to the Emperor's Decree of 2nd January 1814, after the invasion of France, he had rejoined the colours and had been given the command of a Mameluke Company of the Guard. In spite of his great seniority, he ranked junior to Parquin because, under a regulation peculiar to the Guard, a French officer was always senior to any foreign officer of the same rank.

The raising and march of these new troops provides an interesting illustration of Napoleon's efforts to strengthen his weakened army in face of the Allied invasion.

The detachment reached the Army on 10th February, the day before the Battle of Montmirail, and Parquin's company went straight into action the following day. General Baron Edouard de Colbert de Chabanais, commander of the 1st Cavalry Division of the Guard,[3] ordered him to charge the left of a Russian square, which was being charged on the right by General Baron Letort, commanding the Dragoons of the Guard,[4] with a squadron of dragoons. The charges were successful in breaking the Russian square and *chasseurs* and dragoons met in the middle. The Russians had been so confident that their square would hold that they had put their knapsacks on the ground. The victorious French gave them time to pick them up and deposit their muskets in their place.

Parquin is silent about his own activities during the ensuing three weeks, and it is likely that his company spent most of its time marching rather than fighting. On 2nd March the major part of the Prussian army under the command of Blücher and a Russian corps which marched with them crossed the Marne, says Parquin, at Chateau-Thierry, and blew up an arch of the bridge there to delay the French pursuit. Napoleon established his advanced headquarters in the house of the Master of Posts in the street where Parquin's company and other Guard cavalry were accommodated. On 3rd March the engineers to repair the bridge arrived and Napoleon moved at 10 am into a bivouac on the bank of the Marne to watch the reconstruction of the bridge. General Bertrand, who had succeeded Duroc as Grand Marshal of the Palace, was responsible for the work, and Napoleon sent for him and asked him how long it would take. Bertrand said four hours. 'I will give you six,' said the Emperor, and as the clock in Chateau-Thierry struck 4 pm the bridge was finished.

General Colbert had ordered Parquin to be ready that morning with a hundred troopers of the Old Guard to go on a mission, the details of which would would be given to him during the day by the Emperor himself. He found himself in command of a composite squadron consisting of four troops, each from a different regiment of the Guard, which were respectively, *Chasseurs à Cheval*, Lancers, Dragoons, and Mamelukes. The idea was to make the force he commanded appear to be very much larger than it actually was.

At 4 pm Parquin rode with his squadron to the bridge and reported to the Emperor, who said to him: 'Captain, follow up the enemy and take some prisoners: I need them.' Knowing that there were three roads from Chateau-Thierry, leading to Soissons, La Ferté, and Rheims, he asked, 'By which road, Sire?' 'By the Soissons road.' Parquin immediately led his squadron off in sections of four at a walk over the newly repaired bridge. When he reached the far bank he allowed his men to accept, without stopping, bread, brandy, ham, and sausages, that the inhabitants of Chateau-Thierry offered them—overjoyed at being rid of the Russians and Prussians, who had behaved badly in this open and peaceable town.

About seven miles beyond Chateau-Thierry, on the road to Soissons, the march of Parquin's squadron was brought to a halt by flames from the houses of a hamlet which the enemy had set on fire. The inhabitants had apparently fled, but Parquin had the vicinity searched in case there was an old man about who could give him some information about the enemy troops. Whilst engaged in this search, a sergeant of the *Chasseurs* of the Guard came and told him that in the last house in the village, the only one not reached by the flames, he had discovered stragglers of the Russian Army, stretched out near the kitchen fire and apparently waiting for their food to cook. He added that he had had some men of his troop with him and had captured these enemy infantrymen. He effected the capture in rather a clever fashion. He ordered his *chasseurs* to put their loaded carbines against the window panes, aimed in the general direction of the hearth, round which the Russians were sitting, and above their heads. The crash of the volley, with bullets whistling round their ears, terrified the Russians, and before they had time to recover the sergeant entered the room with drawn sabre, followed by the men of his detachment and seized the lot. Parquin says that if it was not that France was being invaded, he would have enjoyed capturing a monstrous saucepan in which some thirty chickens had been cooked, together with hams, potatoes, etc. The bread was cut and ready, and the *chasseur* troop of the squadron sat down to a delicious meal.

According to the strict rules of war, and in the exceptional position in which Parquin was placed, he should have shot immediately these Russian grenadiers of General Sacken's Corps, because they had been caught in a village set on fire by the enemy. However, the Emperor had saved their lives by giving him an order to take prisoners. Parquin extended this generosity by permitting them to share in the supper that they had prepared. He did not have the heart to deprive them of the repast that had brought them bad luck, because, as they said, it was the desire not to be separated from the precious dish containing their company supper that had made them stop behind their column. They had intended to catch up by a night march, but the inopportune arrival of the French squadron had spoilt their project.

From the information given by the prisoners. Parquin was convinced that he was on the track of the enemy, who were retreating hastily in the direction of Soissons. After this short halt, he continued his march, leaving his prisoners in charge of a sergeant commanding his rearguard. At about 10 pm he received information from his scouts that the enemy was occupying the large town of Ouchy-le-Chateau, about three miles away and ten miles from Soissons. He immediately sent back information to General Colbert, whom he knew was following him with a brigade of the cavalry the Guard, that the enemy rearguards had their outposts outside Ouchy-le-Chateau, that the enemy were occupying the town, and that bivouac fires showed that they were in strength. At the same time he notified Colbert that he was about to carry out the order given him by the Emperor, and asked him to support him with some squadrons of cavalry, because, after the enemy had recovered from their surprise, they might harrass his withdrawal in strength.

Having taken this precaution, Parquin fed men and horses, and then led his squadron at a walk along the unpaved margin of the road. Soon he saw the enemy, only a hundred yards away and heard a German vedette challenge '*Wer da?*' (Who goes there?). Parquin immediately ordered his squadron to gallop, and, overrunning vedette, picquet, and main guard, the troopers swept into Ouchy-le-Chateau, achieving a complete surprise. The alarm spread rapidly as the French cavalry broke into Russian and Prussian bivouacks and the enemy soldiers were roughly awakened by the sabres and lance heads of the *chasseurs* and lancers, and by the carbine and pistol shots of the dragoons and mamelukes. These weapons, characteristic of the different types of cavalry, gave the enemy the impression, as was intended, that they were being attacked by several regiments. Many of the Russian and Prussian soldiers were killed in the attack, and Parquin took about a hundred prisoners, including two colonels and many other officers.

The enemy did not recover in time to molest Parquin's rapid withdrawal, and his prisoners were immediately taken to the Emperor for interrogation. From them Napoleon learned the fatal news that General Moreau, commandant of Soissons, had opened the gates of the town to the enemy on simple summons, and thereby saved Blücher's army from almost certain destruction. 'That name', said Napoleon, 'has always brought me bad luck.' He was referring to the other General Moreau who was banished for conspiracy in 1804 and subsequently defected to the enemy.

On 5th March General Colbert ordered Parquin to carry out a reconnaissance with his improvised squadron on the road towards Fismes. He moved with one troop forward as an advanced guard and the other three concentrated on the road behind. The advanced guard troop encountered some Cossack scouts and, following these, the officer commanding the troop got lured into a tricky defile, at the other side of which enemy troops were drawn up. Parquin had to support the advanced guard with the other three troops, but, finding himself faced by forces far superior to his own, it was obvious that he would have to withdraw; in any case, he had been ordered to get information and not to fight. This was information of prime importance for, though he did not know it, these were the leading troops of Winzingerode's Russian Corps which had recently joined Blücher and had been directed to attack Napoleon's right rear.

Parquin gave orders for a withdrawal through the defile. This was a slow process and by the time he got clear of it, the enemy had ouflanked him and about five hundred Cossacks were across the Soissons road. Parquin charged and broke through, but his losses were heavy, for he had two officers wounded and forty-three troopers killed, wounded, or missing. He himself had a lance wound in the arm. But the information he brought back was well worth the casualties.

These two actions show admirably what could be achieved by one squadron of light cavalry boldly handled. In both cases Parquin's task was to get information, and his brilliant handling of his small force shows how justified was Colbert's confidence in him. The immediate result was Napoleon's victory at the Battle of Craonne.

Parquin distinguished himself again when, at Saint Dizier on 27th March, Napoleon won his last victory. A Russian battery of eighteen guns, lined up in the open, was causing considerable casualties, and Colbert ordered him to charge home on this battery with his squadron, regardless of loss. Parquin got within a hundred yards of the guns, but, with grapeshot thinning the ranks of his squadron, he ordered two troops to swing right and two left, at the same time extending to skirmishing order. This must have been a well rehearsed tactical drill, and as Parquin's troops swept round the flanks of the battery, a wide gap was left between them. Into the gap, and straight at and over the guns, thundered the Red Lancers of the Guard. A Russian cuirassier division now counter-attacked to try and recapture the guns. But Colbert was ready with his reserve, and General Milhaud charged and routed the cuirassiers with his 3rd and 6th Dragoons of the Guard.

In his report to Napoleon on the day's fighting, General Count Sebastiani de la Porta, commanding the Cavalry of the Guard, said: 'I have been a cavalry officer, Sire, for twenty years, but I do not recall ever having seen a charge more brilliant than that made by the advanced guard squadron.'

This charge was executed by light cavalry and at the gallop. At the risk of being accused of poaching on the preserves of Chapter 2, one of the most famed charges by the heavy cavalry affords an interesting comparison. The occasion was the Battle of Eckmühl on 22nd April 1809, in the concluding stages of the initial operations against the Archduke Charles.

It was nearly dark when heavy masses of French cuirassiers formed for the decisive attack. The Austrians saw them coming and thirty-two squadrons of their cavalry drew up to oppose them. Marching against this mass of horsemen were six squadrons of Würtemberg light cavalry on the right front, twenty-four of Nansouty's cuirassiers and carabiniers to the left rear of the Würtembergers, sixteen squadrons of Saint-Sulpice's cuirassiers behind Nansouty, and about fourteen squadrons of Bavarian light cavalry as a reserve. The rival forces totalled some 13,000 to 15,000 cavalry.[5]

The Austrian cavalry were coming forward at a trot. There was a clash when their leading light cavalry were driven back by the Würtembergers, but these latter were in turn routed by the Austrian reserve cavalry. Meanwhile the cuirassiers and carabiniers on their heavy Norman and Flemish horses were coming forward at a walk. When only a hundred yards separated them from the Austrians, the carabiniers in Nansouty's centre halted and fired a volley, and at the same time the cuirassiers were ordered to trot. The carabiniers slung their carbines, drew their swords, and also trotted. Whilst the French were still trotting, the Austrians swept into them at a gallop; but before Saint-Sulpice's regiments could join in, the Austrians were beaten and flying.[6]

General Count Bismarck, then commanding a squadron in the King's Light Horse of the Würtemberg Cavalry Division, took part in the action and describes the attack by the French heavy cavalry as follows:

'In the meantime the cuirassier divisions had followed at a trot, and opposed the attack of the reserve cavalry in a manner so brilliant that Lannes's infantry, who were advancing on the heights, stopped to clap their hands and cheer the cuirassiers.

'The blow by the cuirassiers was delivered on a front of two regiments; the other regiments followed the first two at the distance of a squadron frontage. These cuirassiers paid particular attention to keeping close formation and they never moved at a pace faster than a trot. One heard the officers constantly calling out, "Close up, cuirassiers, close up!" in the tone of an observation rather than a command. The attack was not made in columns, as the term is usually understood; the charge was made in a succession of lines at short distances.

'As all the orders were repeated by officers in descending scale of command, the slightest order produced a hubbub of voices, but this was far from creating a bad impression.

'A little before the moment of impact, the generals and colonels gave a final order: "*En avant! Marche! Marche!*"; and this was repeated by the cuirassiers themselves, but without increasing the pace. This "*En avant!*", or "Forward", is equivalent to the "Hurrah" of the Russians: it is a means of excitation.'[7]

Parquin, as a result of the reorganisation of the army after the Restoration, was transferred to the 11th Cuirassiers, and it was in this regiment that he charged at Quatre Bras and Waterloo. He was probably nowhere near his beloved Emperor, who, as he rode away from the field where the Old Guard had been tumbled into defeat by a long line of red-coated infantry, said to his ADC, General Count de la Billarderie Flahaut, '*Cela à touiours été ainsi depuis Crécy*' ('It has always been the same since Crecy').[8]

This chapter has been largely dependent on the *Souvenirs de Capitaine Parquin*, Introduction by F. Masson, 1892.
Specific references are:

1. Parquin, op. cit.
2. Henry Lachouque, adapted by Anne S. K. Brown, *The Anatomy of Glory*, 1961
3. ibid.
4. ibid.
5. F. Loraine Petre, *Napoleon and the Archduke Charles*, 1909
6. ibid.
7. Commandant Saski, *Campagne de 1809*, 1899
8. *Journal of the Society for Army Historical Research*, Vol. XII, No. 46, p. 111. Flahault told this to Lord Acton, who repeated it in an address in 1877. (Flahaut was French Ambassador in England in 1860–1862.)

INDEX